NOV   2017

IMAGE COMICS, INC.
Robert Kirkman—Chief Operating Officer
Erik Larsen—Chief Financial Officer
Todd McFarlane—President
Marc Silvestri—Chief Executive Officer
Jim Valentino—Vice President

Eric Stephenson—Publisher
Corey Murphy—Director of Sales
Jeff Boison—Director of Publishing Planning & Book Trade Sales
Chris Ross—Director of Digital Sales
Jeff Stang—Director of Specialty Sales
Kat Salazar—Director of PR & Marketing
Branwyn Bigglestone—Controller
Kali Dugan—Senior Accounting Manager
Sue Korpela—Accounting & HR Manager
Drew Gill—Art Director
Heather Doornink—Production Director
Leigh Thomas—Print Manager
Tricia Ramos—Traffic Manager
Briah Skelly—Publicist
Aly Hoffman—Events & Conventions Coordinator
Sasha Head—Sales & Marketing Production Designer
David Brothers—Branding Manager
Melissa Gifford—Content Manager
Drew Fitzgerald—Publicity Assistant
Vincent Kukua—Production Artist
Erika Schnatz—Production Artist
Ryan Brewer—Production Artist
Shanna Matuszak—Production Artist
Carey Hall—Production Artist
Esther Kim—Direct Market Sales Representative
Emilio Bautista—Digital Sales Representative
Leanna Caunter—Accounting Analyst
Chloe Ramos-Peterson—Library Market Sales Representative
Marla Eizik—Administrative Assistant
IMAGECOMICS.COM

EAST OF WEST

JONATHAN HICKMAN
WRITER

NICK DRAGOTTA
ARTIST

FRANK MARTIN
COLORS

RUS WOOTON
LETTERS

EAS

W

OF

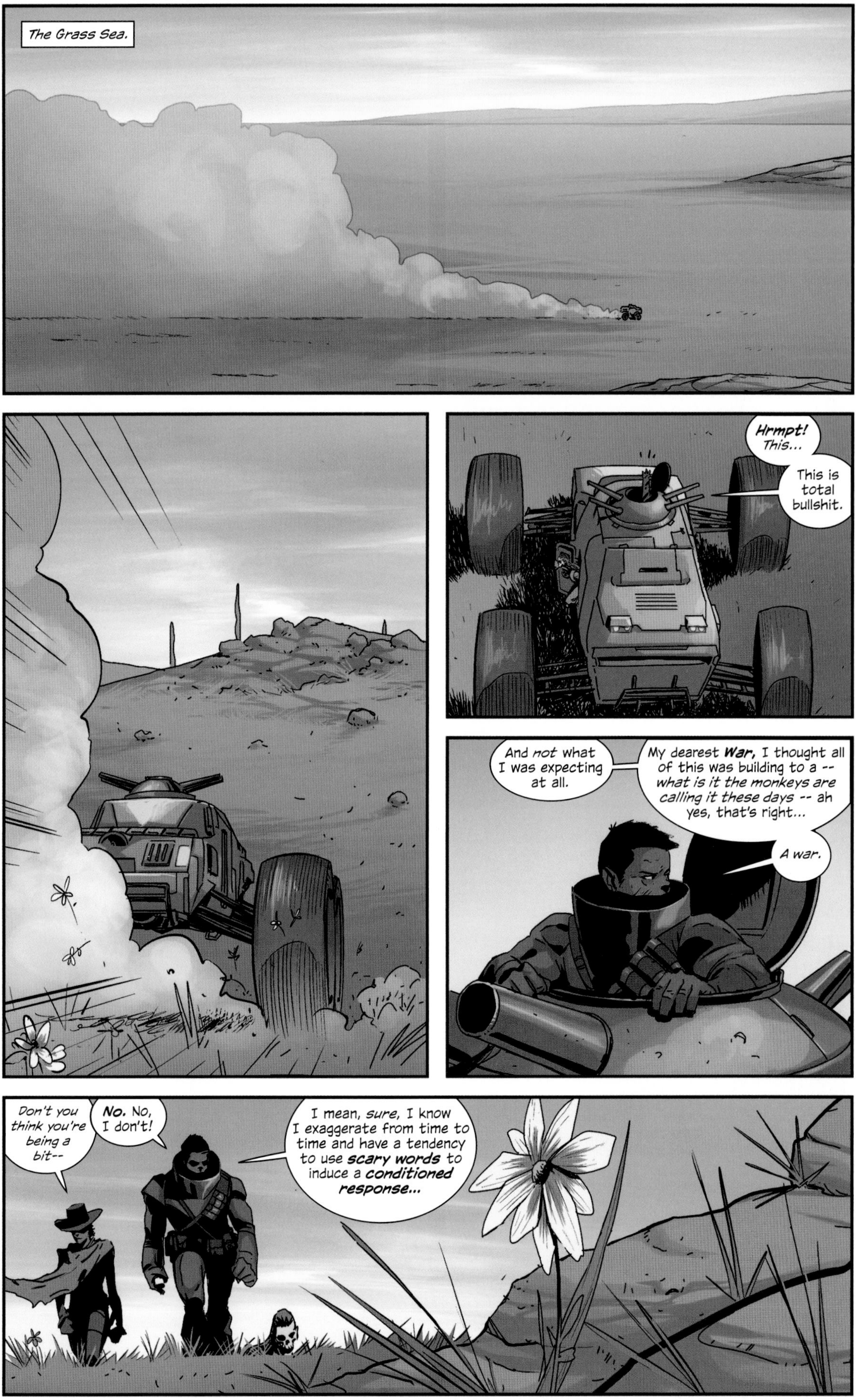
The Grass Sea.
Hrmpt! This...
This is total bullshit.
And not what I was expecting at all.
My dearest War, I thought all of this was building to a -- what is it the monkeys are calling it these days -- ah yes, that's right...
A war.
Don't you think you're being a bit--
No. No, I don't!
I mean, sure, I know I exaggerate from time to time and have a tendency to use scary words to induce a conditioned response...

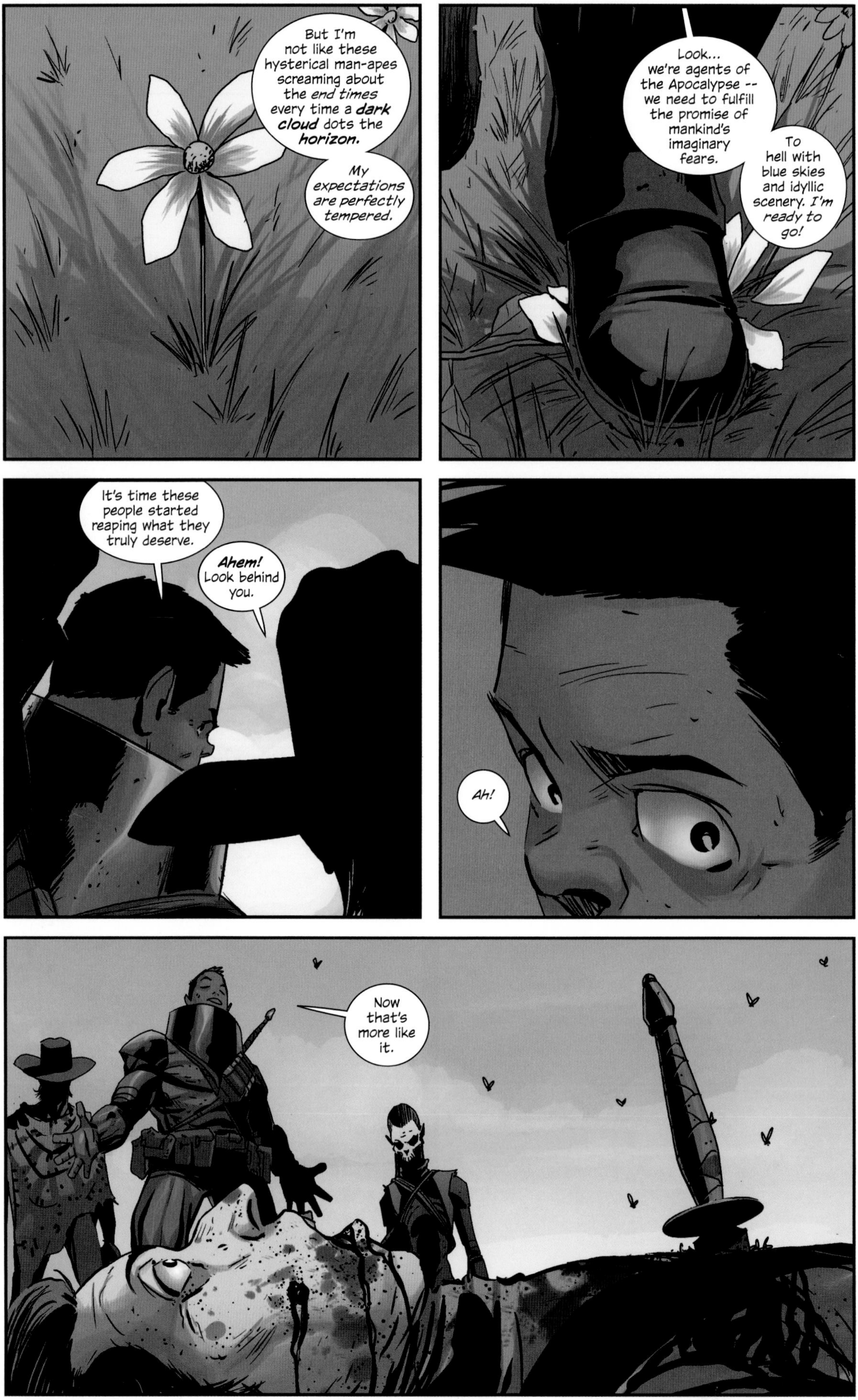
But I'm not like these hysterical man-apes screaming about the *end times* every time a ***dark cloud*** dots the ***horizon.***
My expectations are perfectly tempered.
Look... we're agents of the Apocalypse -- we need to fulfill the promise of mankind's imaginary fears.
To hell with blue skies and idyllic scenery. *I'm ready to go!*
It's time these people started reaping what they truly deserve.
Ahem! Look behind you.
Ah!
Now that's more like it.

2066

THE APOCALYPSE: YEAR THREE

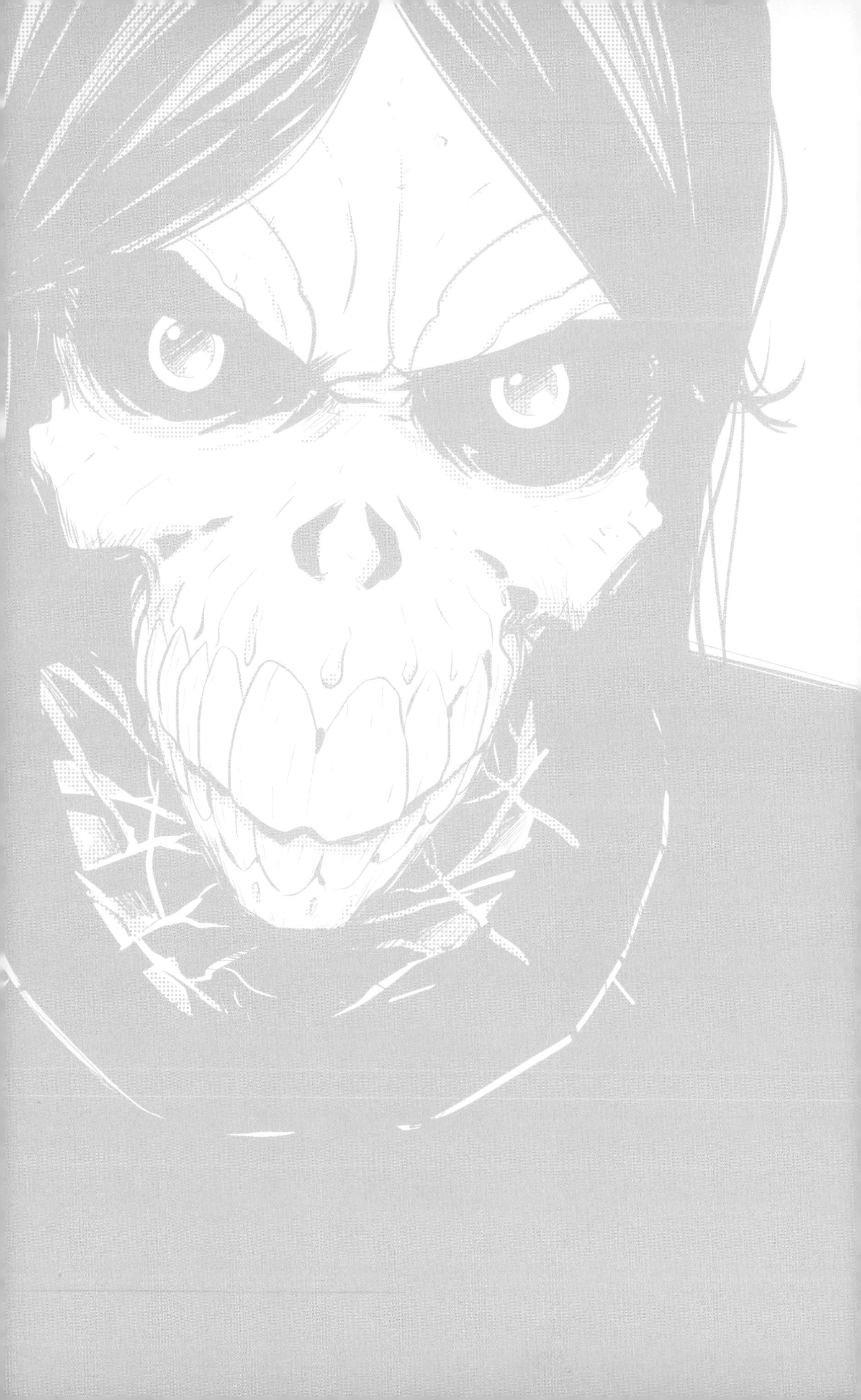

30

THIRTY:
THE MACHINE
CITY MUST **FALL**

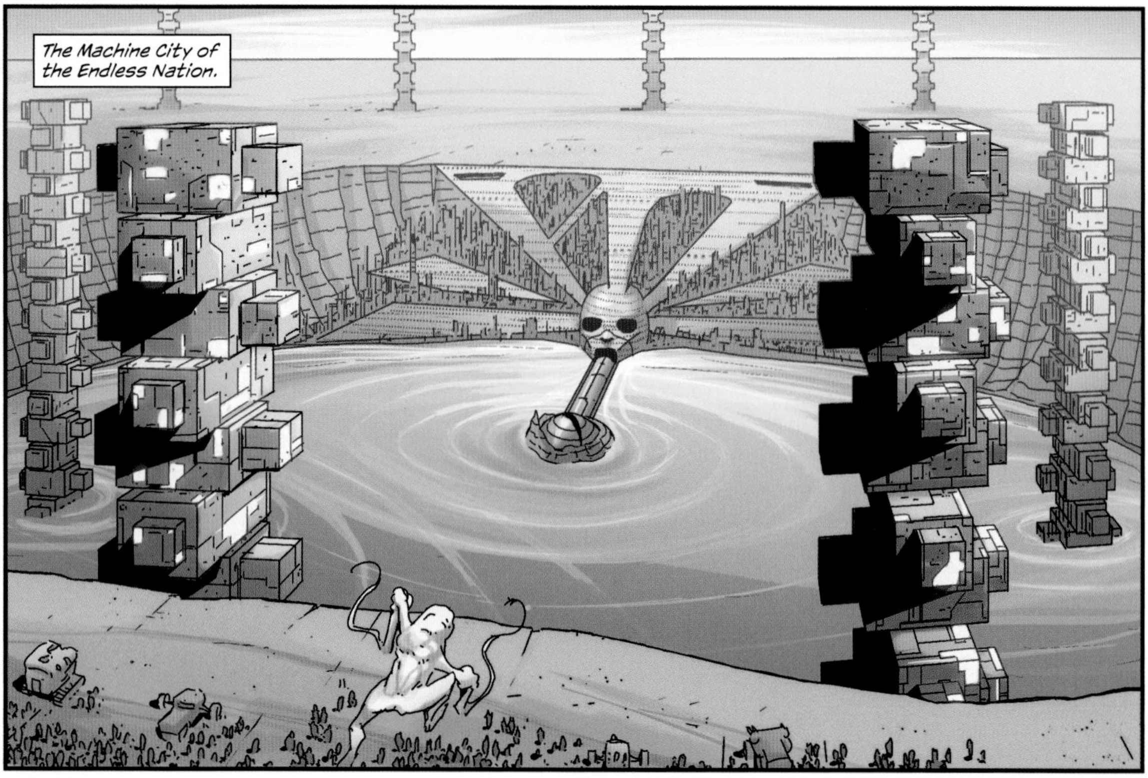
The Machine City of the Endless Nation.

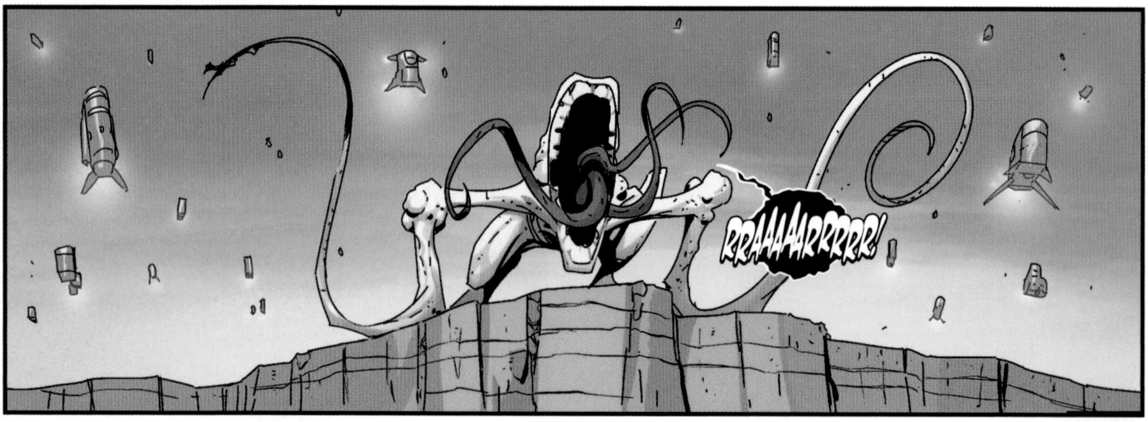
RRAAAAARRRRR!

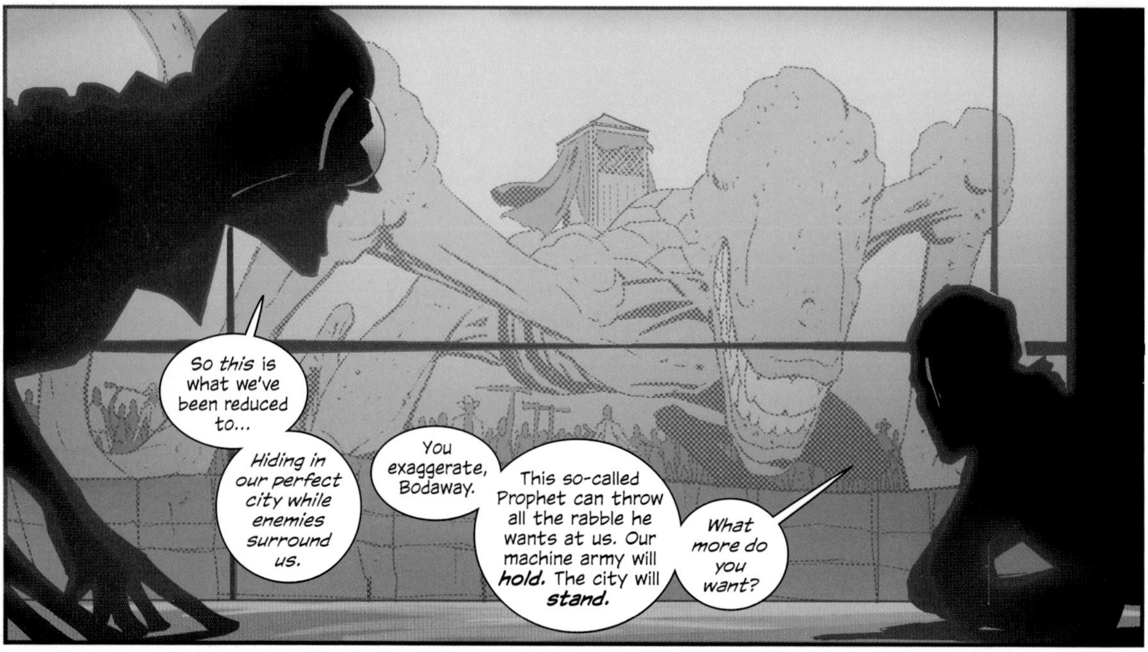
So this is what we've been reduced to...
Hiding in our perfect city while enemies surround us.
You exaggerate, Bodaway.
This so-called Prophet can throw all the rabble he wants at us. Our machine army will hold. The city will stand.
What more do you want?

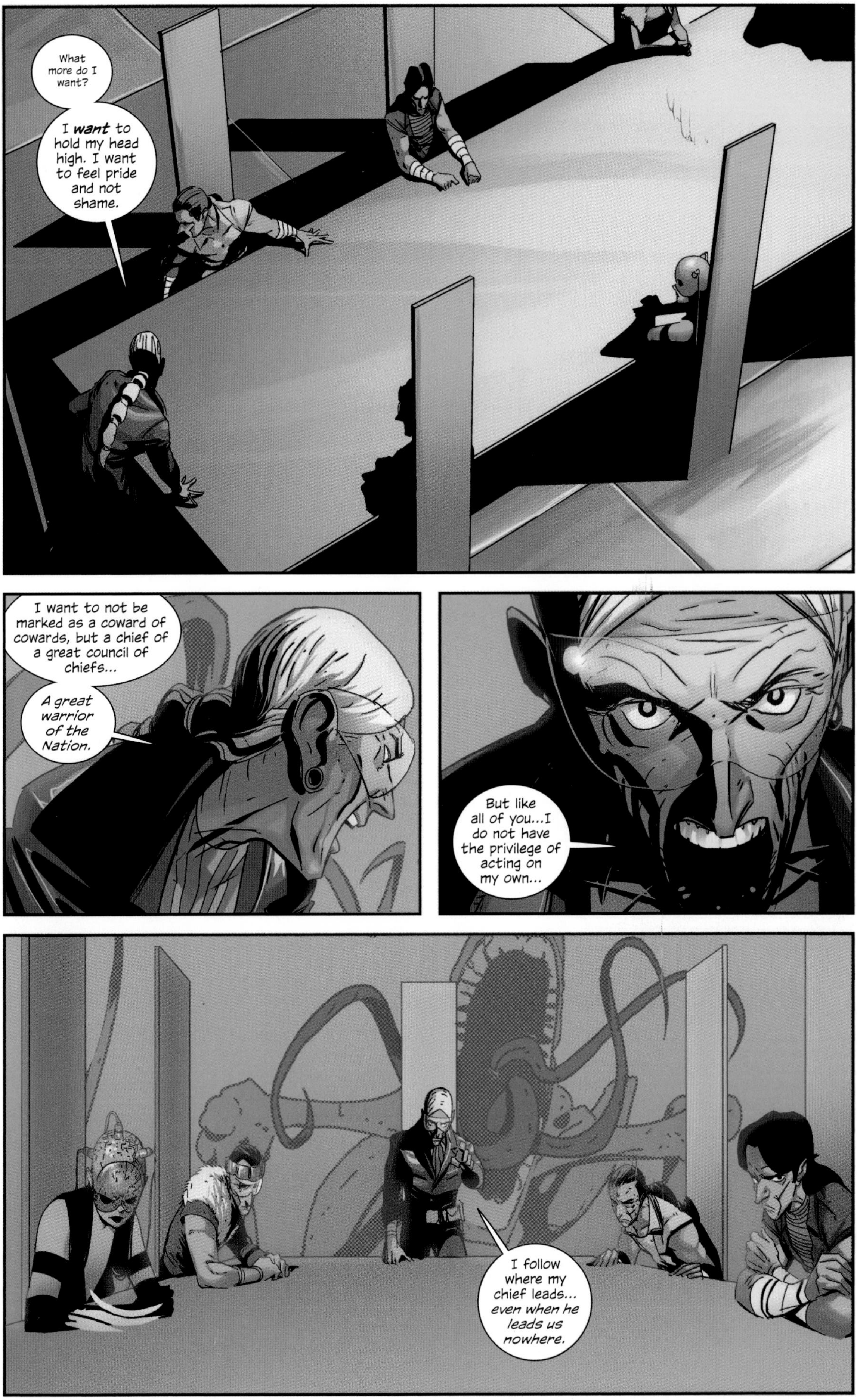
What more do I want?
I *want* to hold my head high. I want to feel pride and not shame.
I want to not be marked as a coward of cowards, but a chief of a great council of chiefs...
A great warrior of the Nation.
But like all of you...I do not have the privilege of acting on my own...
I follow where my chief leads... *even when he leads us nowhere.*

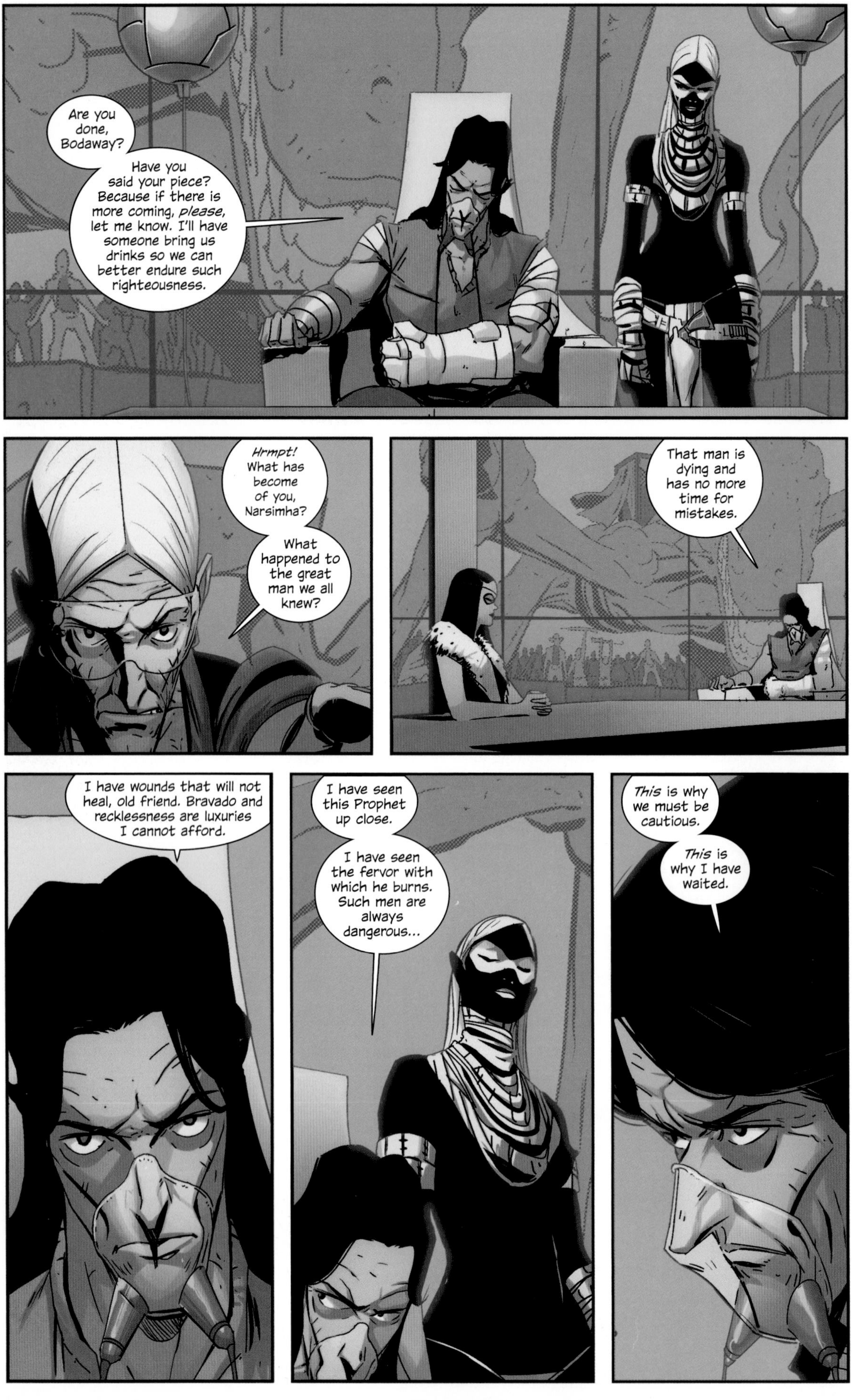
Are you done, Bodaway?
Have you said your piece? Because if there is more coming, *please*, let me know. I'll have someone bring us drinks so we can better endure such righteousness.
Hrmpt! What has become of you, Narsimha?
What happened to the great man we all knew?
That man is dying and has no more time for mistakes.
I have wounds that will not heal, old friend. Bravado and recklessness are luxuries I cannot afford.
I have seen this Prophet up close.
I have seen the fervor with which he burns. Such men are always dangerous...
This is why we must be cautious.
This is why I have waited.

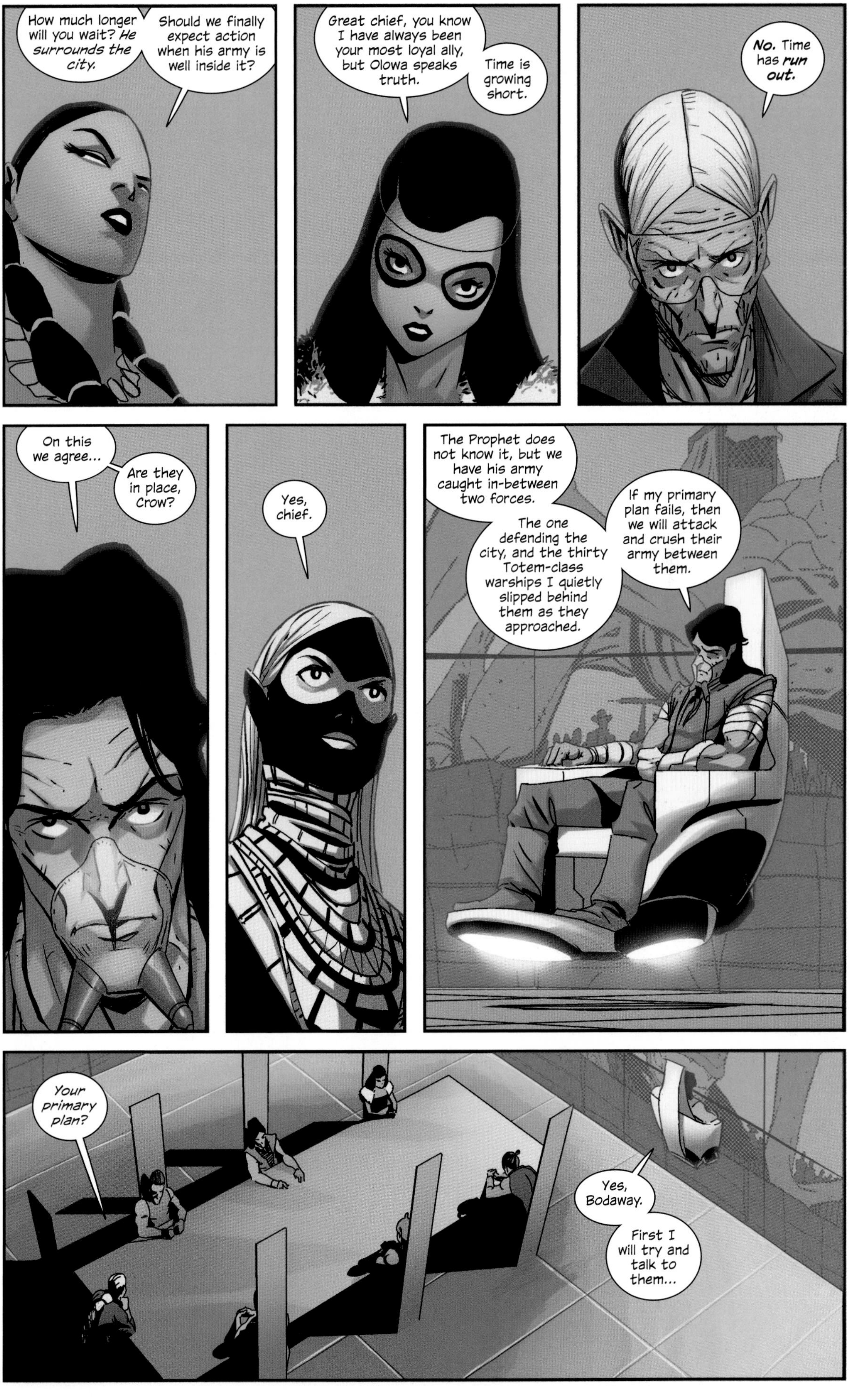
How much longer will you wait? *He surrounds the city.*
Should we finally expect action when his army is well inside it?
Great chief, you know I have always been your most loyal ally, but Olowa speaks truth.
Time is growing short.
No. Time has ***run out.***
On this we agree...
Are they in place, Crow?
Yes, chief.
The Prophet does not know it, but we have his army caught in-between two forces.
The one defending the city, and the thirty Totem-class warships I quietly slipped behind them as they approached.
If my primary plan fails, then we will attack and crush their army between them.
Your primary plan?
Yes, Bodaway.
First I will try and talk to them...

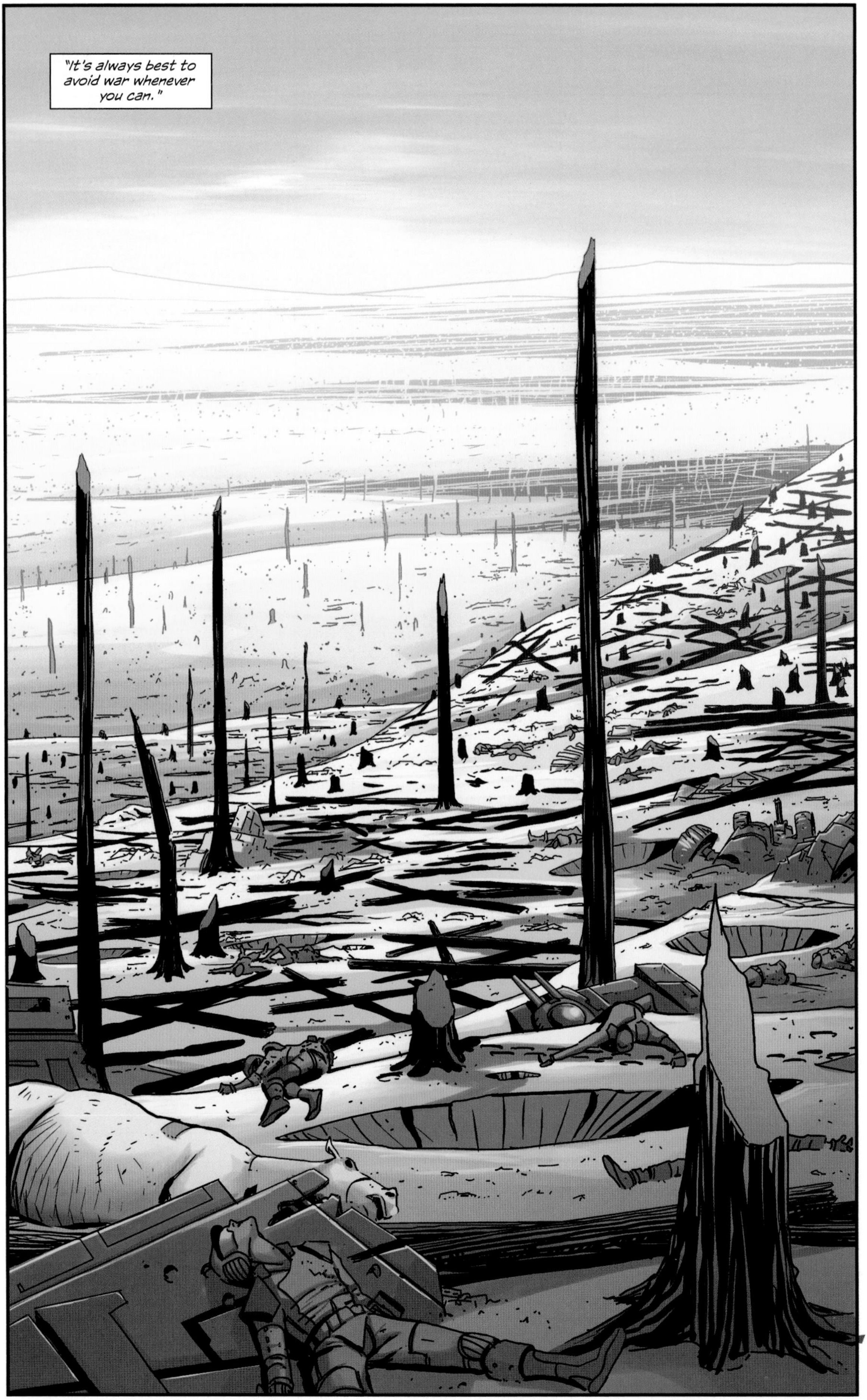
"It's always best to avoid war whenever you can."

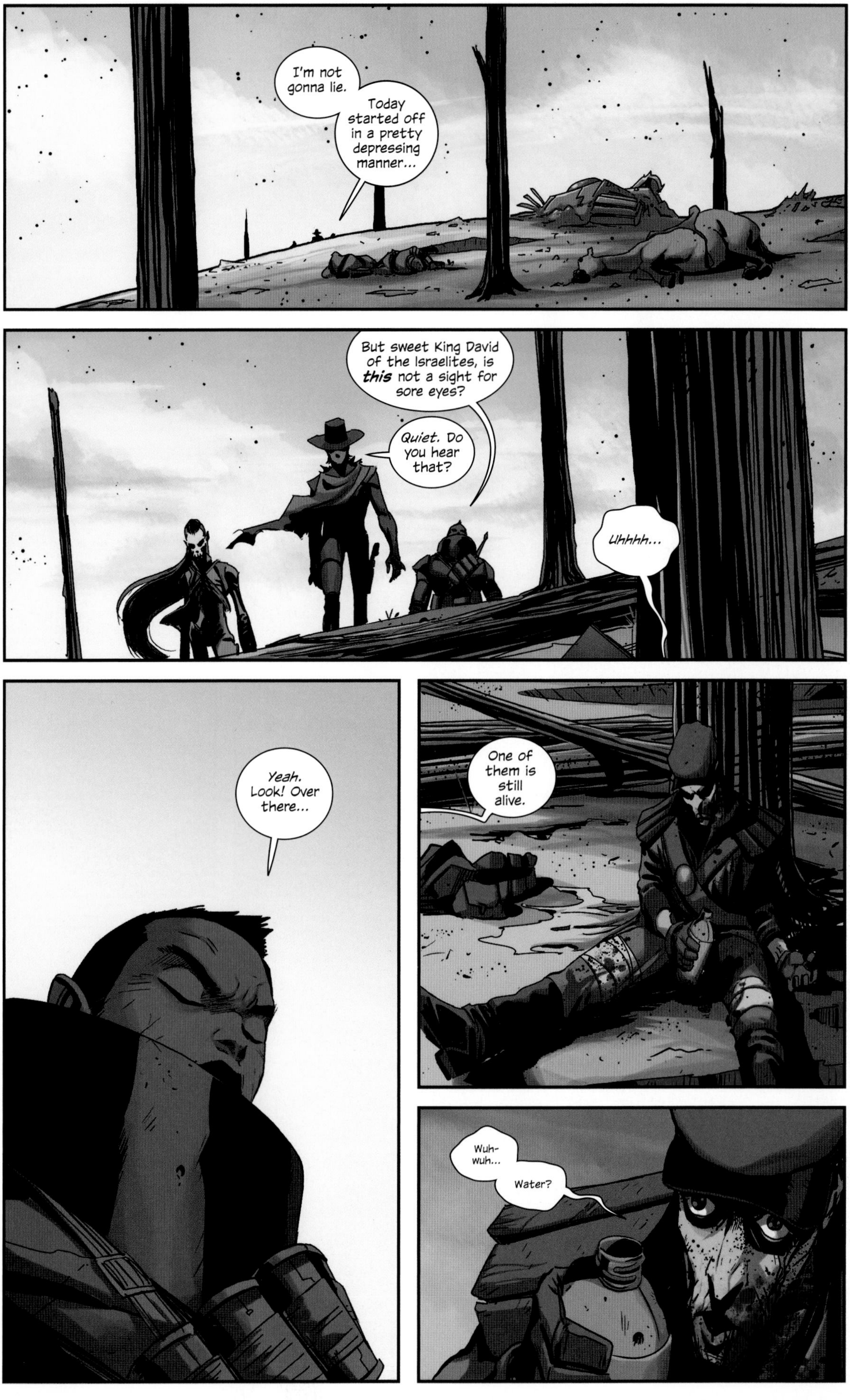
I'm not gonna lie.
Today started off in a pretty depressing manner...
But sweet King David of the Israelites, is *this* not a sight for sore eyes?
Quiet. Do you hear that?
Uhhhh...
Yeah. Look! Over there...
One of them is still alive.
Wuh-wuh...
Water?

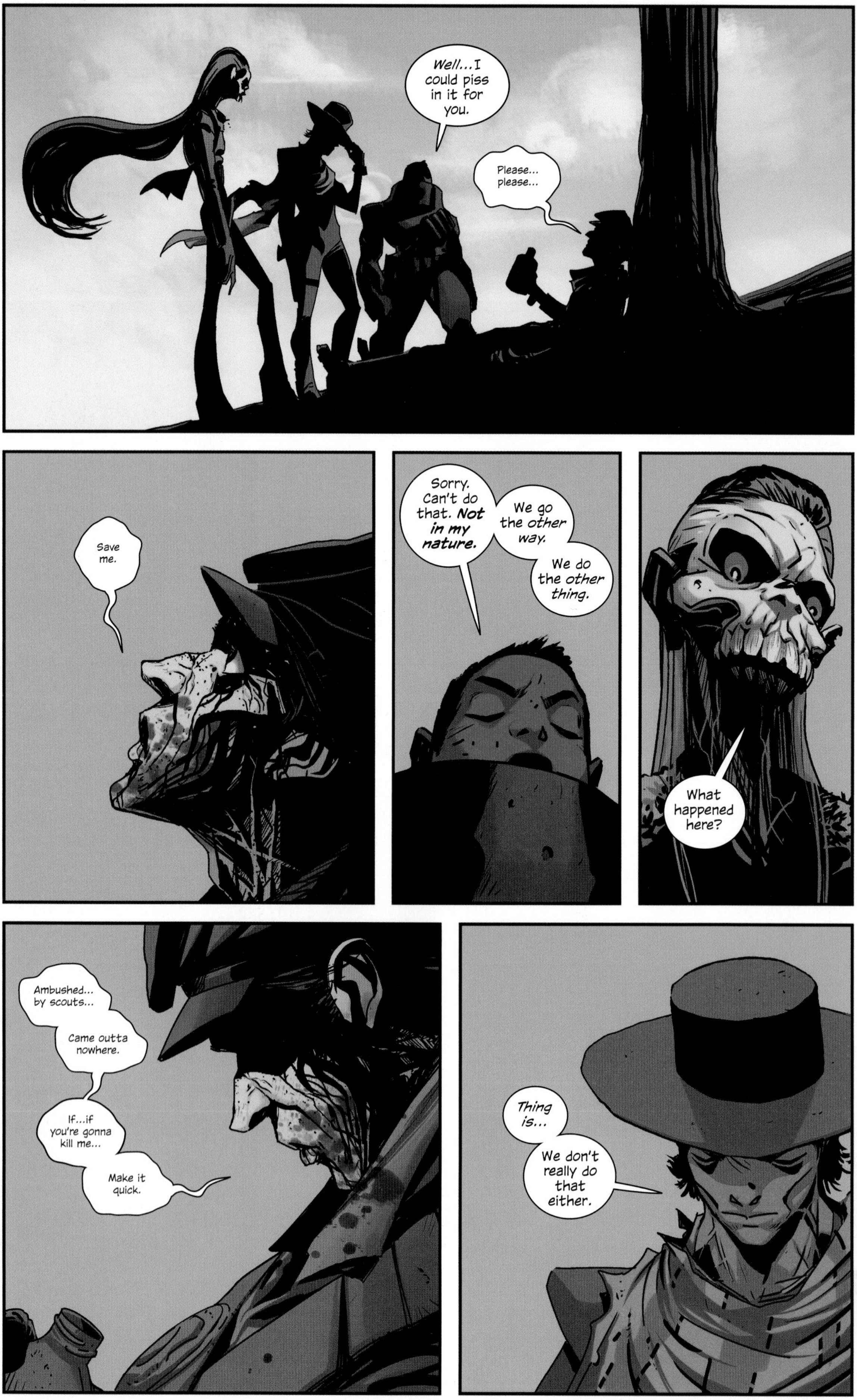

Well...I could piss in it for you.
Please... please...
Save me.
Sorry. Can't do that. Not in my nature.
We go the other way.
We do the other thing.
What happened here?
Ambushed... by scouts...
Came outta nowhere.
If...if you're gonna kill me...
Make it quick.
Thing is...
We don't really do that either.

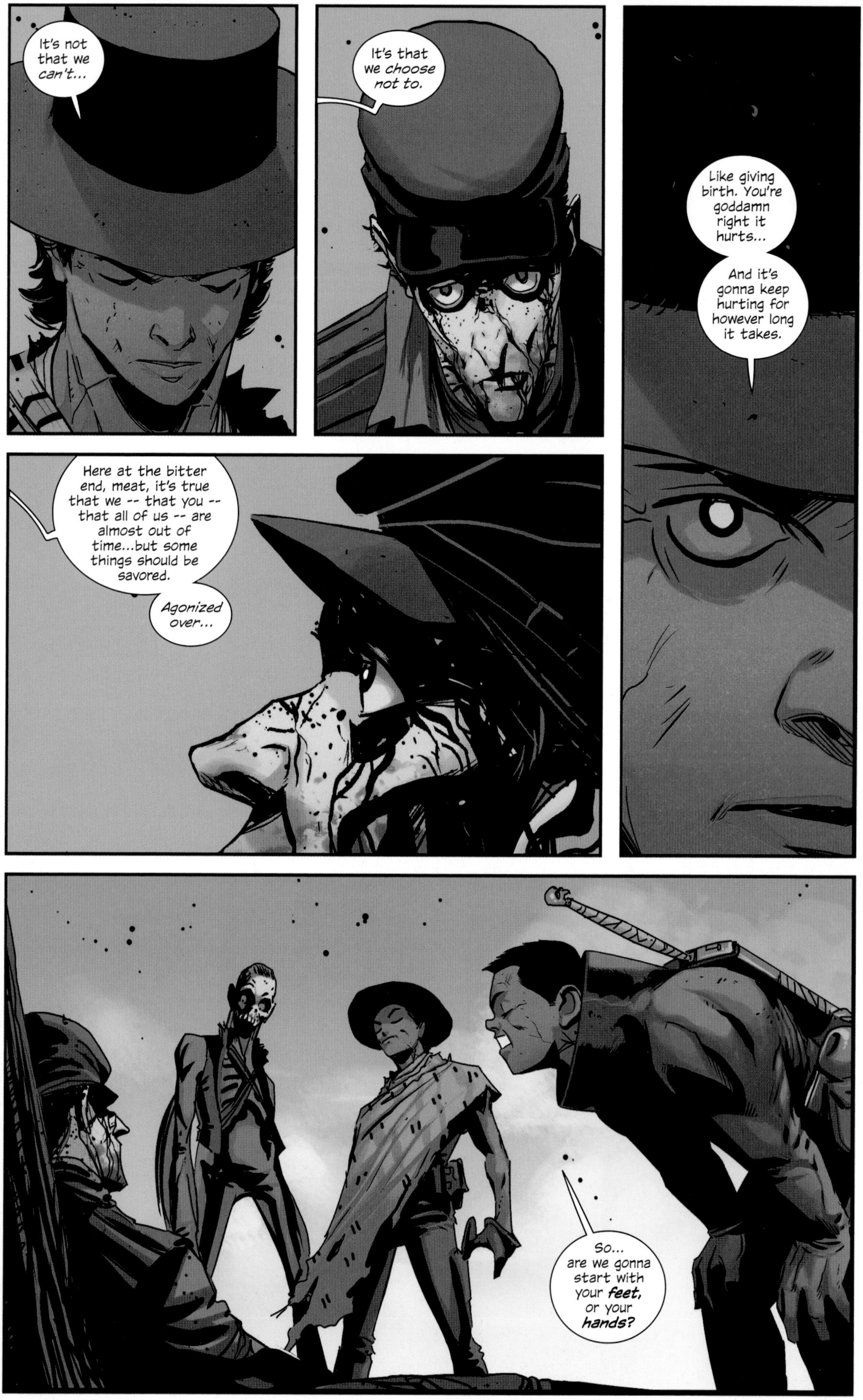
It's not that we *can't*...
It's that we *choose not to.*
Like giving birth. You're goddamn right it hurts...
And it's gonna keep hurting for however long it takes.
Here at the bitter end, meat, it's true that we -- that you -- that all of us -- are almost out of time...but some things should be savored.
Agonized over...
So... are we gonna start with your ***feet,*** or your ***hands?***

CLARITY IS WHAT YOU GET
BEFORE THE **VERY END.**

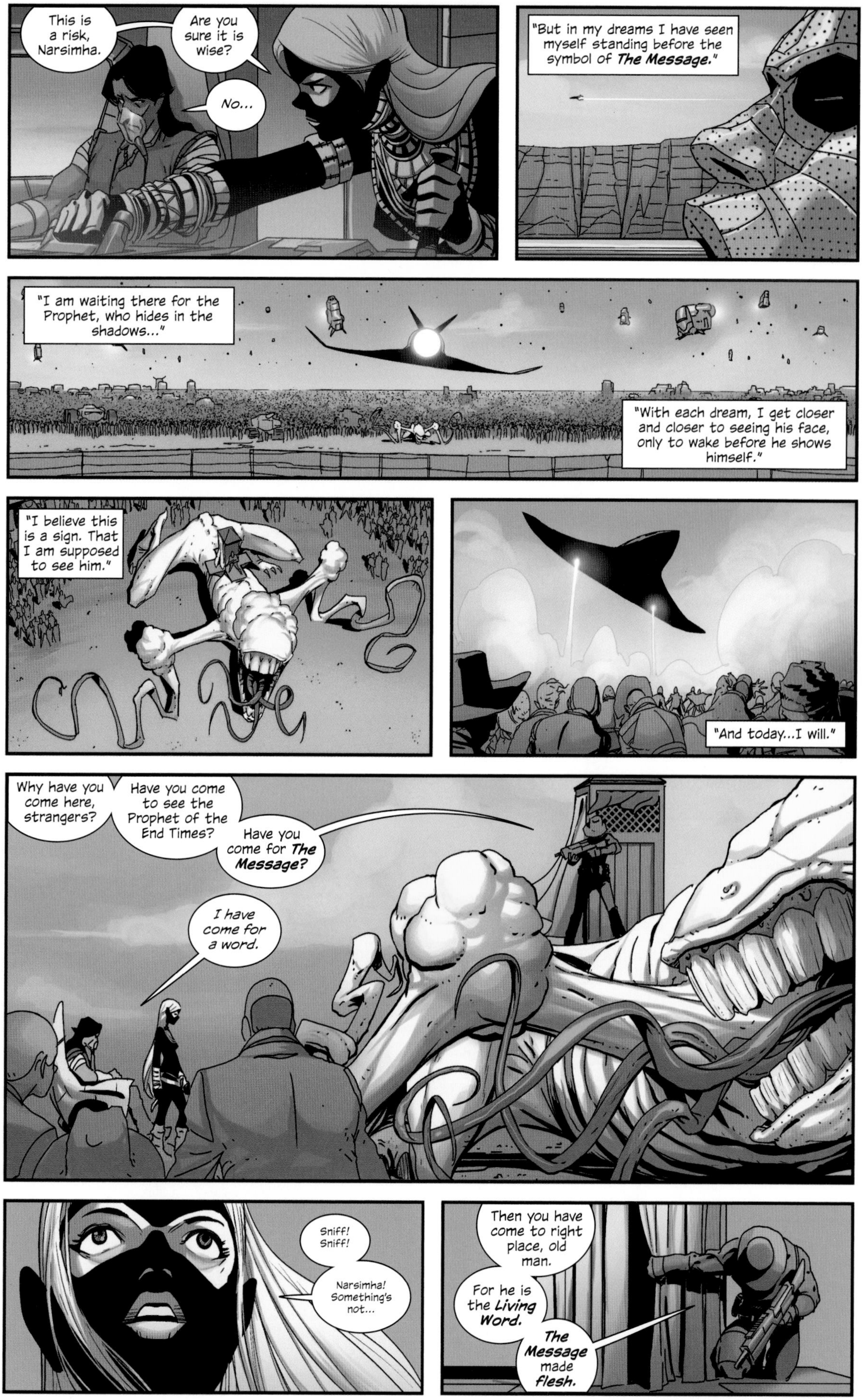
This is a risk, Narsimha.
Are you sure it is wise?
No...
"But in my dreams I have seen myself standing before the symbol of The Message."
"I am waiting there for the Prophet, who hides in the shadows..."
"With each dream, I get closer and closer to seeing his face, only to wake before he shows himself."
"I believe this is a sign. That I am supposed to see him."
"And today...I will."
Why have you come here, strangers?
Have you come to see the Prophet of the End Times?
Have you come for The Message?
I have come for a word.
Sniff! Sniff!
Narsimha! Something's not...
Then you have come to right place, old man.
For he is the Living Word.
The Message made flesh.

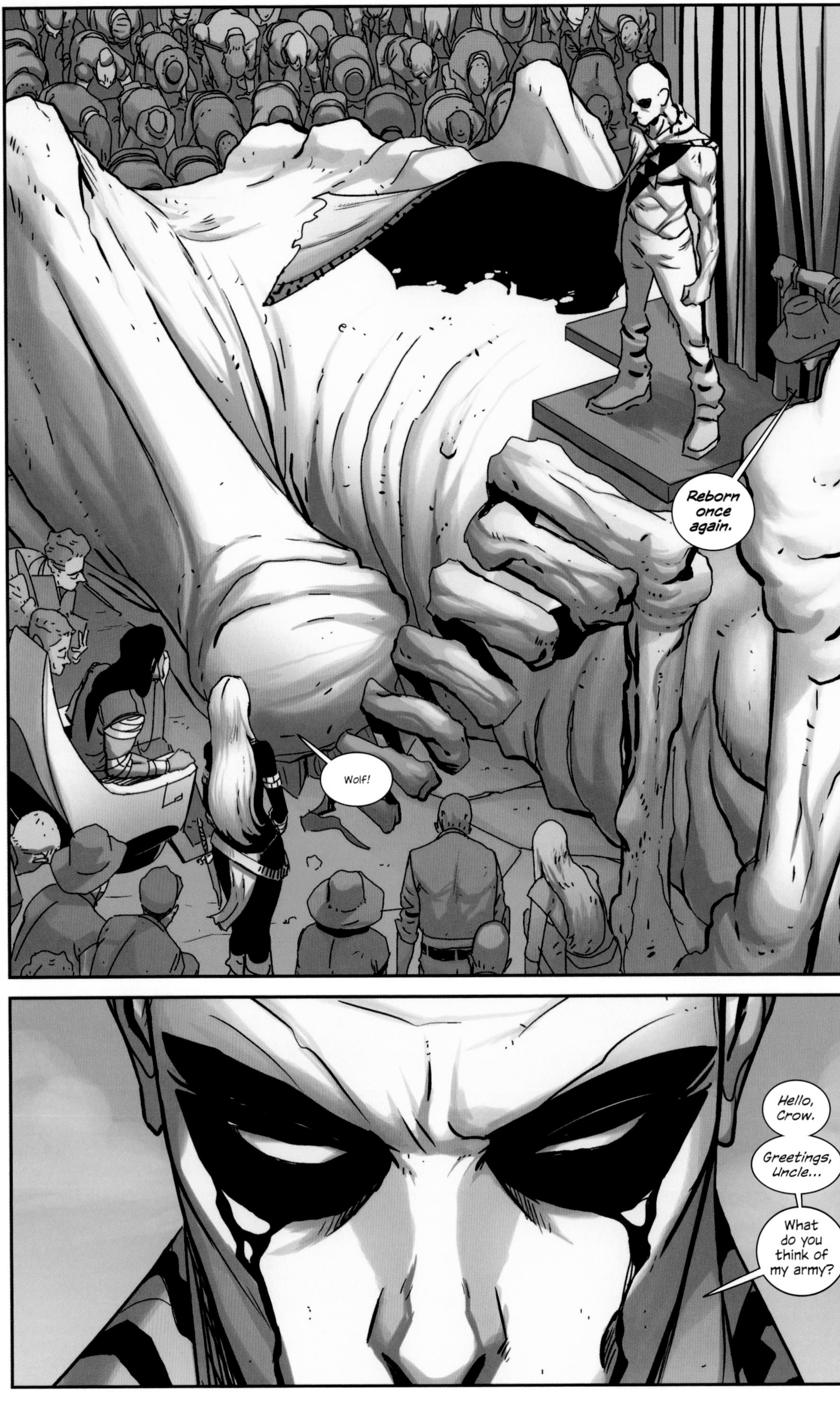
Reborn once again.
Wolf!
Hello, Crow.
Greetings, Uncle...
What do you think of my army?

THIS IS THE **WAY** OF IT.

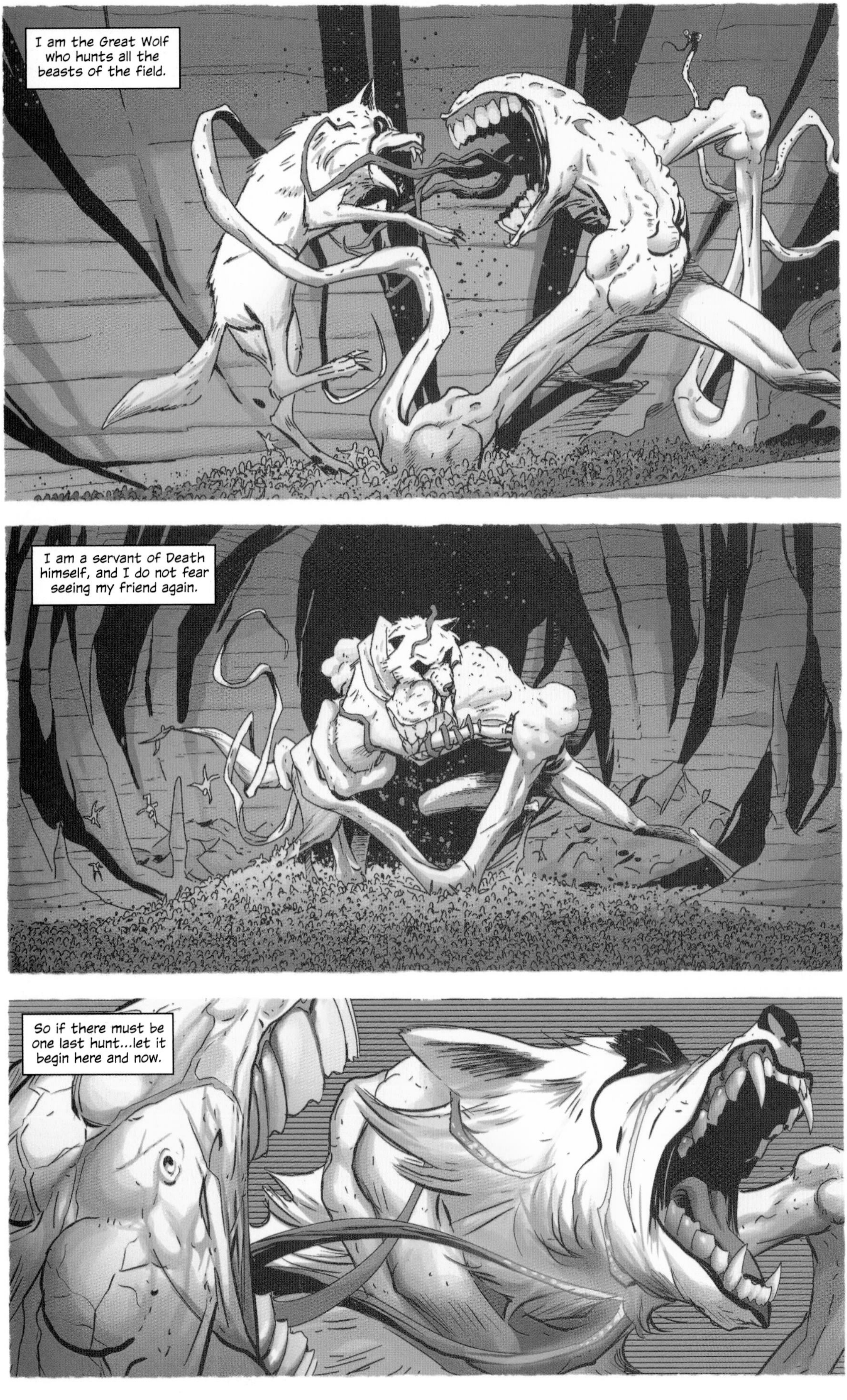
I am the Great Wolf who hunts all the beasts of the field.
I am a servant of Death himself, and I do not fear seeing my friend again.
So if there must be one last hunt...let it begin here and now.

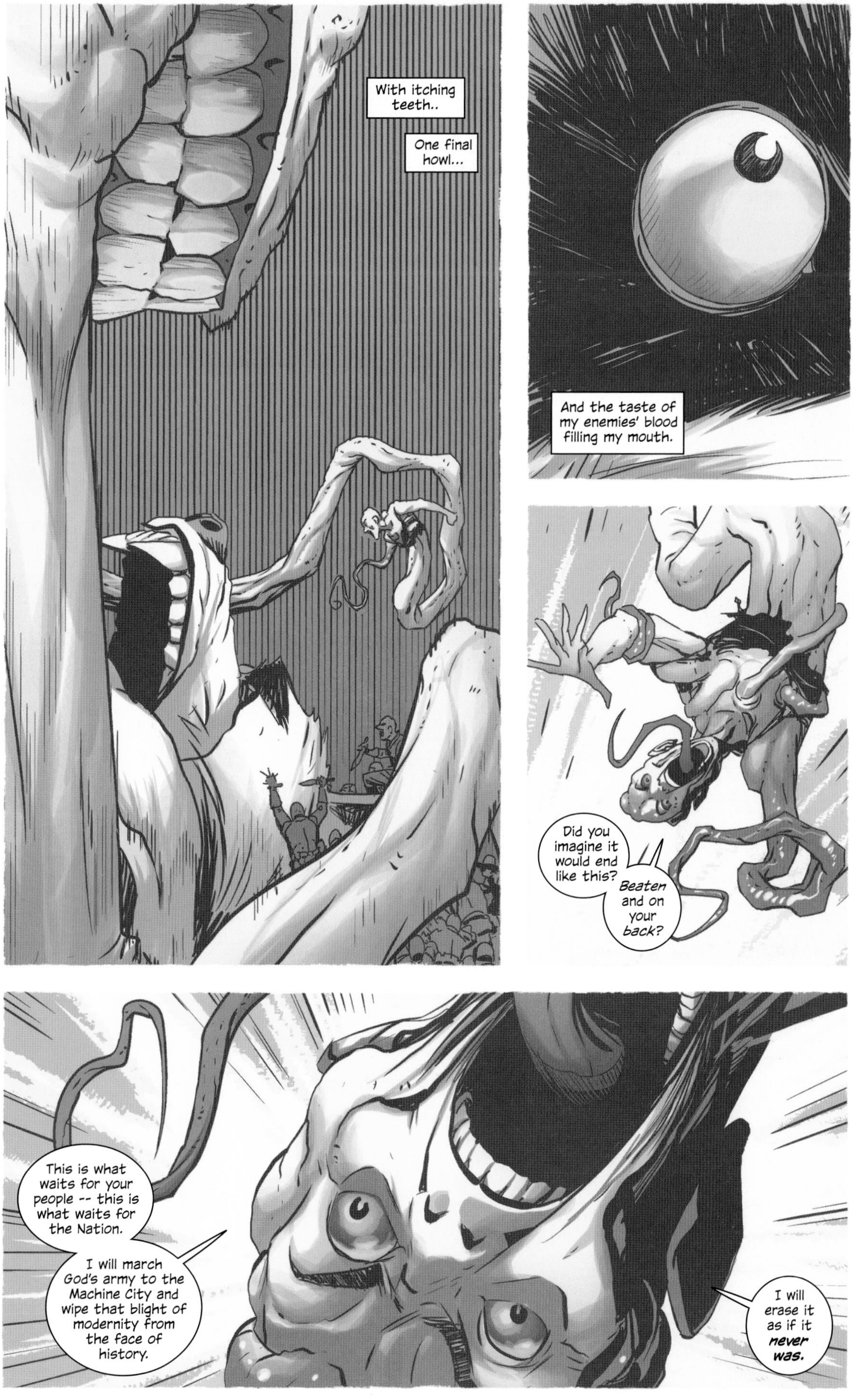
With itching teeth..
One final howl...
And the taste of my enemies' blood filling my mouth.
Did you imagine it would end like this?
Beaten and on your *back?*
This is what waits for your people -- this is what waits for the Nation.
I will march God's army to the Machine City and wipe that blight of modernity from the face of history.
I will erase it as if it ***never was.***

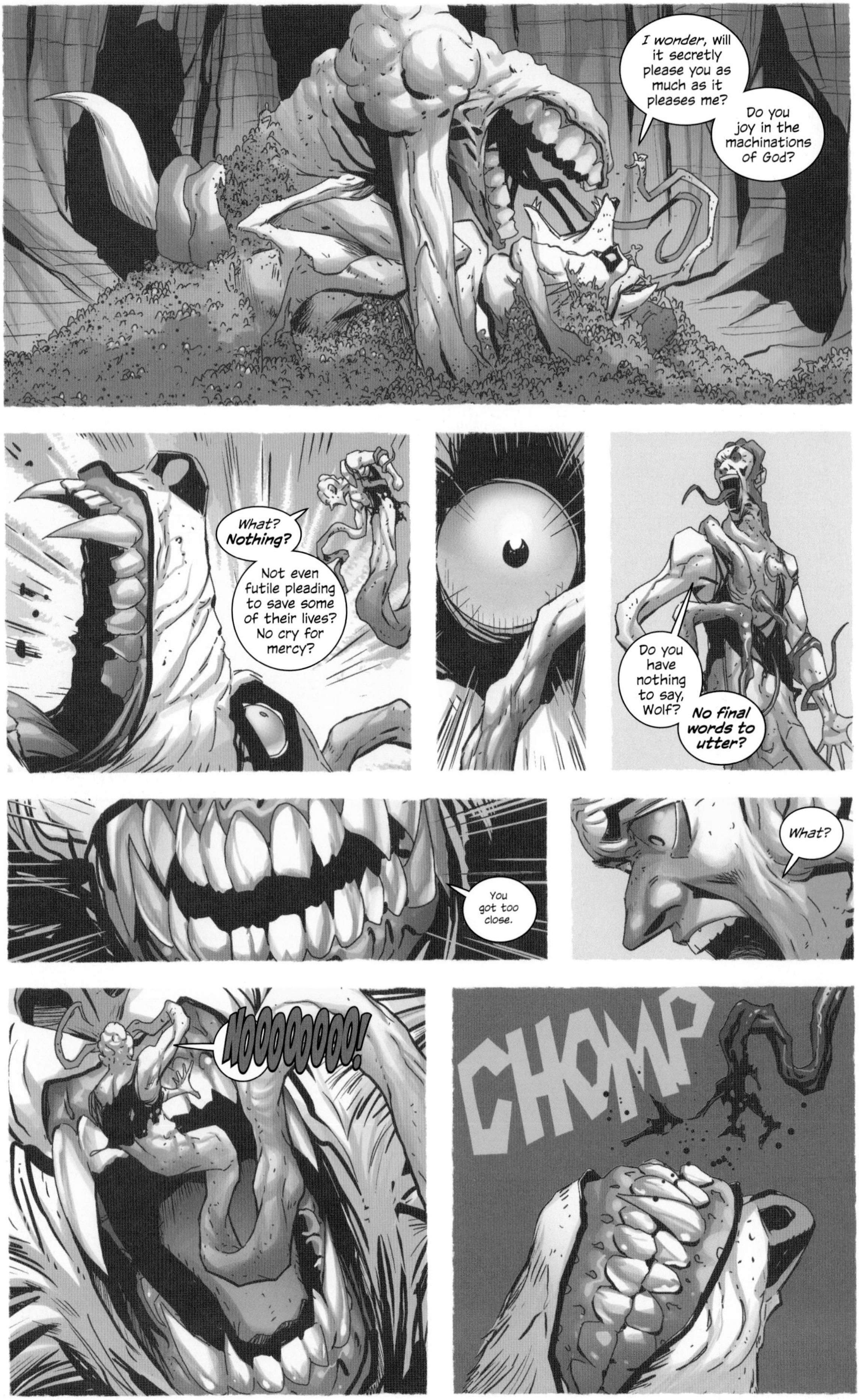

I wonder, will it secretly please you as much as it pleases me?
Do you joy in the machinations of God?
What? ***Nothing?***
Not even futile pleading to save some of their lives? No cry for mercy?
Do you have nothing to say, Wolf?
No final words to utter?
You got too close.
What?
NOOOOOOOO!
CHOMP

CHOMP CHOMP

No!
NO!

GRRRR

He's killed the Prophet!

Strike him!
Strike him down!

Silence, pilgrims!

All of you... on your knees. *Look* with your eyes and see...

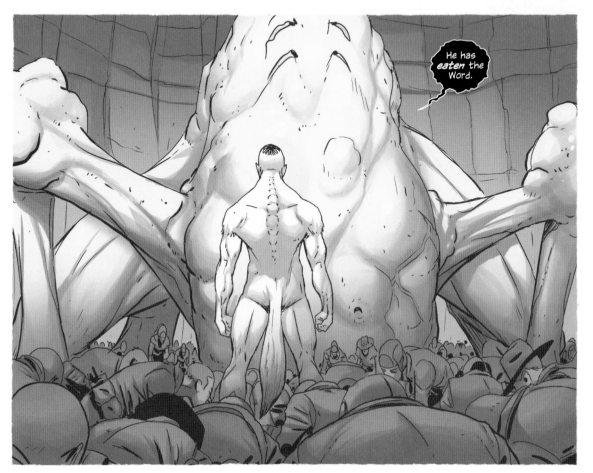

He has *eaten* the Word.

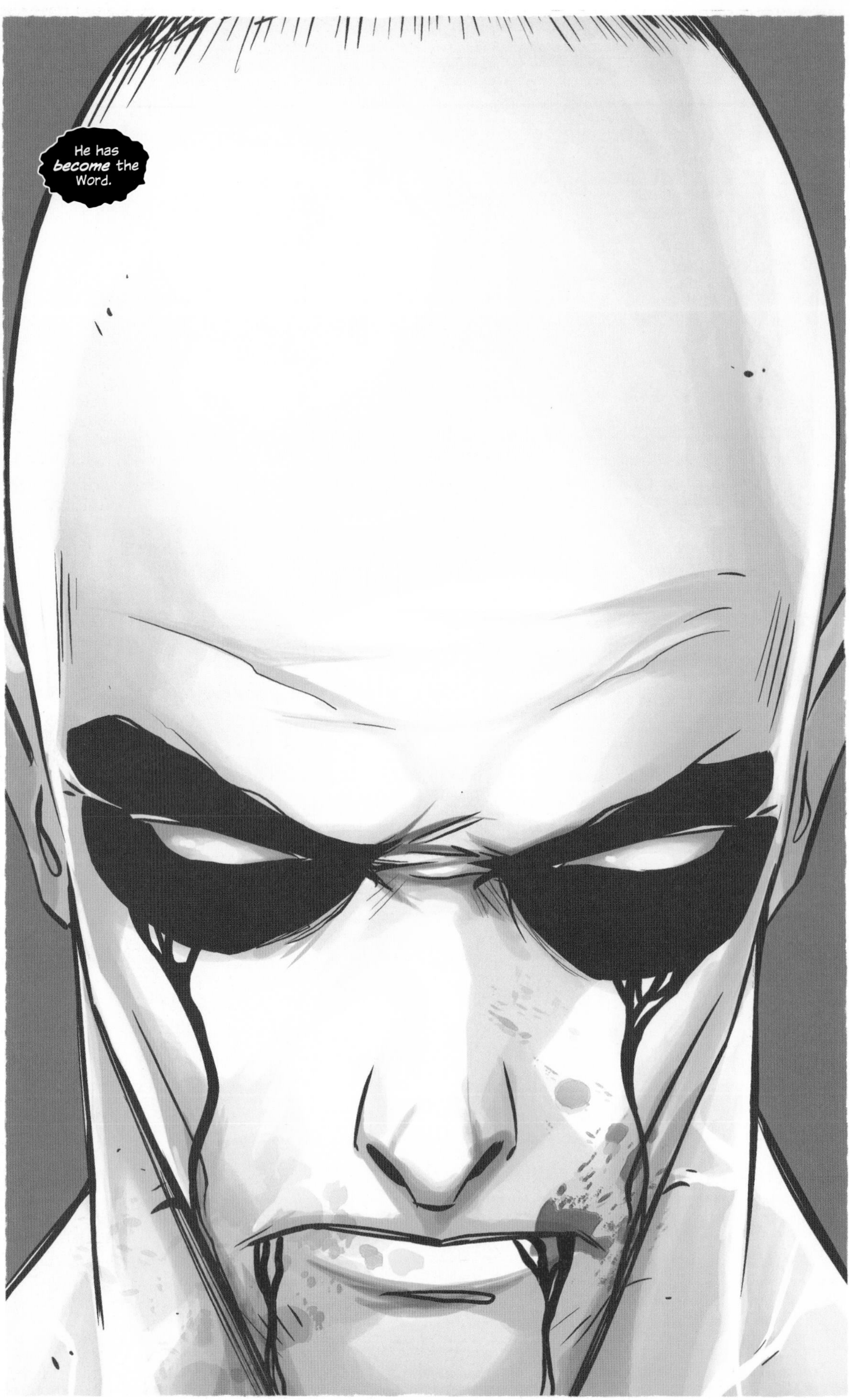
He has *become* the Word.

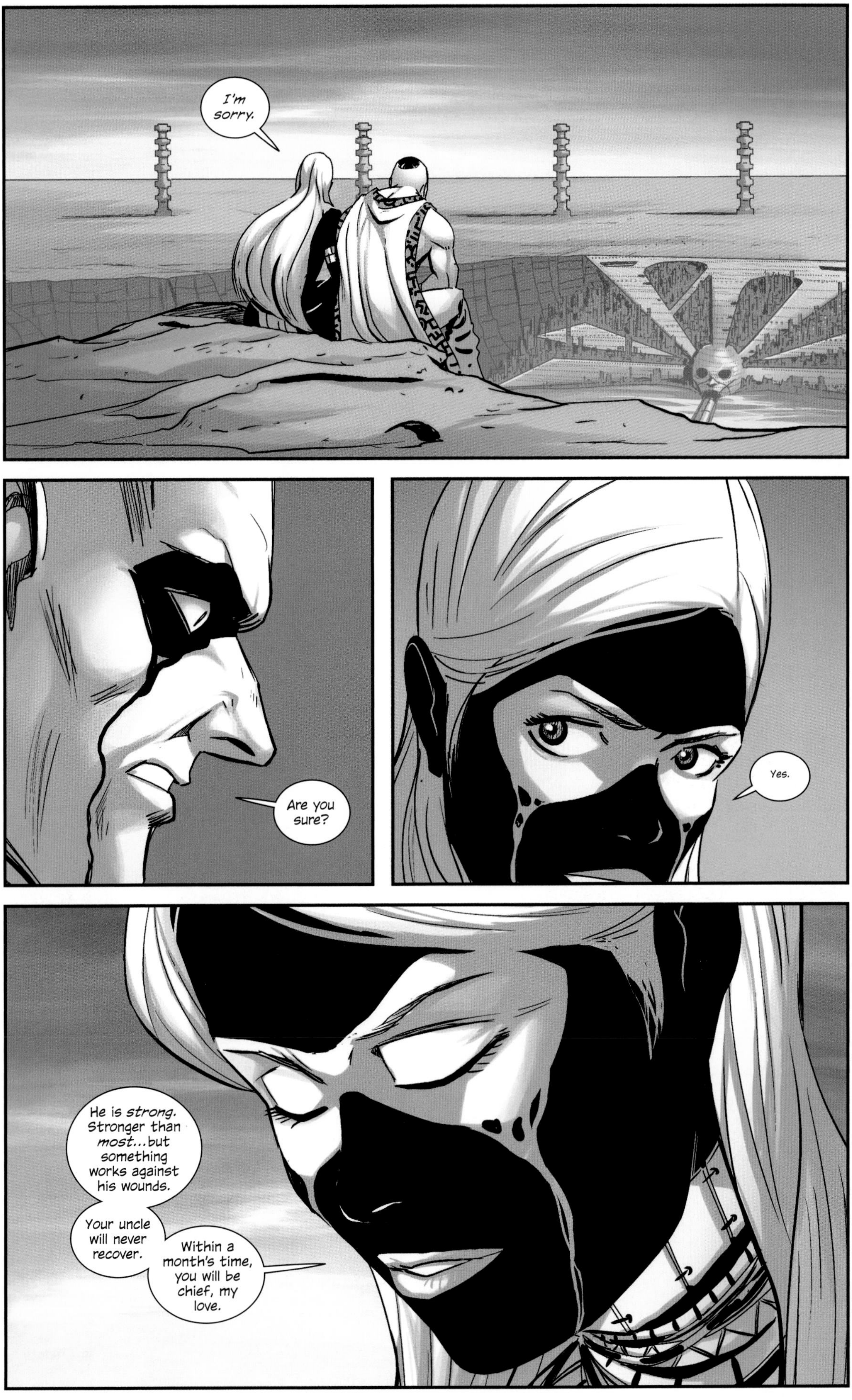
I'm sorry.
Are you sure?
Yes.
He is *strong*. Stronger than *most*...but something works against his wounds.
Your uncle will never recover.
Within a month's time, you will be chief, my love.

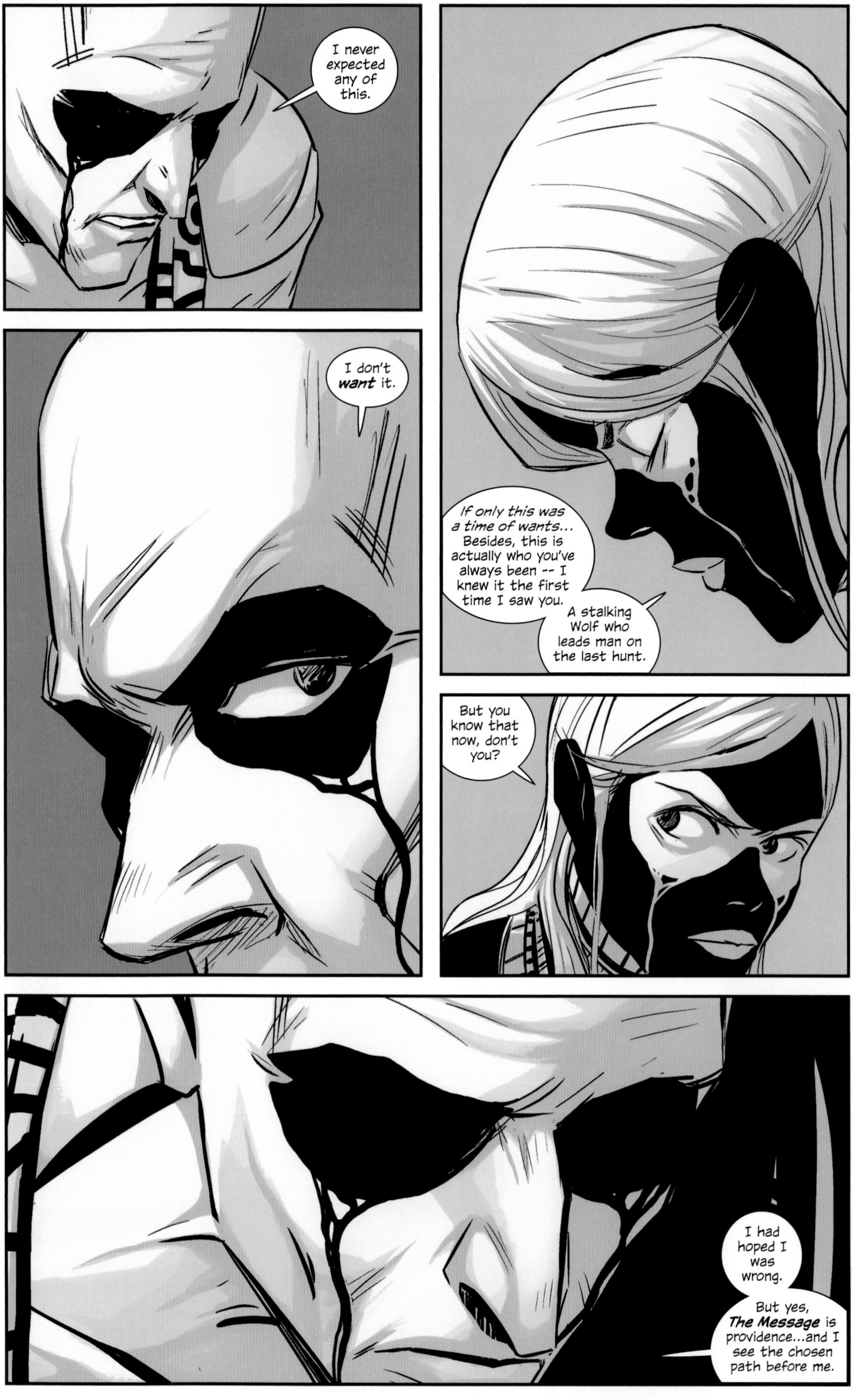
I never expected any of this.
If only this was a time of wants... Besides, this is actually who you've always been -- I knew it the first time I saw you.
A stalking Wolf who leads man on the last hunt.
I don't *want* it.
But you know that now, don't you?
I had hoped I was wrong.
But yes, ***The Message*** is providence...and I see the chosen path before me.

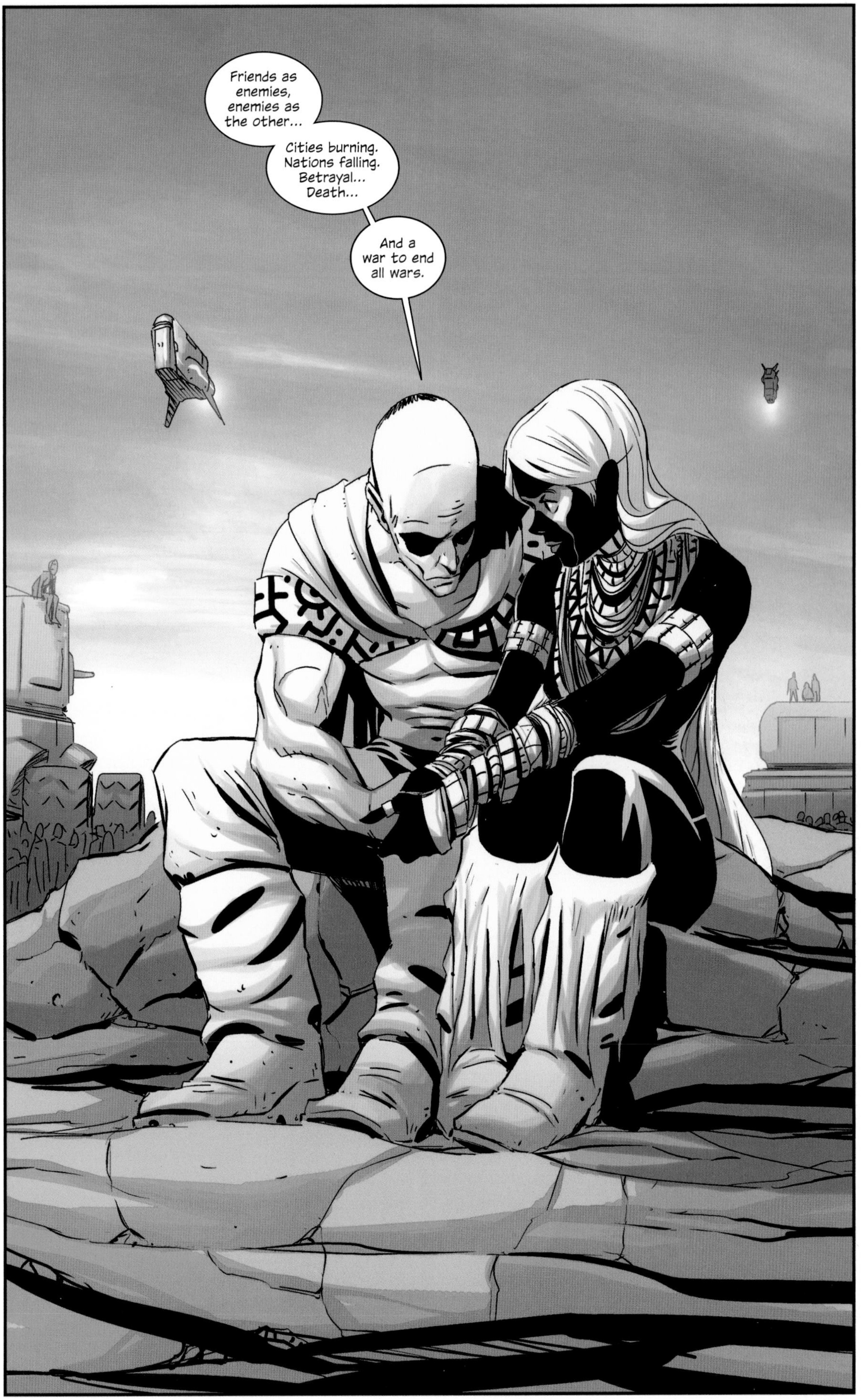
Friends as enemies, enemies as the other...
Cities burning. Nations falling. Betrayal... Death...
And a war to end all wars.

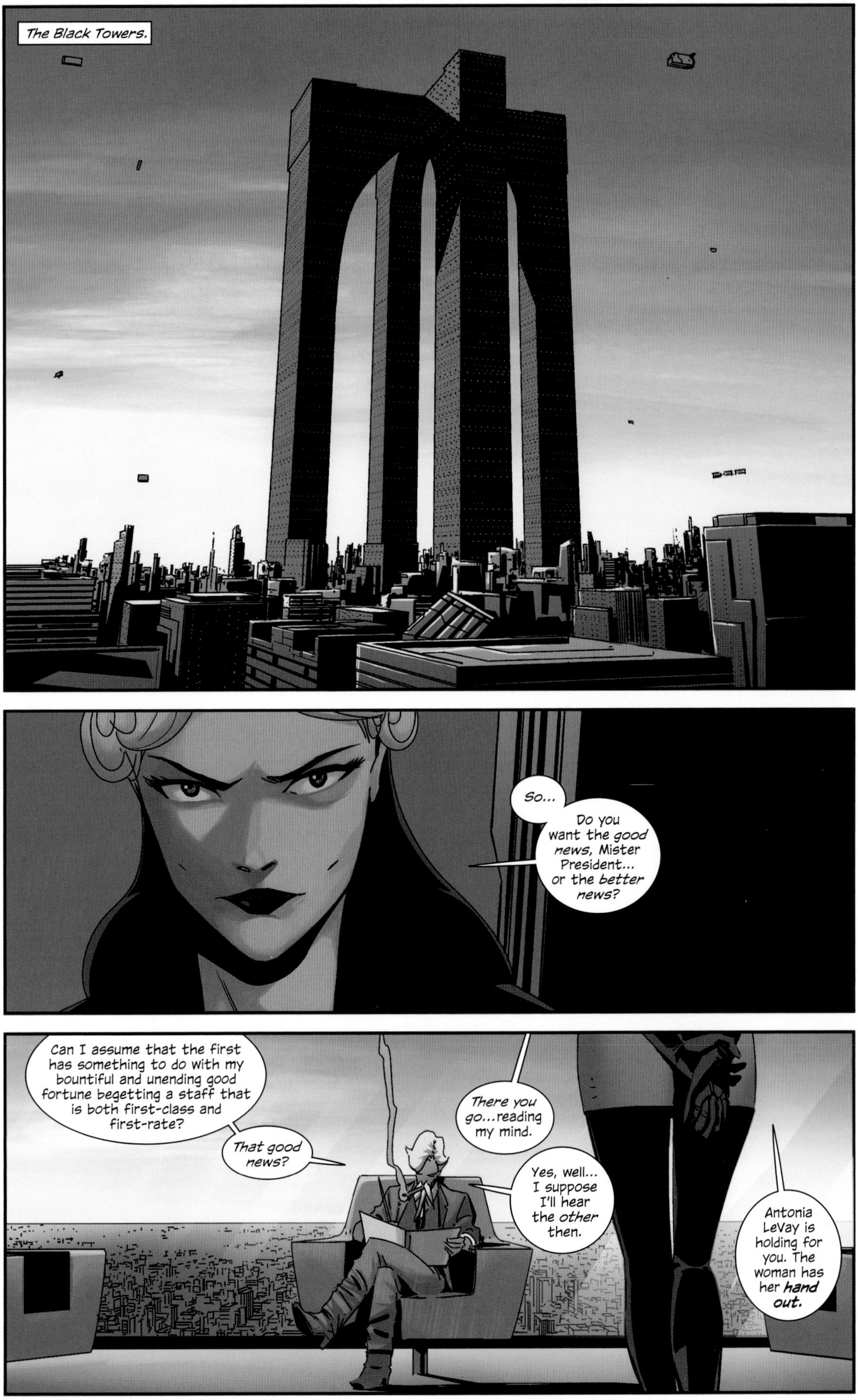
The Black Towers.
So...
Do you want the good news, Mister President... or the better news?
Can I assume that the first has something to do with my bountiful and unending good fortune begetting a staff that is both first-class and first-rate?
That good news?
There you go...reading my mind.
Yes, well... I suppose I'll hear the other then.
Antonia LeVay is holding for you. The woman has her hand out.

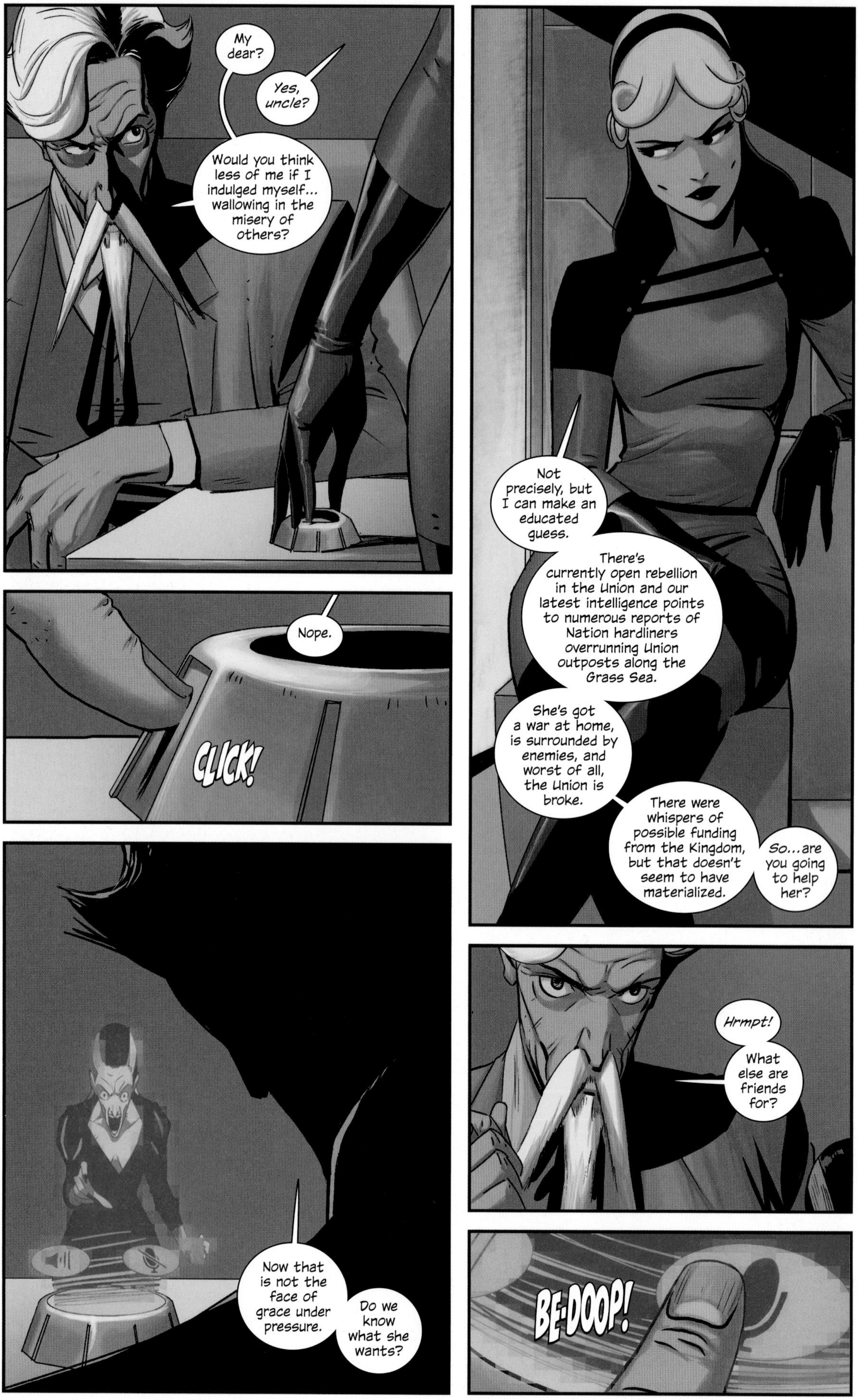
My dear?
Yes, uncle?
Would you think less of me if I indulged myself... wallowing in the misery of others?
Nope.
CLICK!
Now that is not the face of grace under pressure.
Do we know what she wants?
Not precisely, but I can make an educated guess.
There's currently open rebellion in the Union and our latest intelligence points to numerous reports of Nation hardliners overrunning Union outposts along the Grass Sea.
She's got a war at home, is surrounded by enemies, and worst of all, the Union is broke.
There were whispers of possible funding from the Kingdom, but that doesn't seem to have materialized.
So...are you going to help her?
Hrmpt!
What else are friends for?
BE-DOOP!

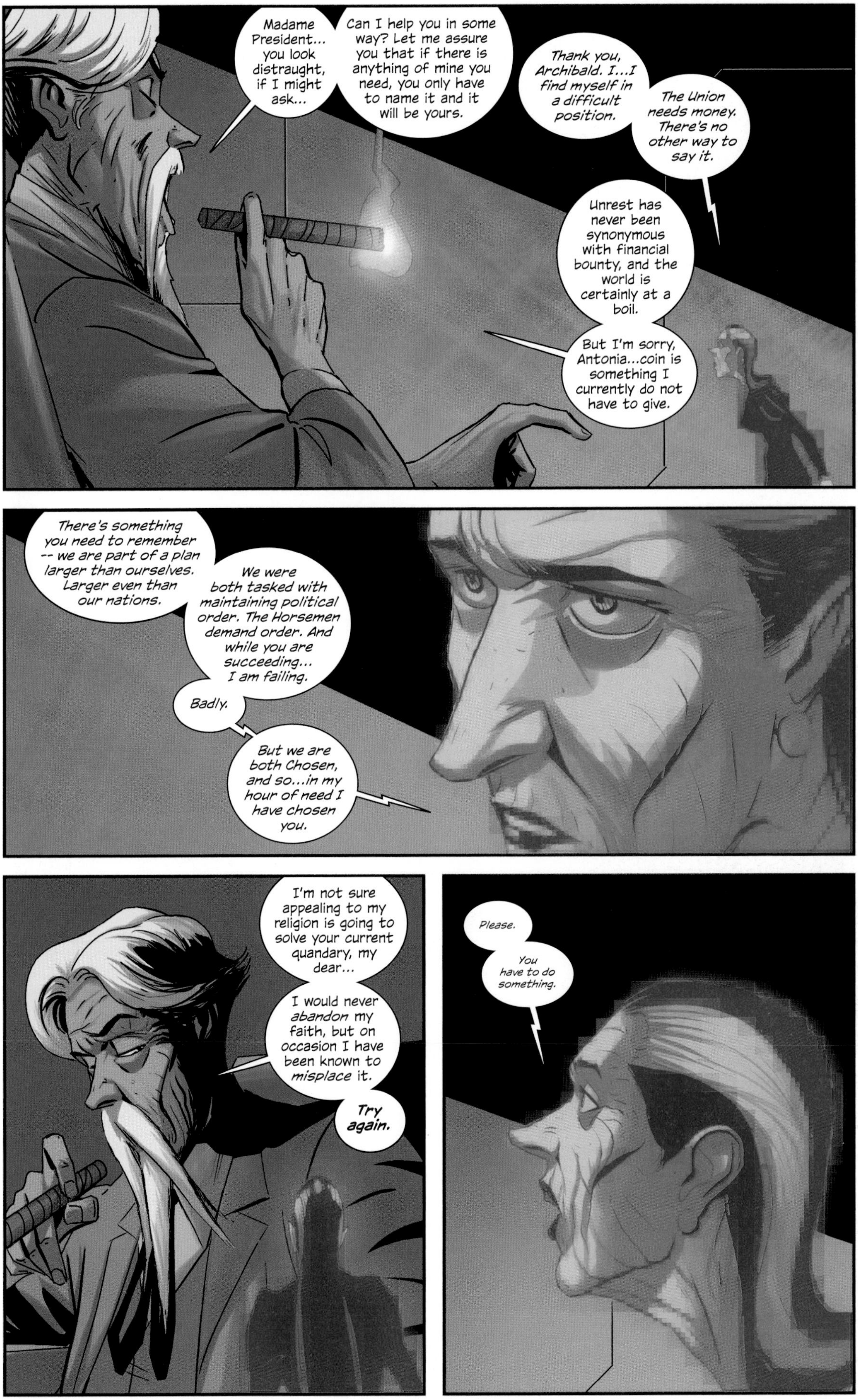
Madame President... you look distraught, if I might ask...
Can I help you in some way? Let me assure you that if there is anything of mine you need, you only have to name it and it will be yours.
Thank you, Archibald. I...I find myself in a difficult position.
The Union needs money. There's no other way to say it.
Unrest has never been synonymous with financial bounty, and the world is certainly at a boil.
But I'm sorry, Antonia...coin is something I currently do not have to give.
There's something you need to remember -- we are part of a plan larger than ourselves. Larger even than our nations.
We were both tasked with maintaining political order. The Horsemen demand order. And while you are succeeding... I am failing.
Badly.
But we are both Chosen, and so...in my hour of need I have chosen you.
I'm not sure appealing to my religion is going to solve your current quandary, my dear...
I would never abandon my faith, but on occasion I have been known to misplace it.
Try again.
Please.
You have to do something.

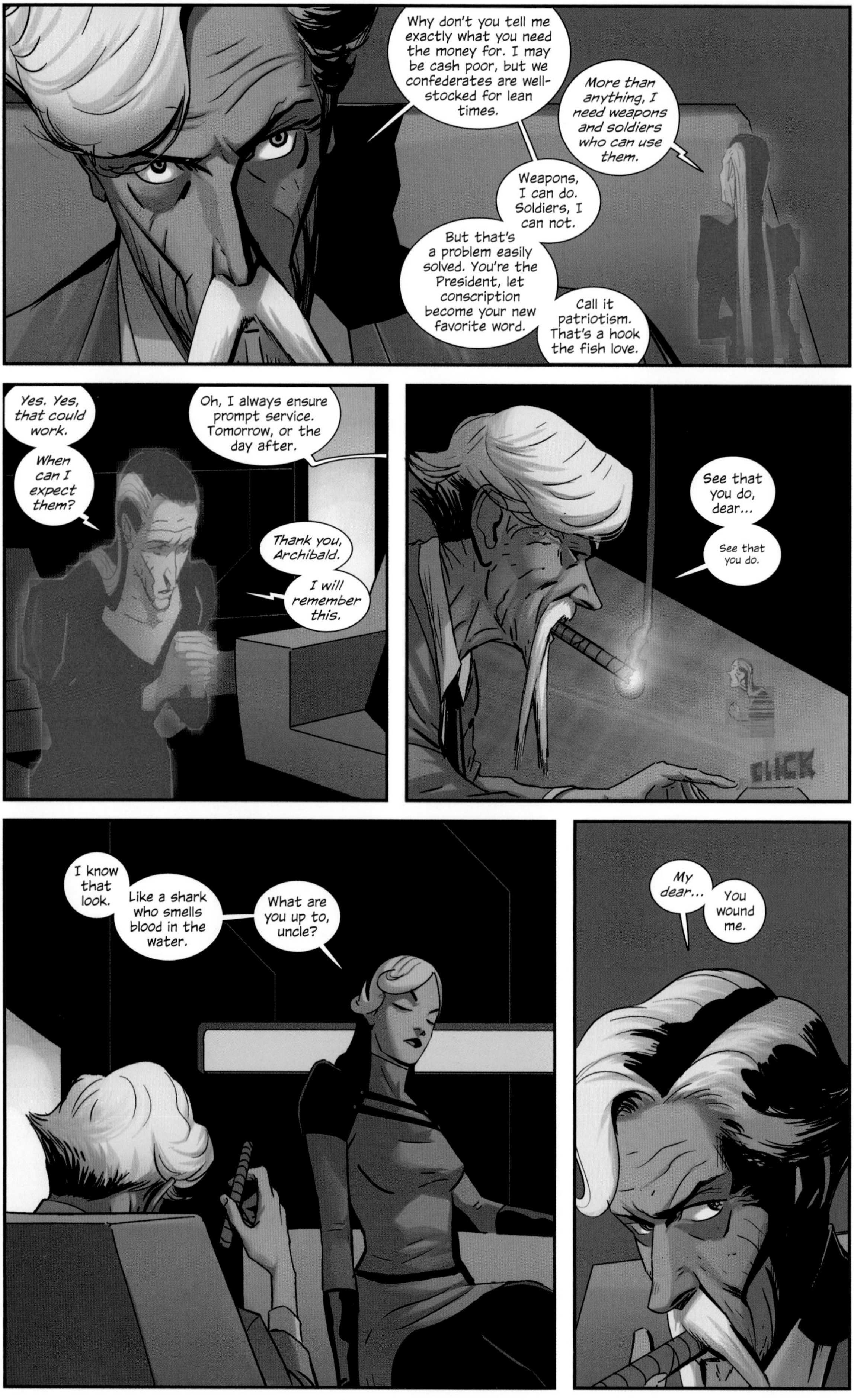
Why don't you tell me exactly what you need the money for. I may be cash poor, but we confederates are well-stocked for lean times.
More than anything, I need weapons and soldiers who can use them.
Weapons, I can do. Soldiers, I can not.
But that's a problem easily solved. You're the President, let conscription become your new favorite word.
Call it patriotism. That's a hook the fish love.
Yes. Yes, that could work.
When can I expect them?
Oh, I always ensure prompt service. Tomorrow, or the day after.
Thank you, Archibald.
I will remember this.
See that you do, dear...
See that you do.
CLICK
I know that look.
Like a shark who smells blood in the water.
What are you up to, uncle?
My dear...
You wound me.

BITE DOWN UNTIL YOU
FEEL **BONE.**

THIRTY-ONE:
WATCH US AS WE
ROB THEM **BLIND**

SUFFER YOUR **SONS** AND
DAUGHTERS

FOR **ONE DAY** THEY WILL
REPLACE YOU.

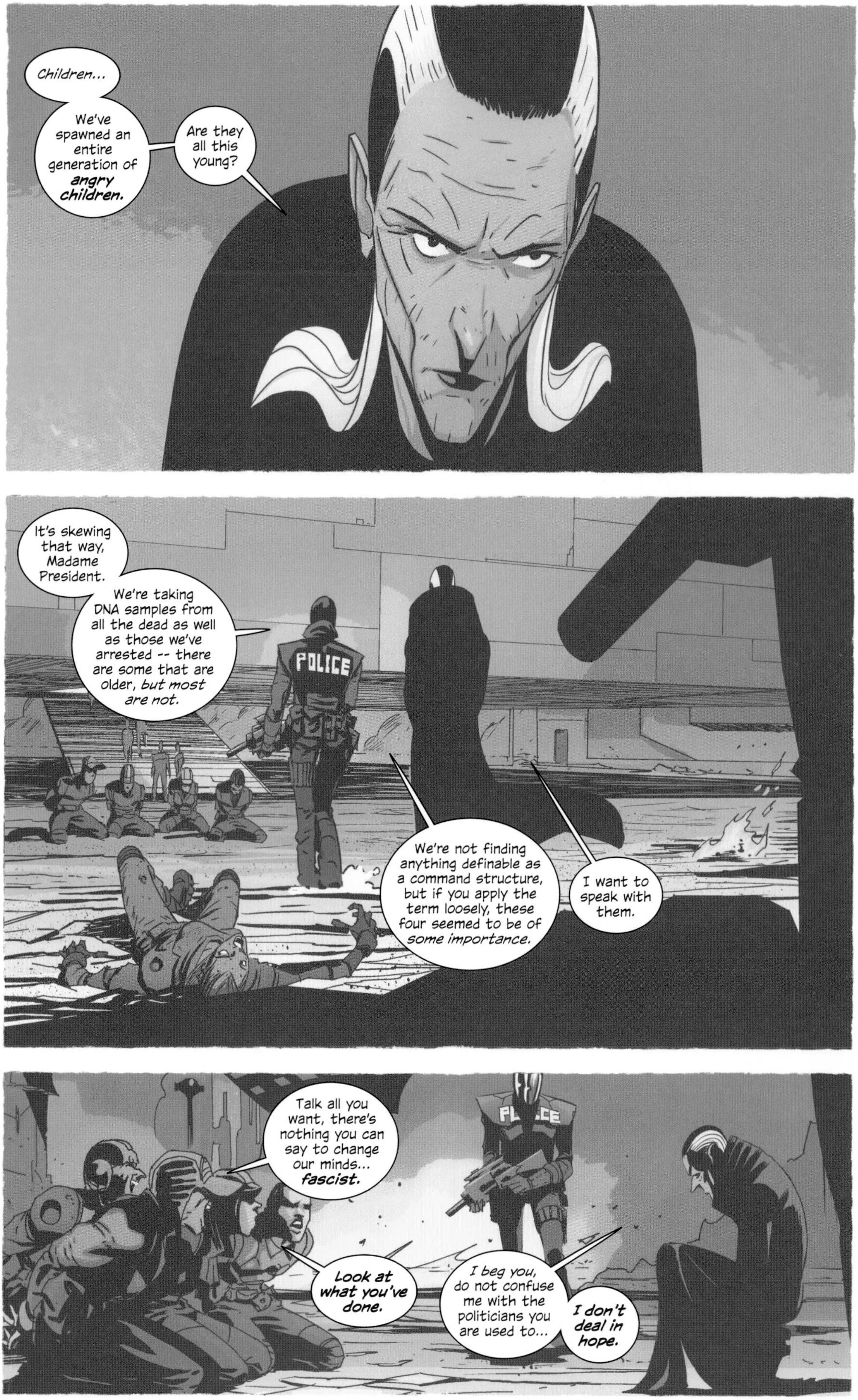
Children...
We've spawned an entire generation of *angry children.*
Are they all this young?
It's skewing that way, Madame President.
We're taking DNA samples from all the dead as well as those we've arrested -- there are some that are older, *but most are not.*
We're not finding anything definable as a command structure, but if you apply the term loosely, these four seemed to be of *some importance.*
I want to speak with them.
Talk all you want, there's nothing you can say to change our minds... ***fascist.***
Look at what you've done.
I beg you, do not confuse me with the politicians you are used to...
I don't deal in hope.

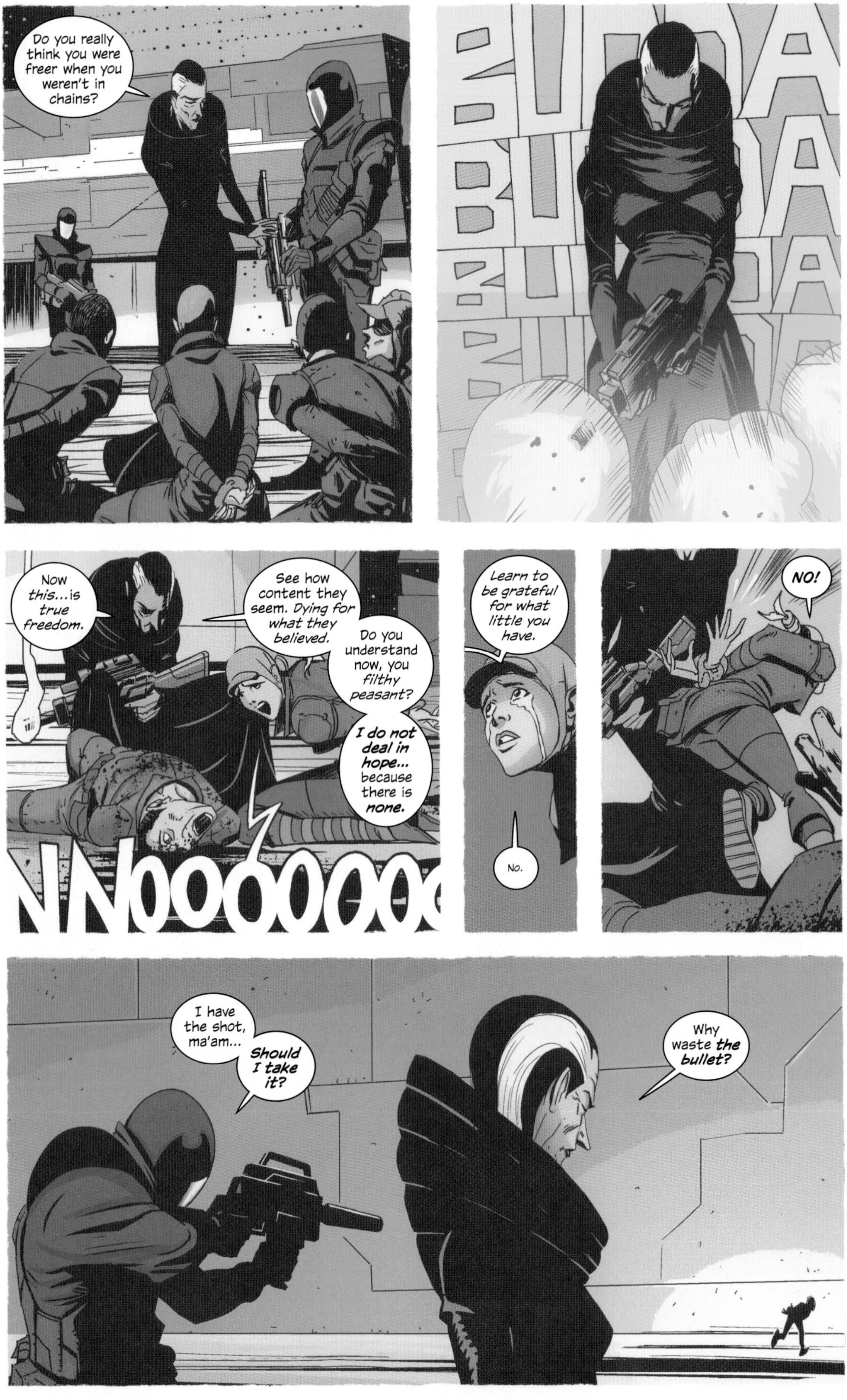
Do you really think you were freer when you weren't in chains?
BUDDA BUDDA BUDDA
Now this...is true freedom.
See how content they seem. Dying for what they believed.
Do you understand now, you filthy peasant?
I do not deal in hope... because there is none.
NNOOOOOO
Learn to be grateful for what little you have.
No.
NO!
I have the shot, ma'am... Should I take it?
Why waste the bullet?

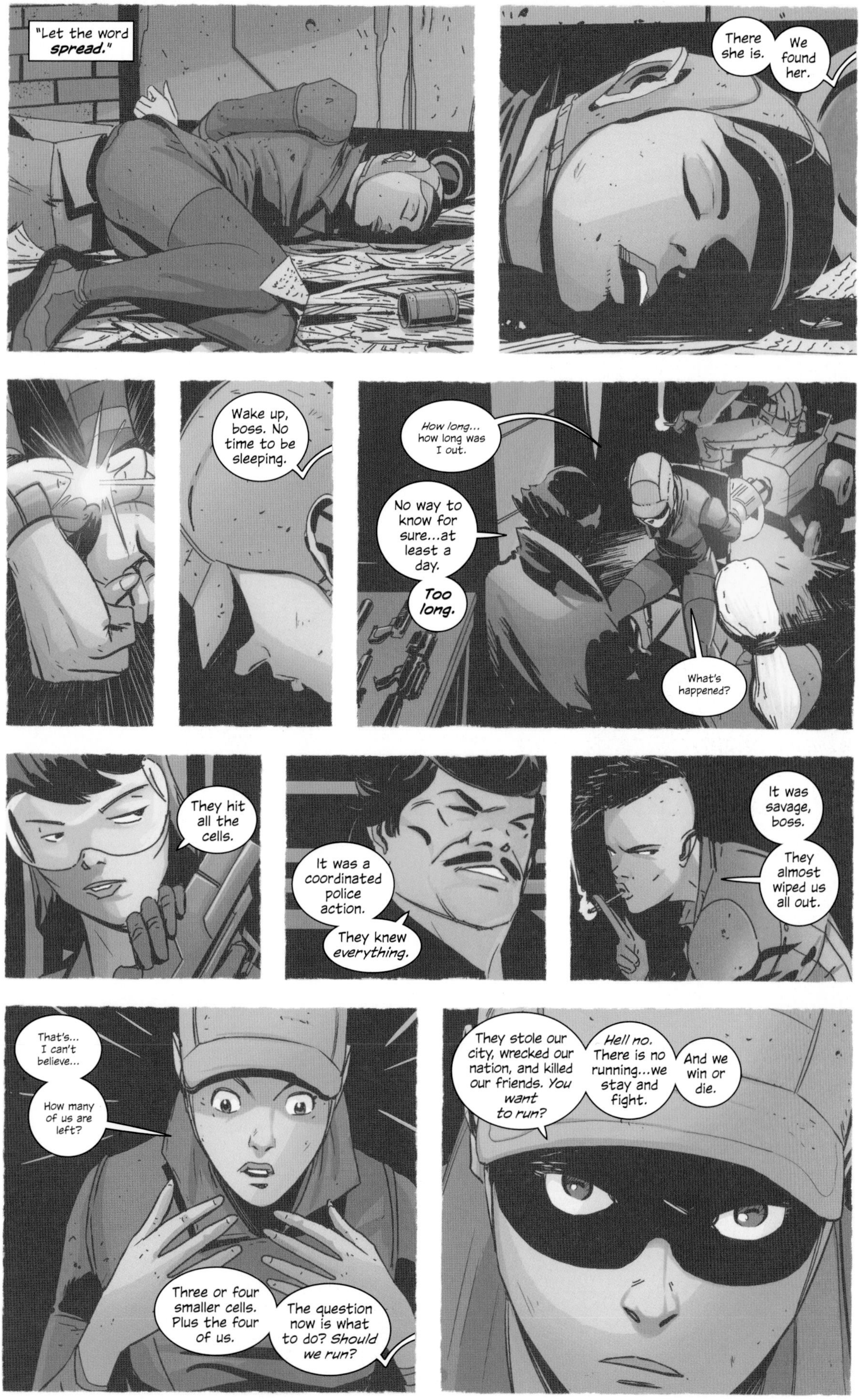
"Let the word *spread*."
There she is.
We found her.
Wake up, boss. No time to be sleeping.
How long... how long was I out.
No way to know for sure...at least a day.
Too long.
What's happened?
They hit all the cells.
It was a coordinated police action.
They knew *everything*.
It was savage, boss.
They almost wiped us all out.
That's... I can't believe...
How many of us are left?
Three or four smaller cells. Plus the four of us.
The question now is what to do? *Should we run?*
They stole our city, wrecked our nation, and killed our friends. *You want to run?*
Hell no. There is no running...we stay and fight.
And we win or die.

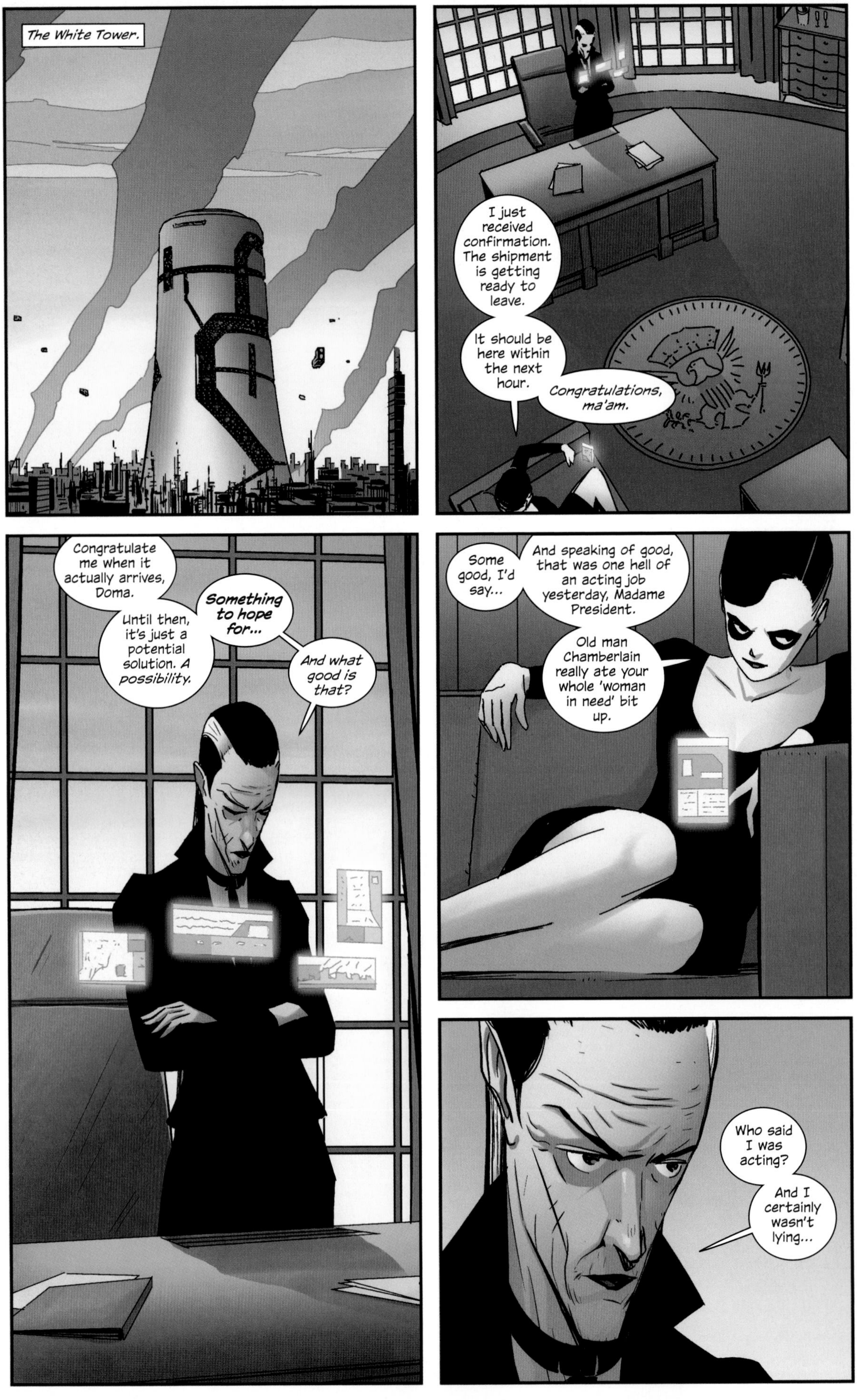
The White Tower.
I just received confirmation. The shipment is getting ready to leave.
It should be here within the next hour.
Congratulations, ma'am.
Congratulate me when it actually arrives, Doma.
Until then, it's just a potential solution. A possibility.
Something to hope for...
And what good is that?
Some good, I'd say...
And speaking of good, that was one hell of an acting job yesterday, Madame President.
Old man Chamberlain really ate your whole 'woman in need' bit up.
Who said I was acting?
And I certainly wasn't lying...

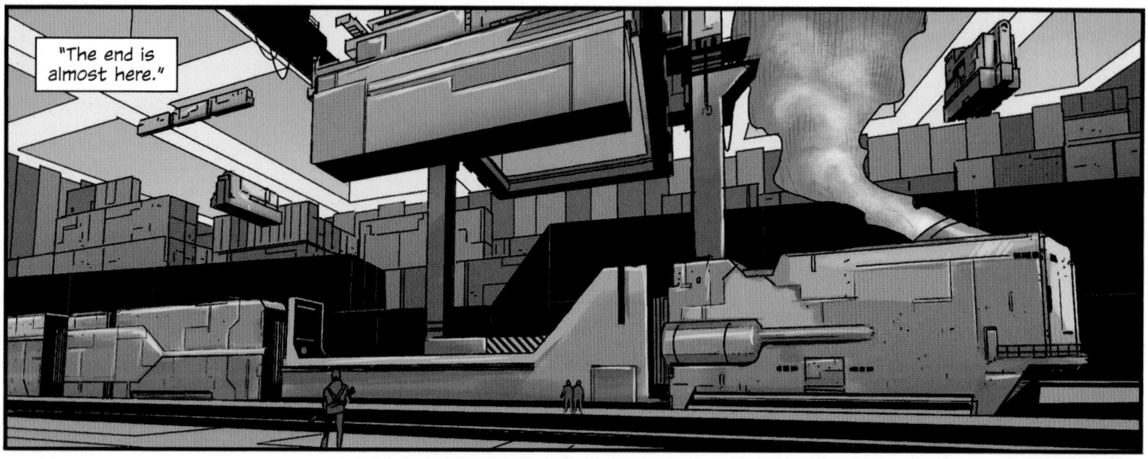
"The end is almost here."

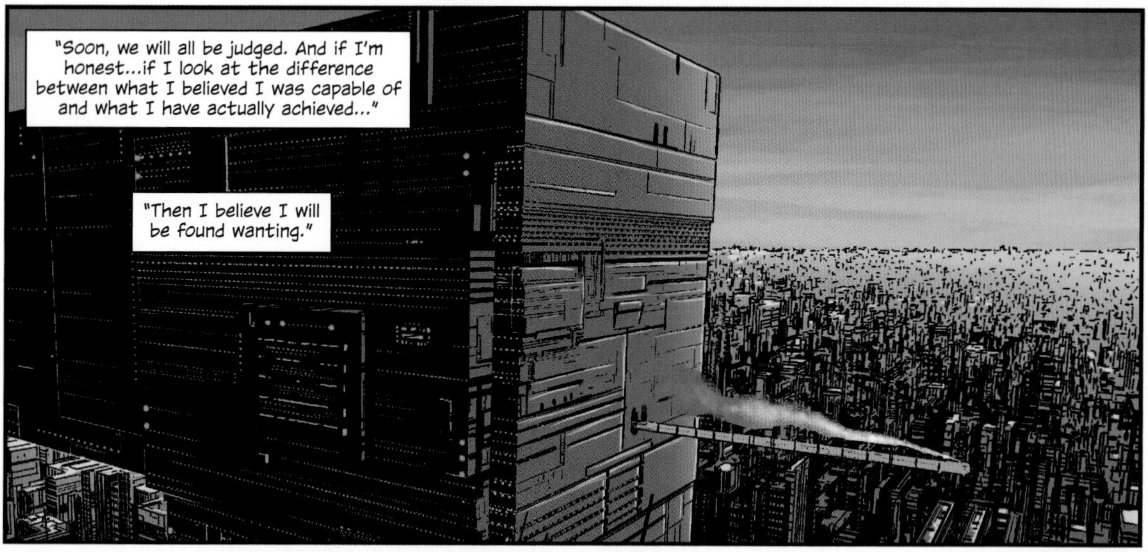
"Soon, we will all be judged. And if I'm honest...if I look at the difference between what I believed I was capable of and what I have actually achieved..."
"Then I believe I will be found wanting."

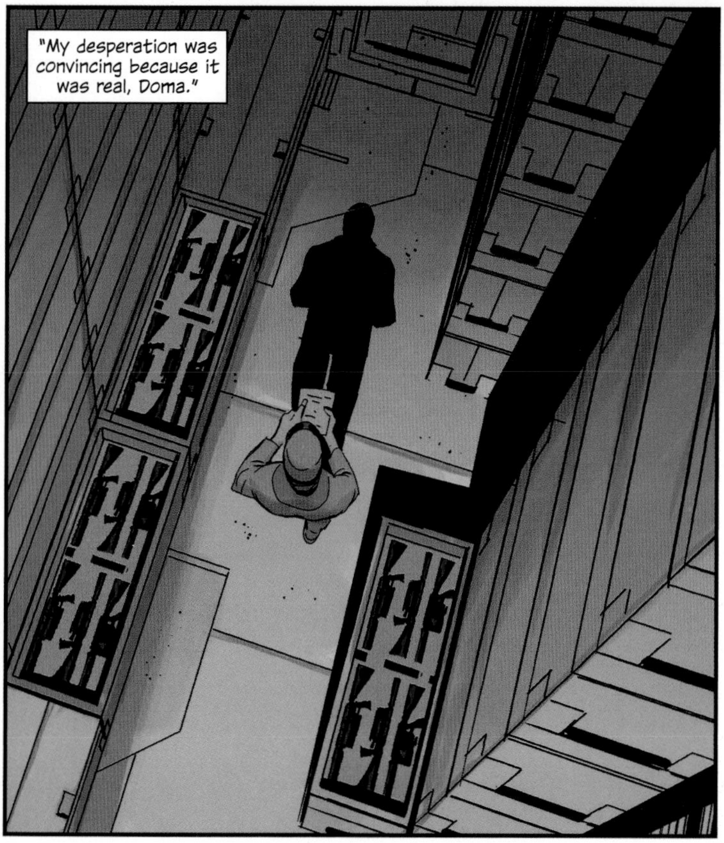
"My desperation was convincing because it was real, Doma."

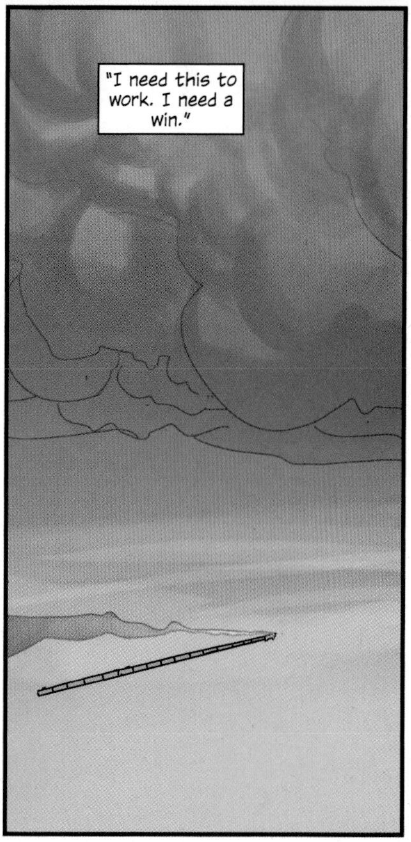
"I need this to work. I need a win."

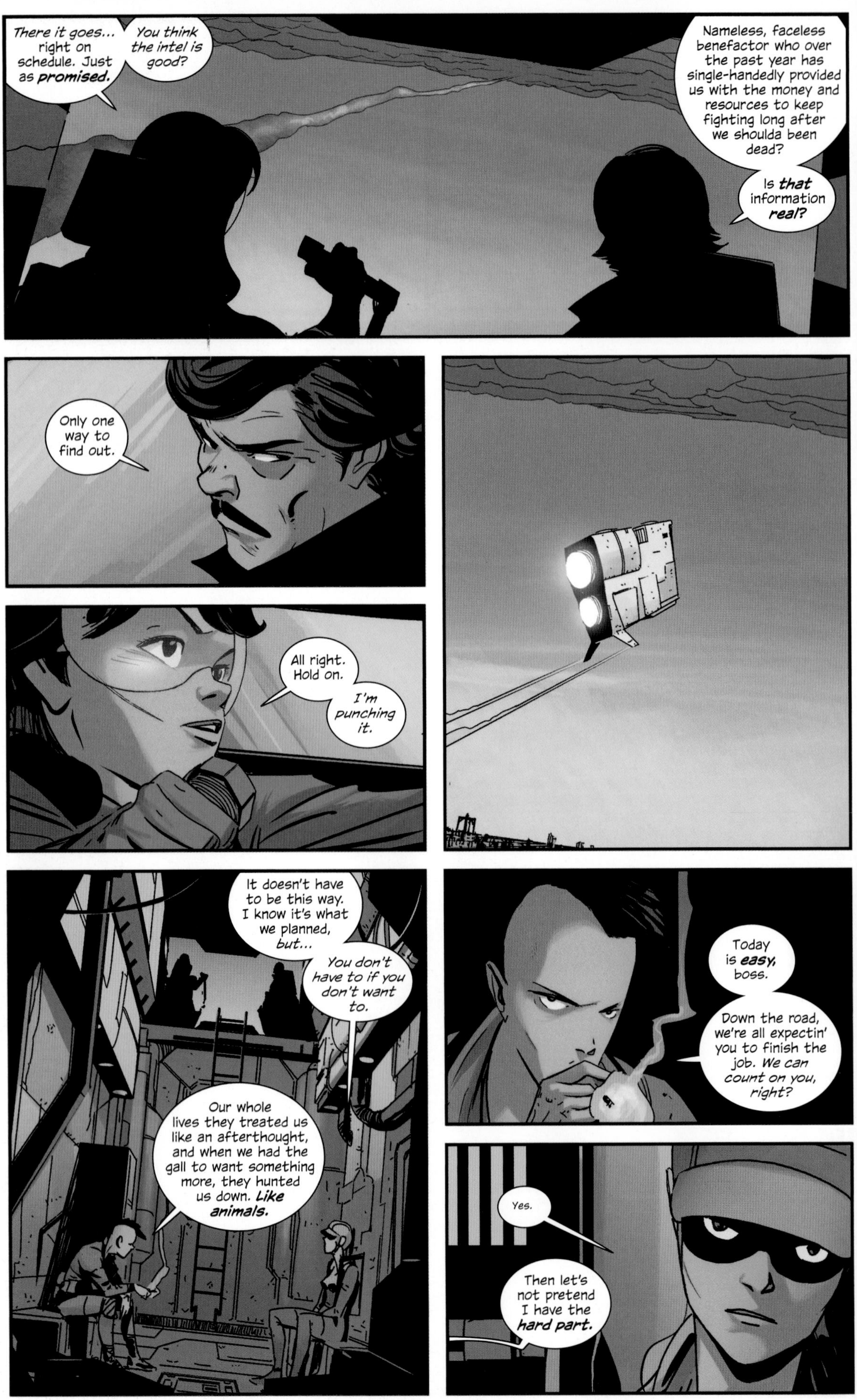
There it goes... right on schedule. Just as **promised.**
You think the intel is good?
Nameless, faceless benefactor who over the past year has single-handedly provided us with the money and resources to keep fighting long after we shoulda been dead?
Is ***that*** information ***real?***
Only one way to find out.
All right. Hold on.
I'm punching it.
It doesn't have to be this way. I know it's what we planned, *but...*
You don't have to if you don't want to.
Our whole lives they treated us like an afterthought, and when we had the gall to want something more, they hunted us down. ***Like animals.***
Today is ***easy,*** boss.
Down the road, we're all expectin' you to finish the job. *We can count on you, right?*
Yes.
Then let's not pretend I have the ***hard part.***

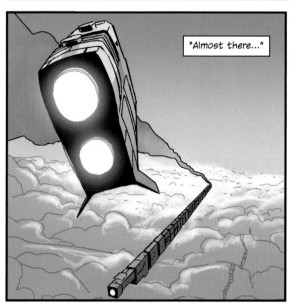

"Almost there..."

"Nice and easy..."

"Just like putting a baby to sleep."

TINK!

Solid?

Yep. Got a green light.

Good luck!

We're locked on.

Time to go.

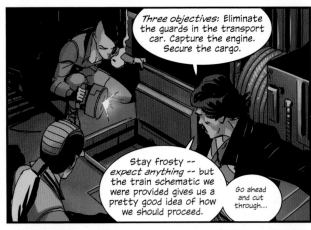

Three objectives: Eliminate the guards in the transport car. Capture the engine. Secure the cargo.

Stay frosty -- expect anything -- but the train schematic we were provided gives us a pretty good idea of how we should proceed.

Go ahead and cut through...

TONG

All clear.

Okay...

Everyone remember to keep their comms active just in case something goes wrong.

Best way into the engine is from topside. There's an access hatch.

Yeah. On it.

Which leaves the cargo hold for me.

The transport car should be the third from the engine, boss.

Work your way through. Make sure there's no one in-between the car and us.

"Here we go."

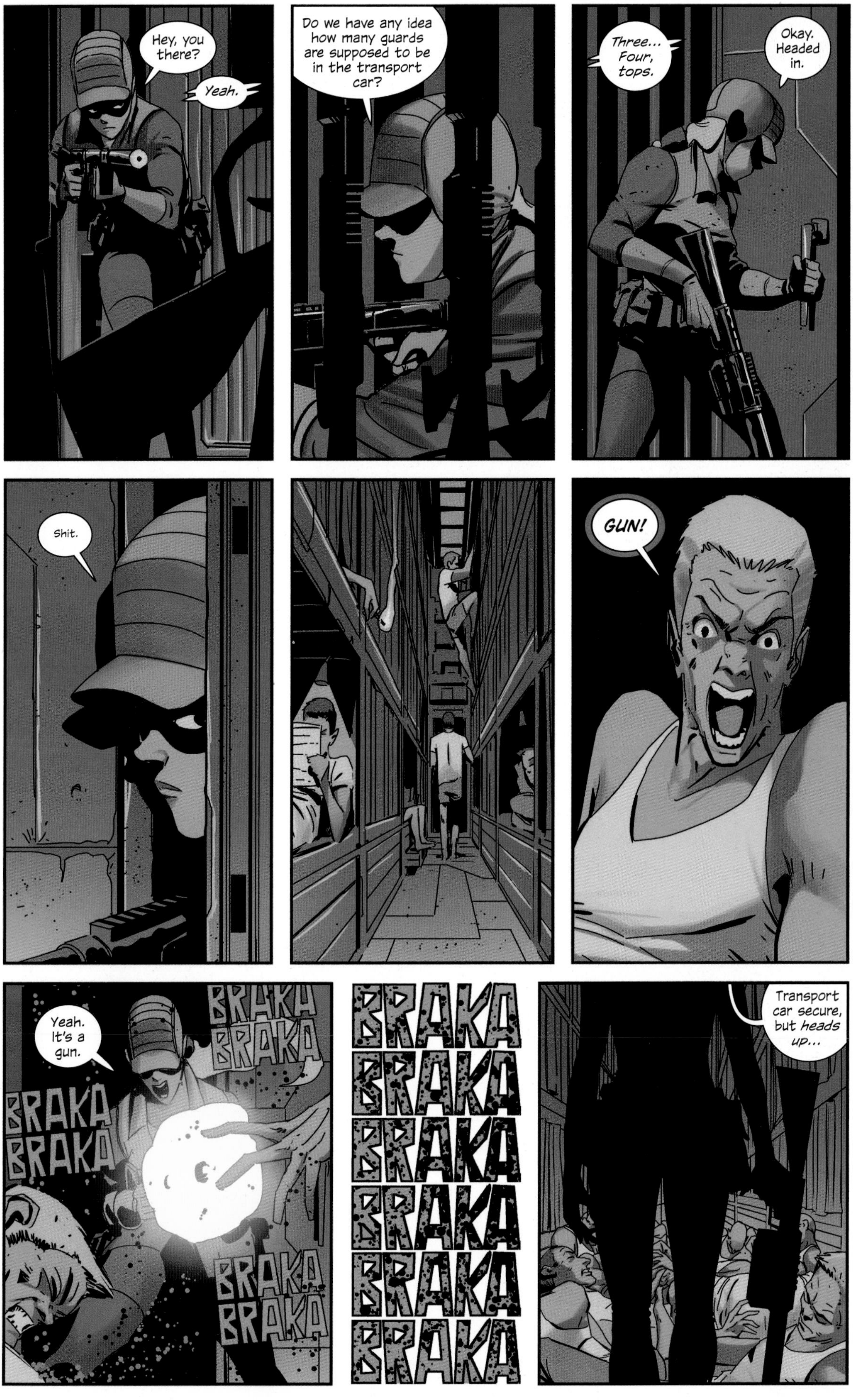
Hey, you there?
Yeah.
Do we have any idea how many guards are supposed to be in the transport car?
Three... Four, tops.
Okay. Headed in.
Shit.
GUN!
Yeah. It's a gun.
BRAKA BRAKA
BRAKA BRAKA
BRAKA BRAKA
BRAKA BRAKA BRAKA BRAKA BRAKA BRAKA
Transport car secure, but *heads up*...

I think one made it out.

Yeah.

I see him.

Not gonna be a problem.

Headed to the engine.

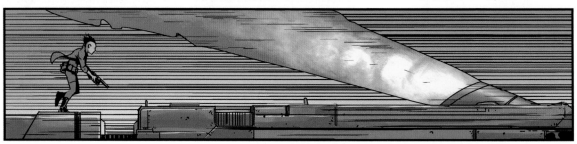

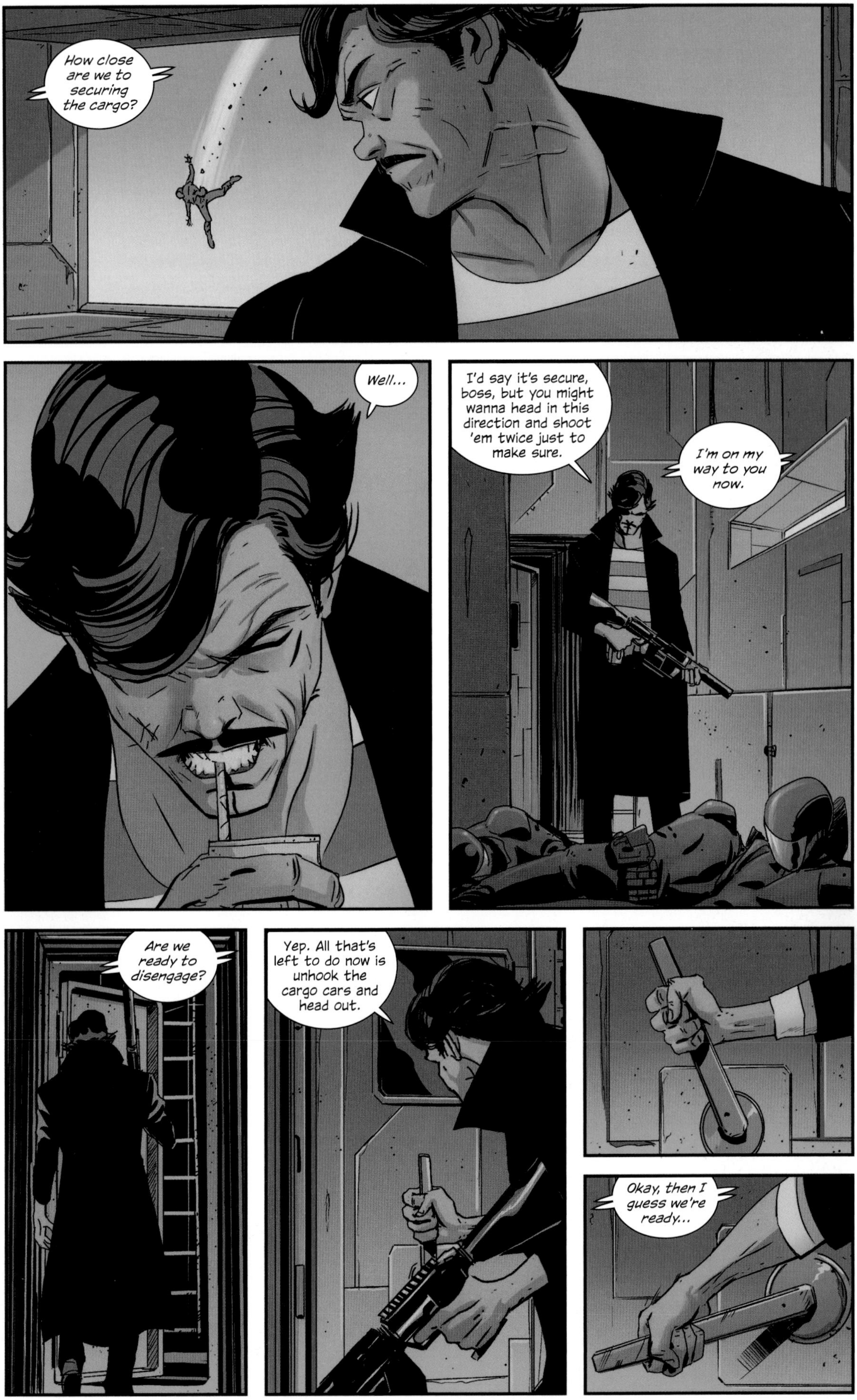
How close are we to securing the cargo?
Well...
I'd say it's secure, boss, but you might wanna head in this direction and shoot 'em twice just to make sure.
I'm on my way to you now.
Are we ready to disengage?
Yep. All that's left to do now is unhook the cargo cars and head out.
Okay, then I guess we're ready...

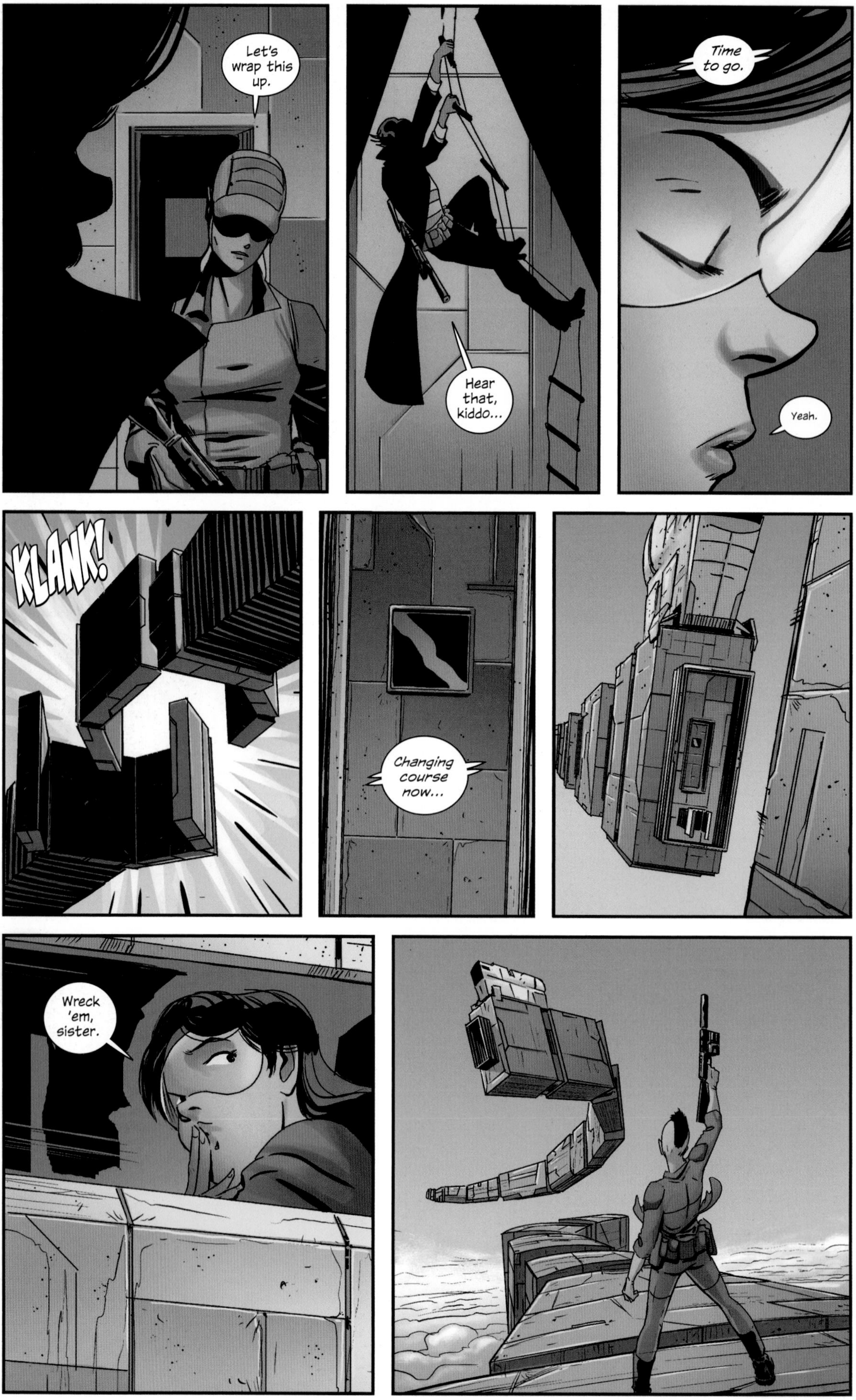
Let's wrap this up.
Hear that, kiddo...
Time to go.
Yeah.
KLANK!
Changing course now...
Wreck 'em, sister.

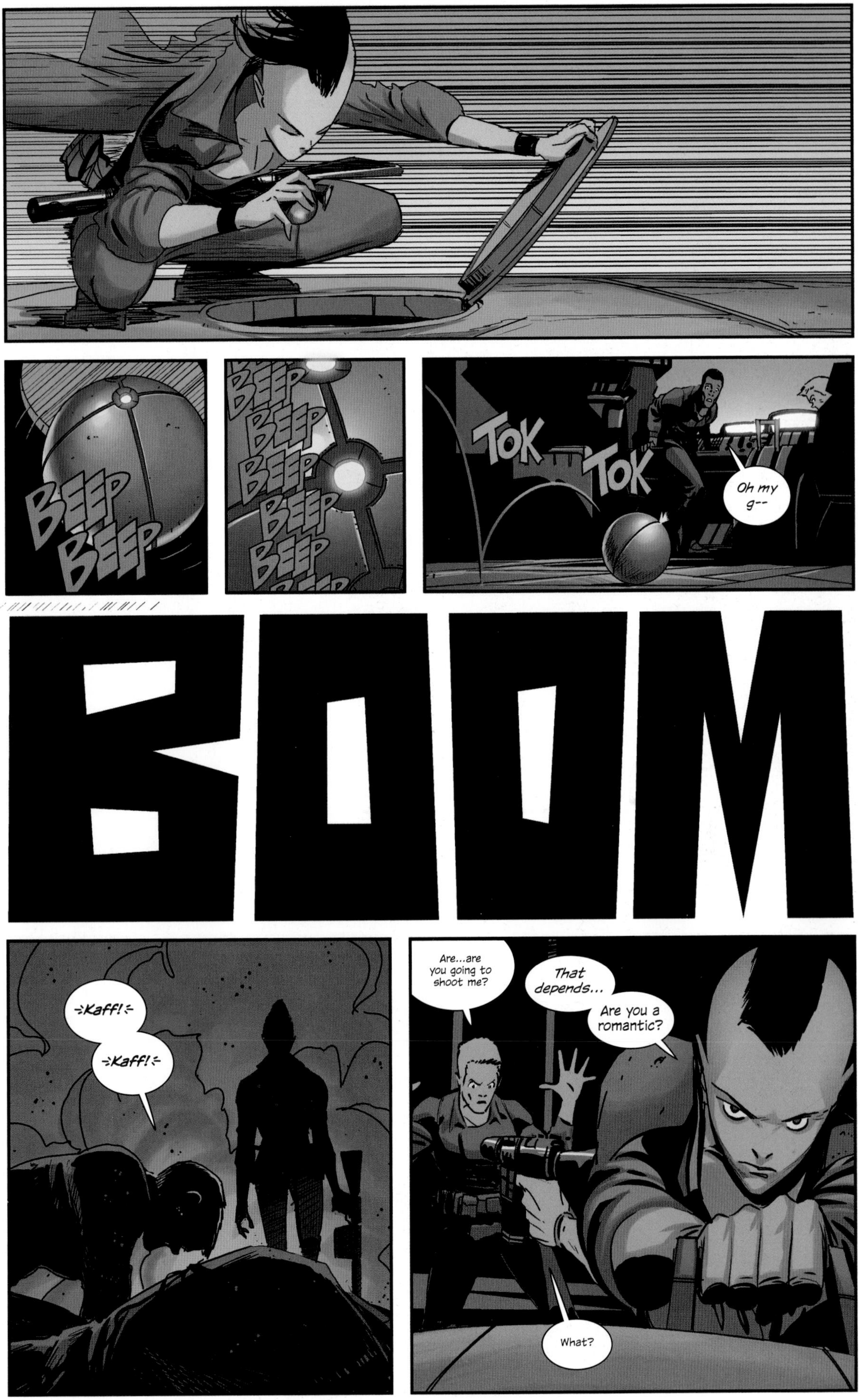
BEEP BEEP
BEEP BEEP BEEP BEEP BEEP
TOK TOK
Oh my g--
BOOM
-Kaff!-
-Kaff!-
Are...are you going to shoot me?
That depends...
Are you a romantic?
What?

PING!

Aaannd I just got confirmation from aviation command...

The shipment has entered our airspace.

Am I allowed to say congratulations now?

Yes... I think you are.

Well, then...

Congratulations, ma'am.

It's like a weight off my chest. Like breathing again after almost drowning.

I must say, Doma, for those such as you and I who are heavily invested in the collapse...I am continually shocked by just how perilous the end times are.

Frankly, when it doesn't make me furious...I find it so very fucking depressing...

But then you have a day like *this.*

TING

When there's a little order to the chaos -- *the clouds part* -- and you know that things are, once again, realigning for your betterment.

So...thank you for your congratulations, Doma...

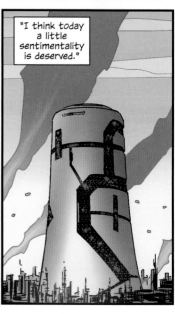

"I think today a little sentimentality is deserved."

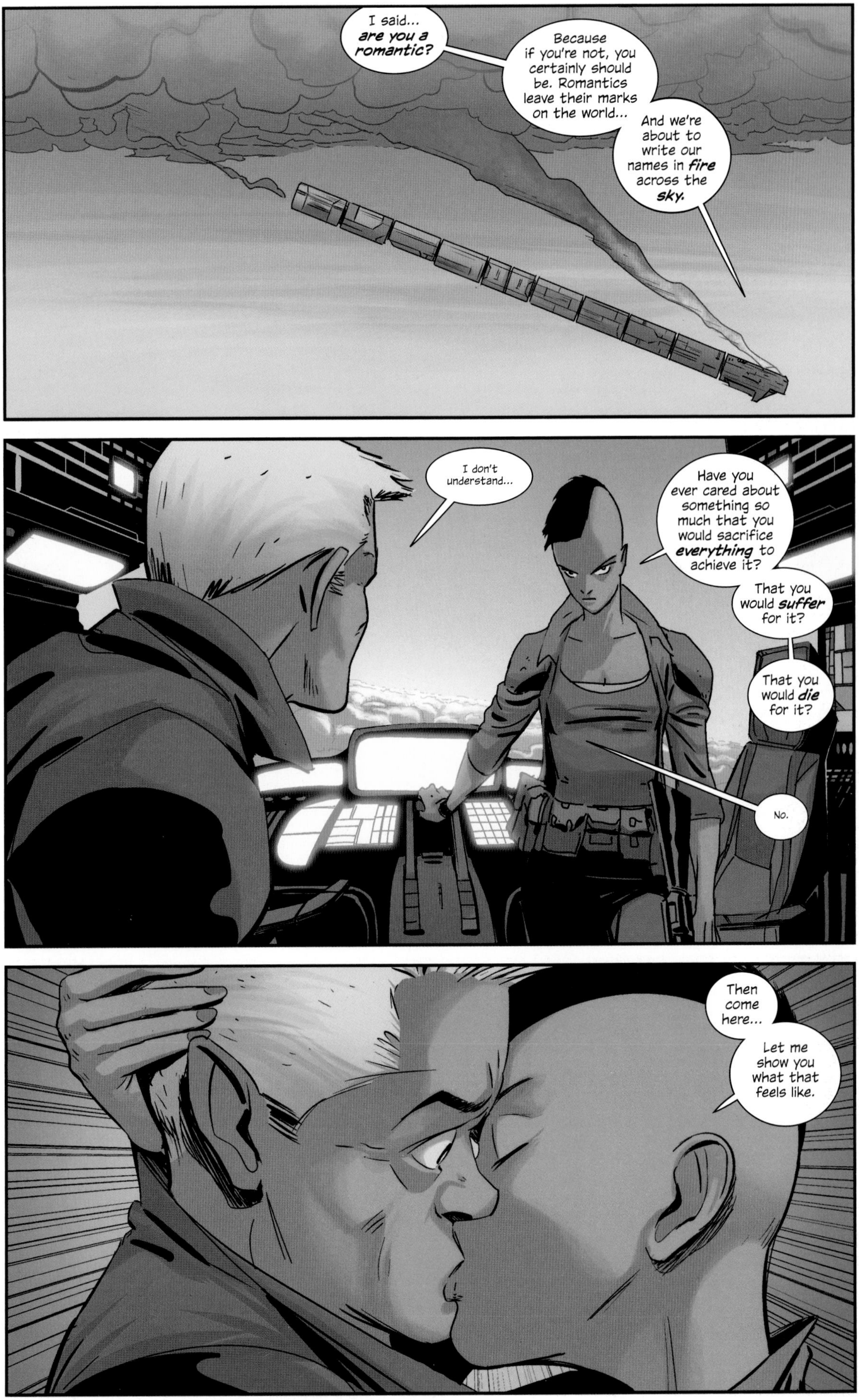
I said... **are you a romantic?**
Because if you're not, you certainly should be. Romantics leave their marks on the world...
And we're about to write our names in ***fire*** across the ***sky.***
I don't understand...
Have you ever cared about something so much that you would sacrifice ***everything*** to achieve it?
That you would ***suffer*** for it?
That you would ***die*** for it?
No.
Then come here...
Let me show you what that feels like.

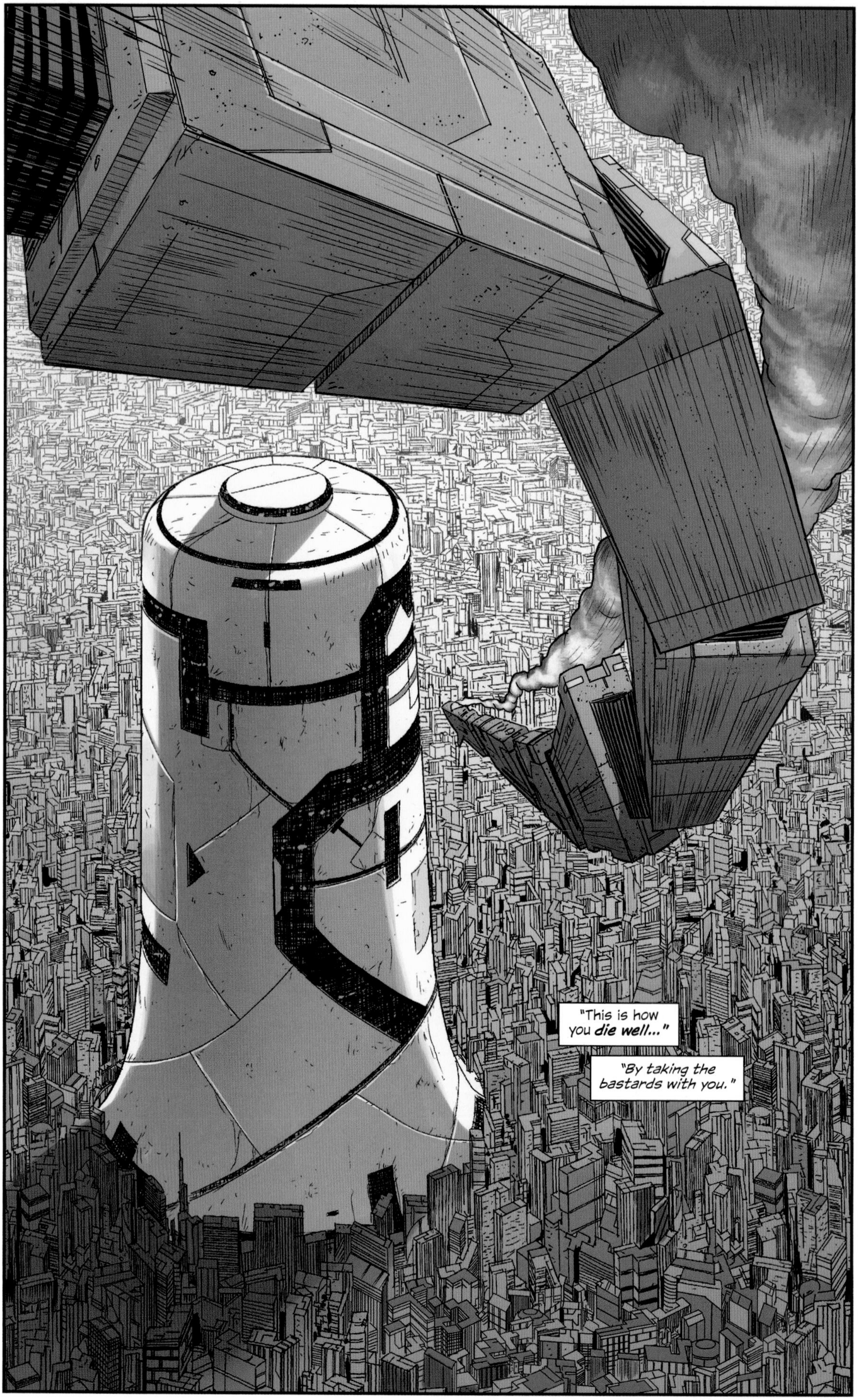
"This is how you **die well...**"
"By taking the bastards with you."

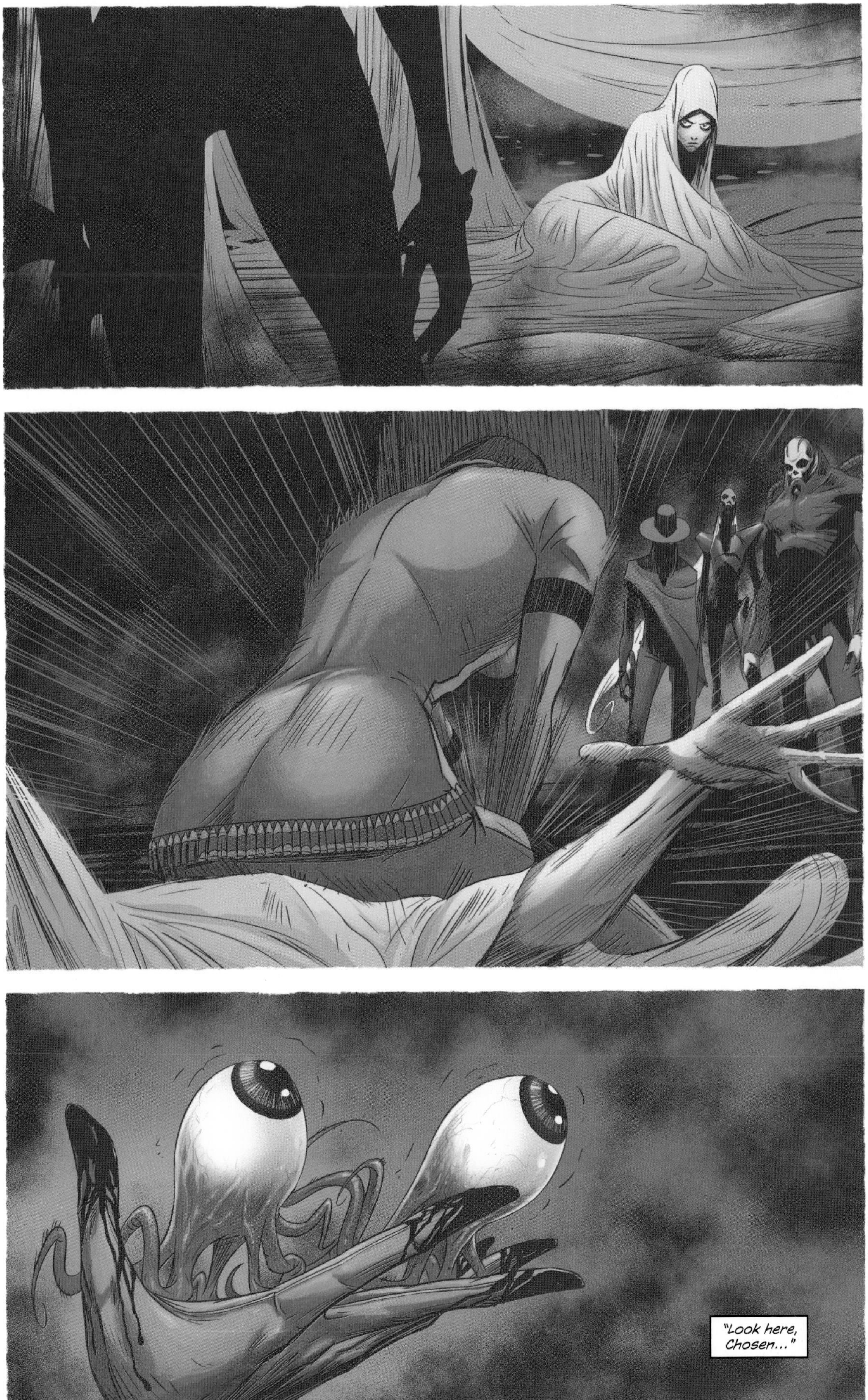
"Look here, Chosen..."

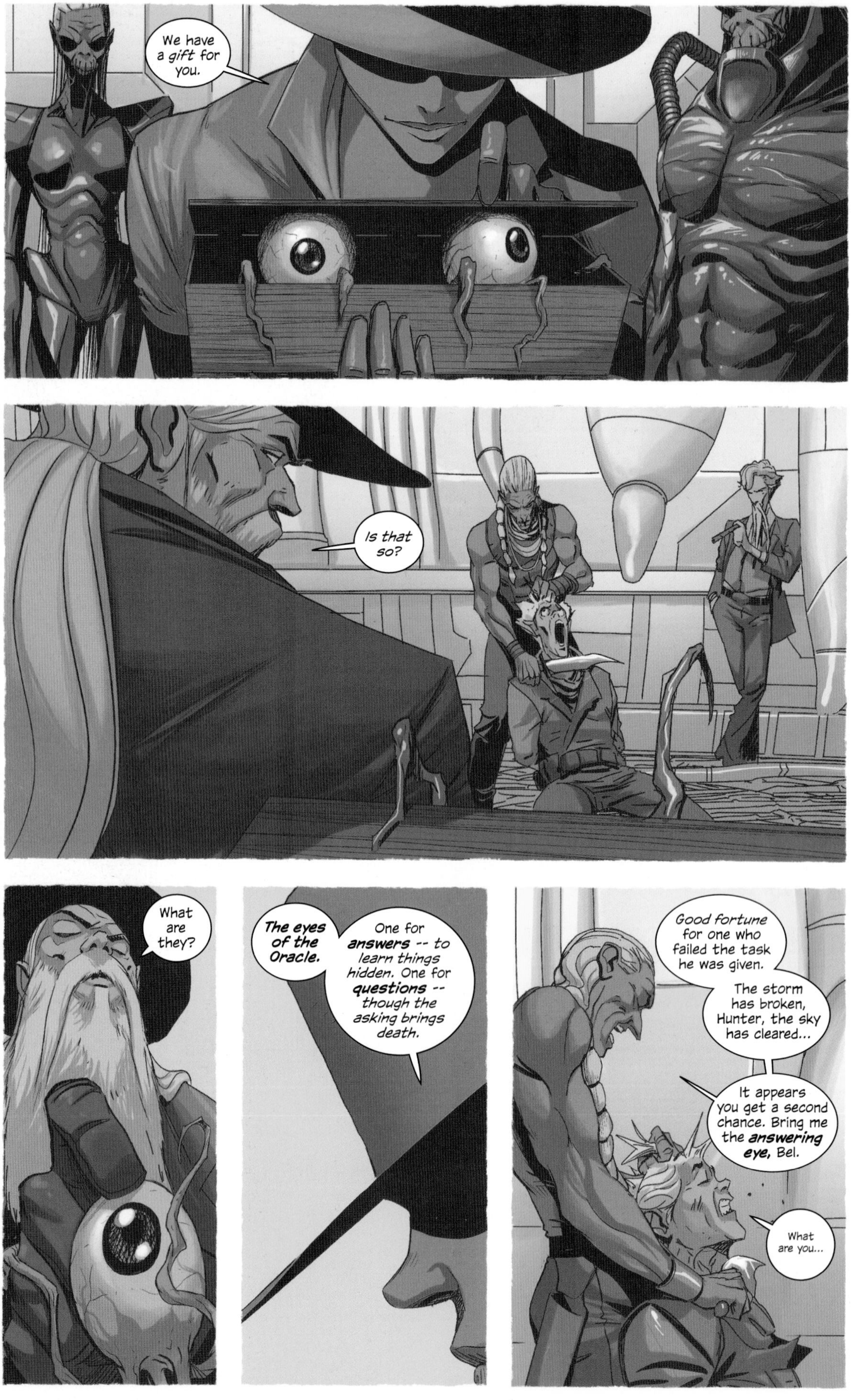
We have a *gift* for you.
Is that so?
What are they?
The eyes of the Oracle.
One for **answers** -- to learn things hidden. One for **questions** -- though the asking brings death.
Good fortune for one who failed the task he was given.
The storm has broken, Hunter, the sky has cleared...
It appears you get a second chance. Bring me the ***answering eye,*** Bel.
What are you...

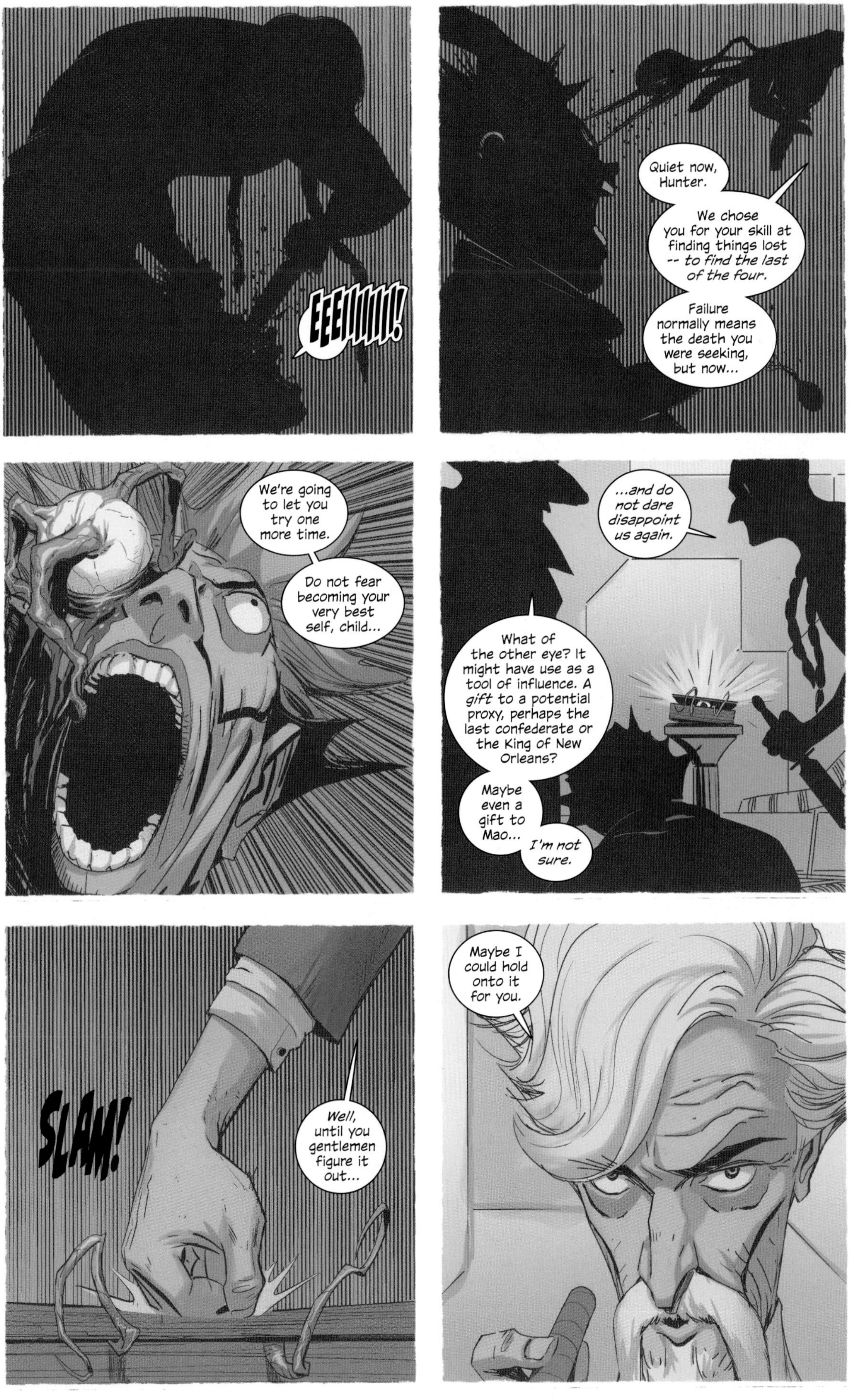
EEEIIIIIII!
Quiet now, Hunter.
We chose you for your skill at finding things lost -- *to find the last of the four.*
Failure normally means the death you were seeking, but now...
We're going to let you try one more time.
Do not fear becoming your very best self, child...
...and do not dare disappoint us again.
What of the other eye? It might have use as a tool of influence. A *gift* to a potential proxy, perhaps the last confederate or the King of New Orleans?
Maybe even a gift to Mao...
I'm not sure.
SLAM!
Well, until you gentlemen figure it out...
Maybe I could hold onto it for you.

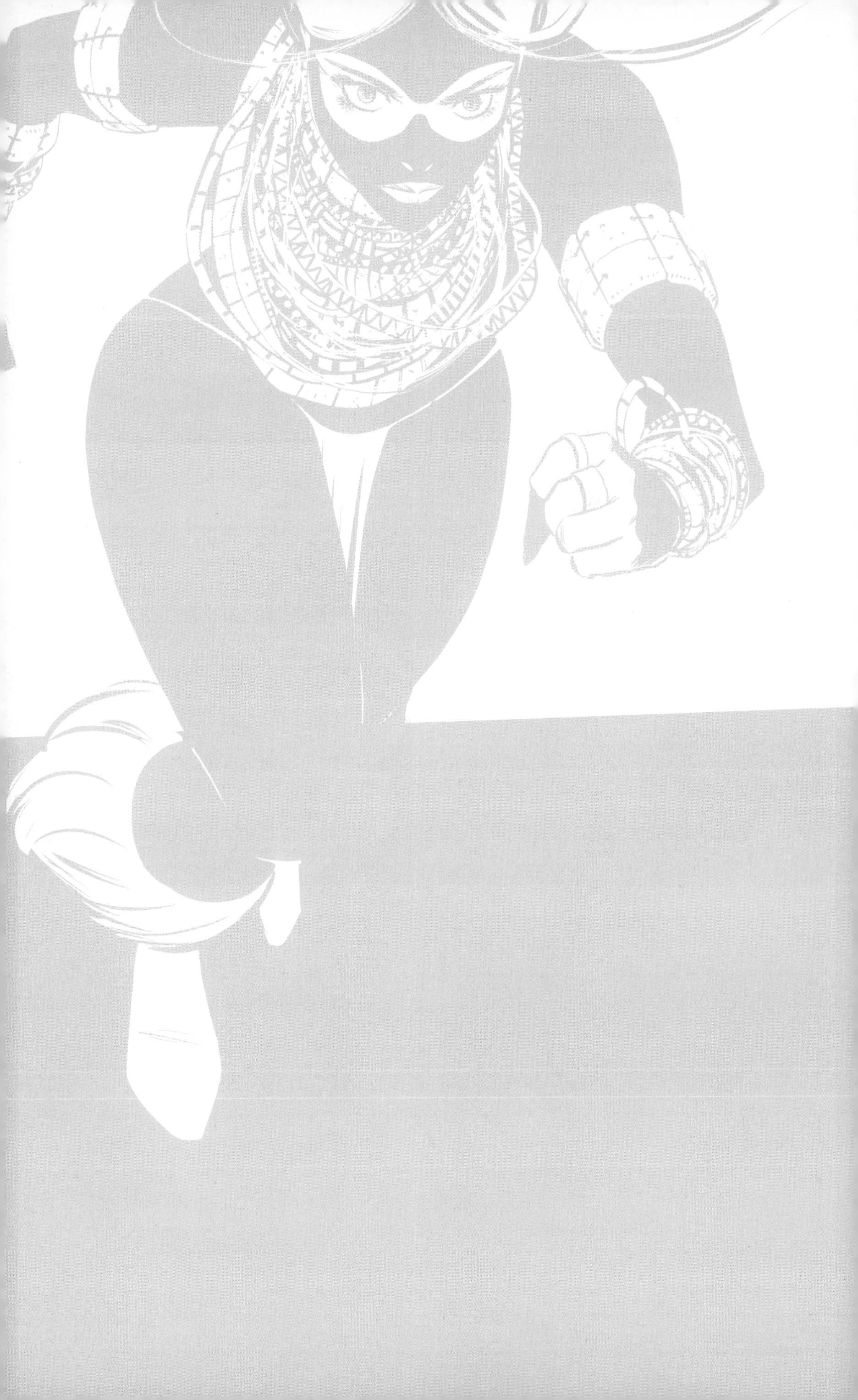

THIRTY-TWO:
THE **MAN** MAKES
A **MOVE**

JUST BECAUSE YOU DON'T
SEE THE **STRINGS.**

DOESN'T MEAN YOU'RE NOT
A **PUPPET.**

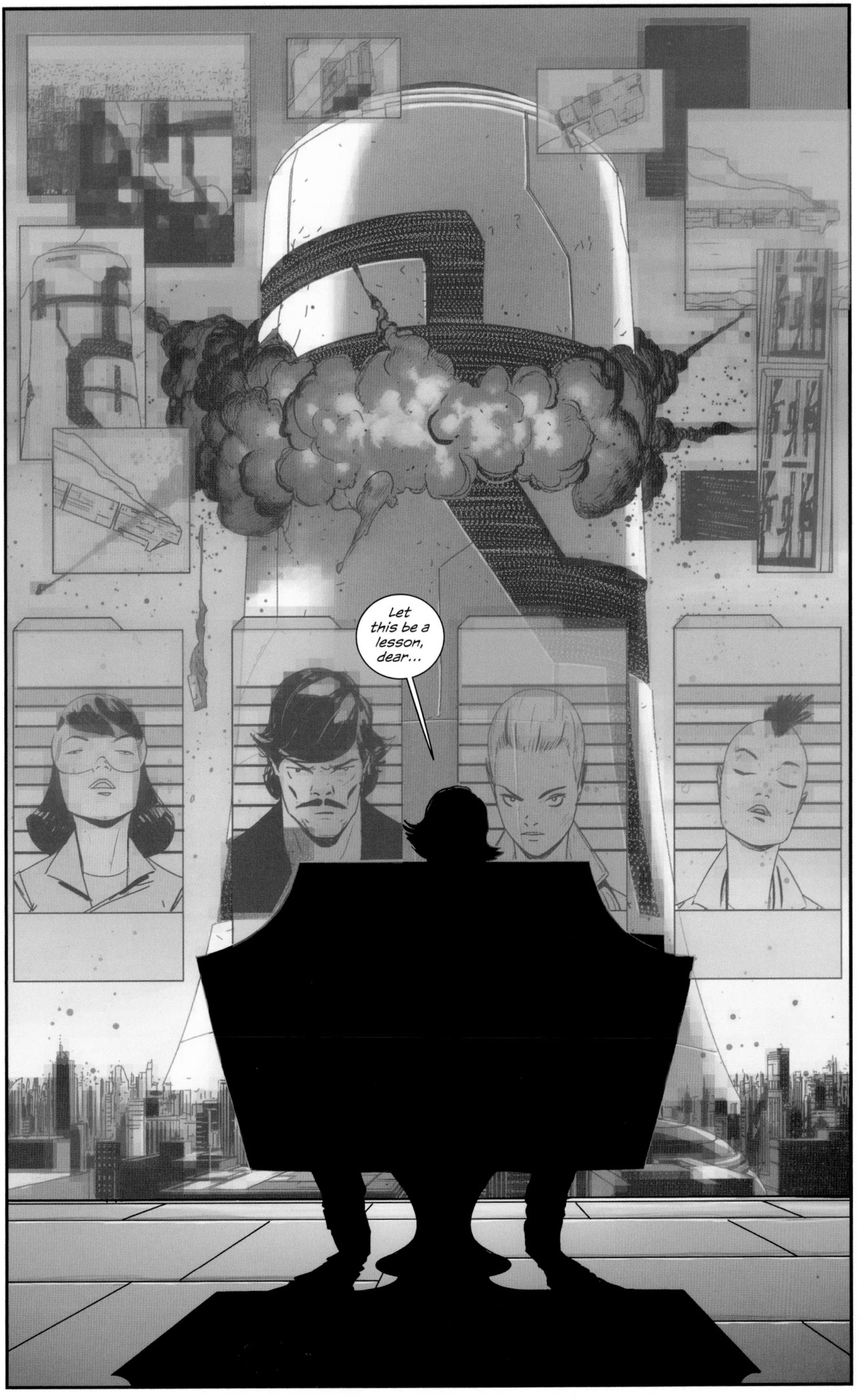
Let this be a lesson, dear...

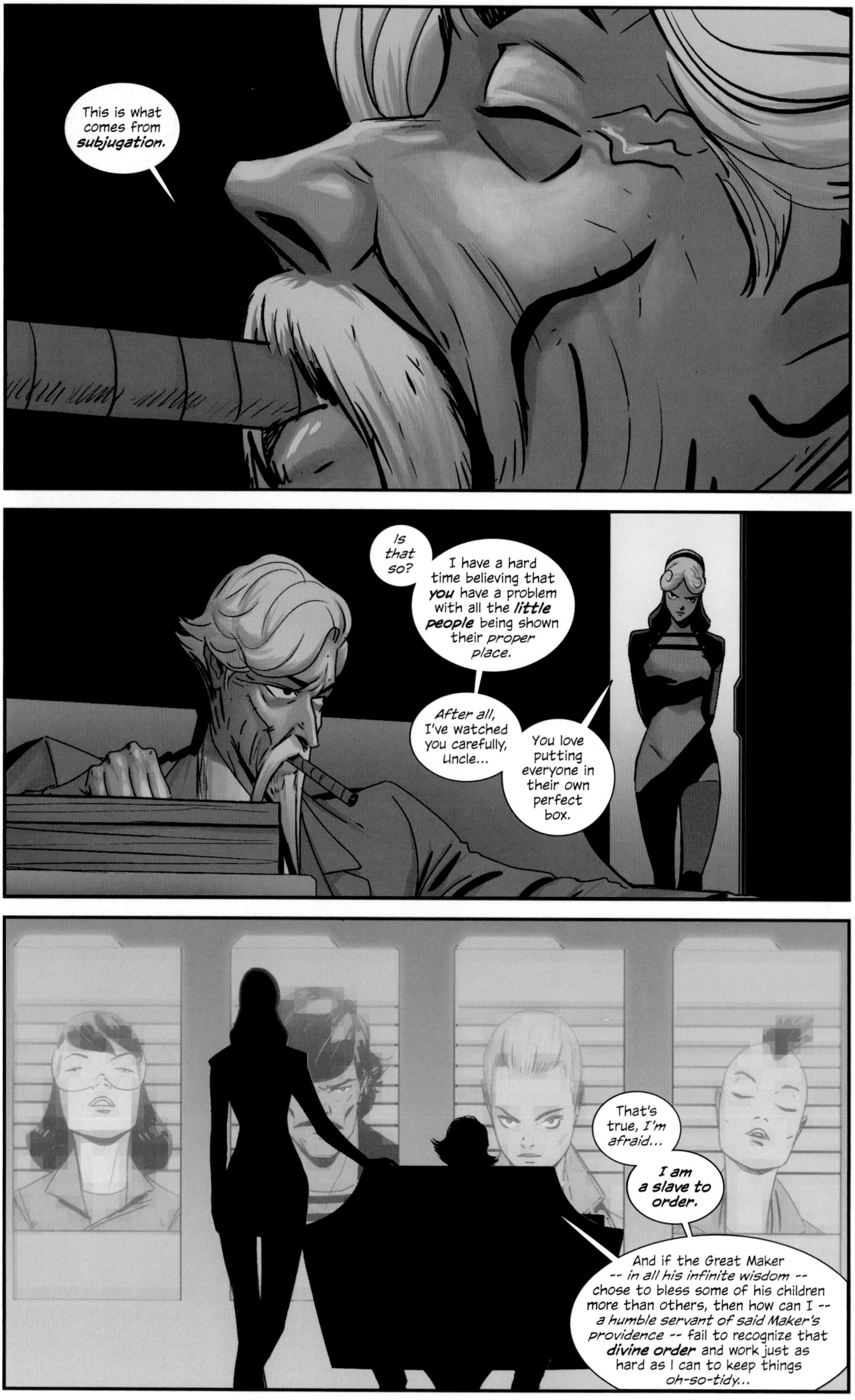
This is what comes from subjugation.
Is that so?
I have a hard time believing that you have a problem with all the little people being shown their proper place.
After all, I've watched you carefully, Uncle...
You love putting everyone in their own perfect box.
That's true, I'm afraid...
I am a slave to order.
And if the Great Maker -- in all his infinite wisdom -- chose to bless some of his children more than others, then how can I -- a humble servant of said Maker's providence -- fail to recognize that divine order and work just as hard as I can to keep things oh-so-tidy...

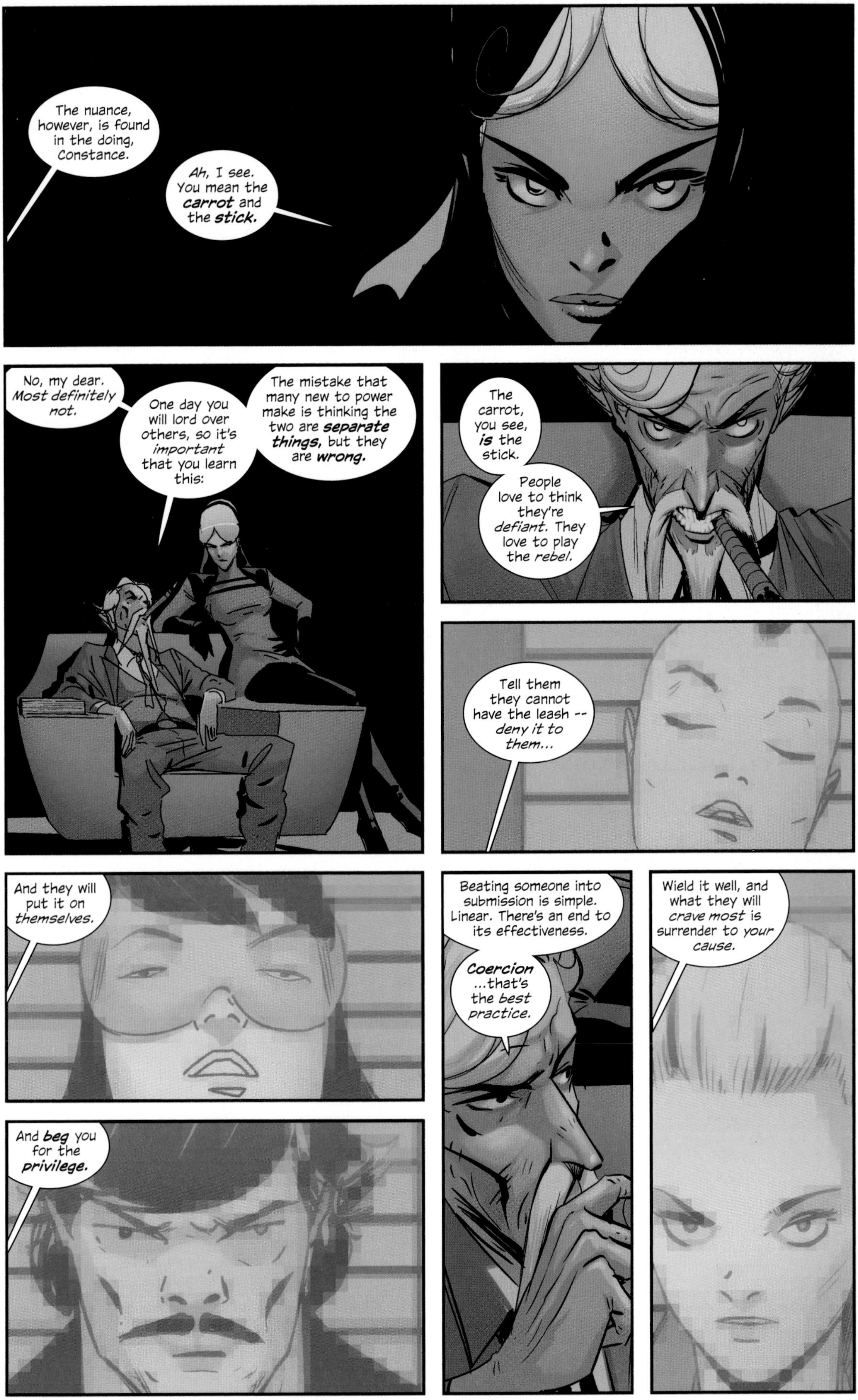
The nuance, however, is found in the doing, Constance.
Ah, I see. You mean the ***carrot*** and the ***stick.***
No, my dear. *Most definitely not.*
One day you will lord over others, so it's *important* that you learn this:
The mistake that many new to power make is thinking the two are ***separate things,*** but they are ***wrong.***
The carrot, you see, ***is*** the stick.
People love to think they're *defiant.* They love to play the *rebel.*
Tell them they cannot have the leash -- *deny it to them...*
And they will put it on *themselves.*
And ***beg*** you for the ***privilege.***
Beating someone into submission is simple. Linear. There's an end to its effectiveness.
Coercion ...that's the *best practice.*
Wield it well, and what they will *crave most* is surrender to *your cause.*

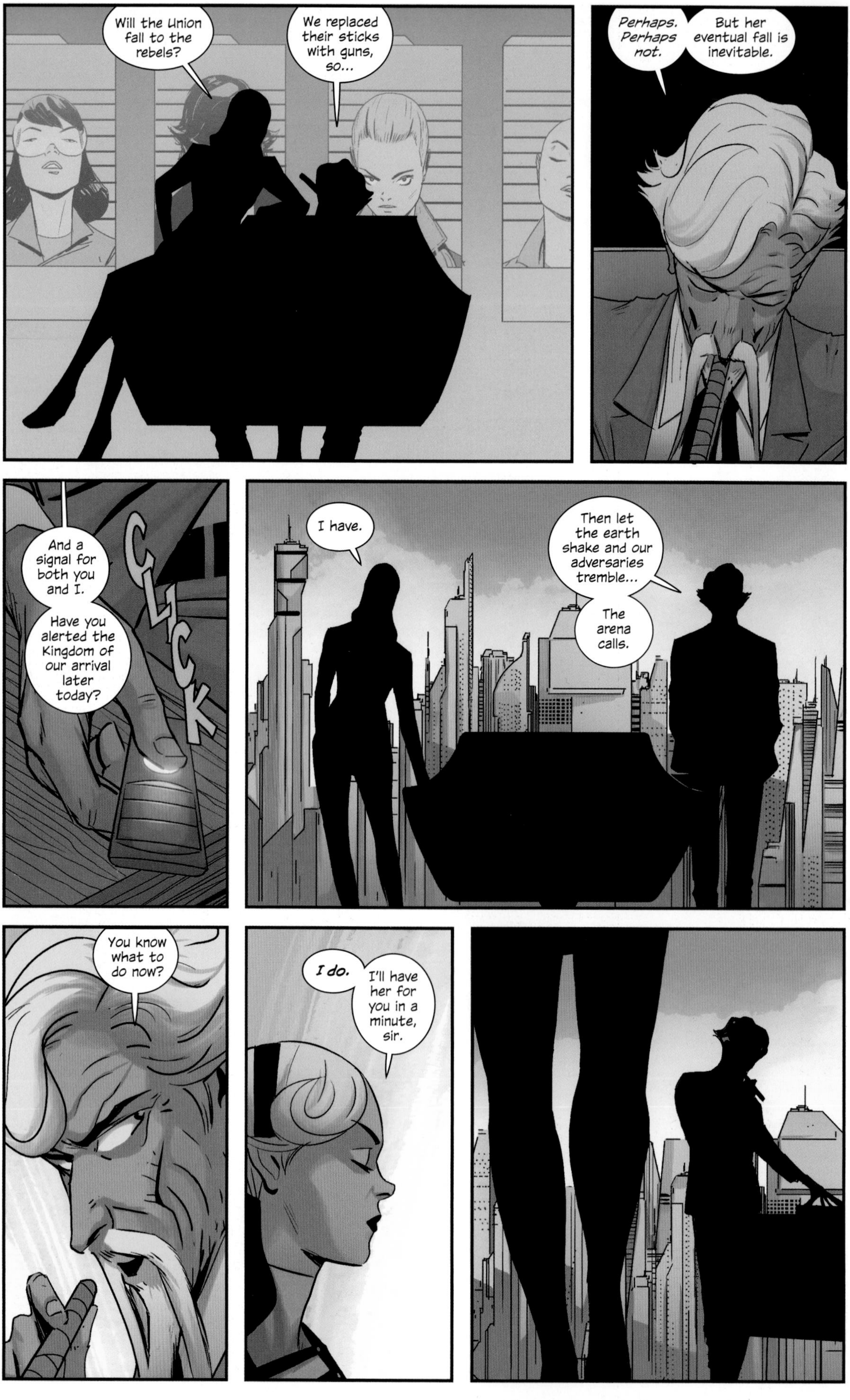
Will the Union fall to the rebels?
We replaced their sticks with guns, so...
Perhaps. Perhaps not.
But her eventual fall is inevitable.
And a signal for both you and I.
Have you alerted the Kingdom of our arrival later today?
CLICK
I have.
Then let the earth shake and our adversaries tremble...
The arena calls.
You know what to do now?
I do.
I'll have her for you in a minute, sir.

?
?
I take it you disagree?
To thine own self, art thou true?
You want to know what you should do?
Is this truly your time? Is your ascendance nigh?
Would a truly clever man give only violence a try?
Listen here, you unfettered, feckless organ...
If you are trying to **deter** me, then you'll have to do better than that.
And if you are trying to **goad** me...

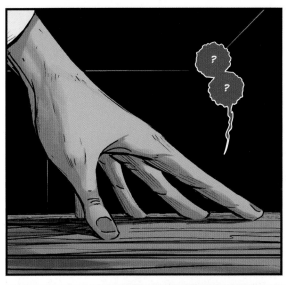

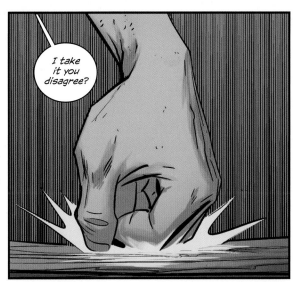

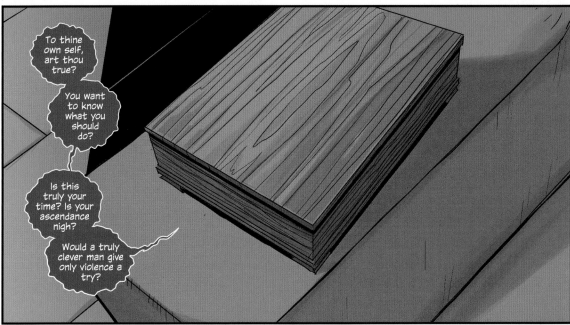

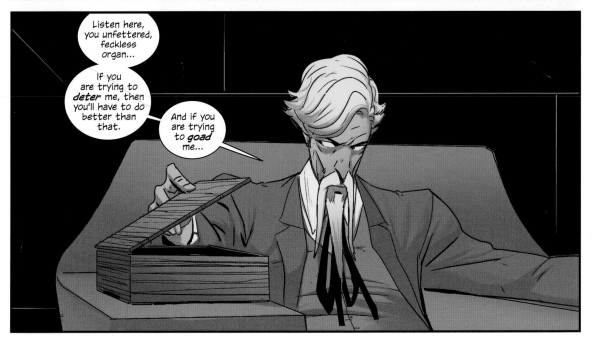

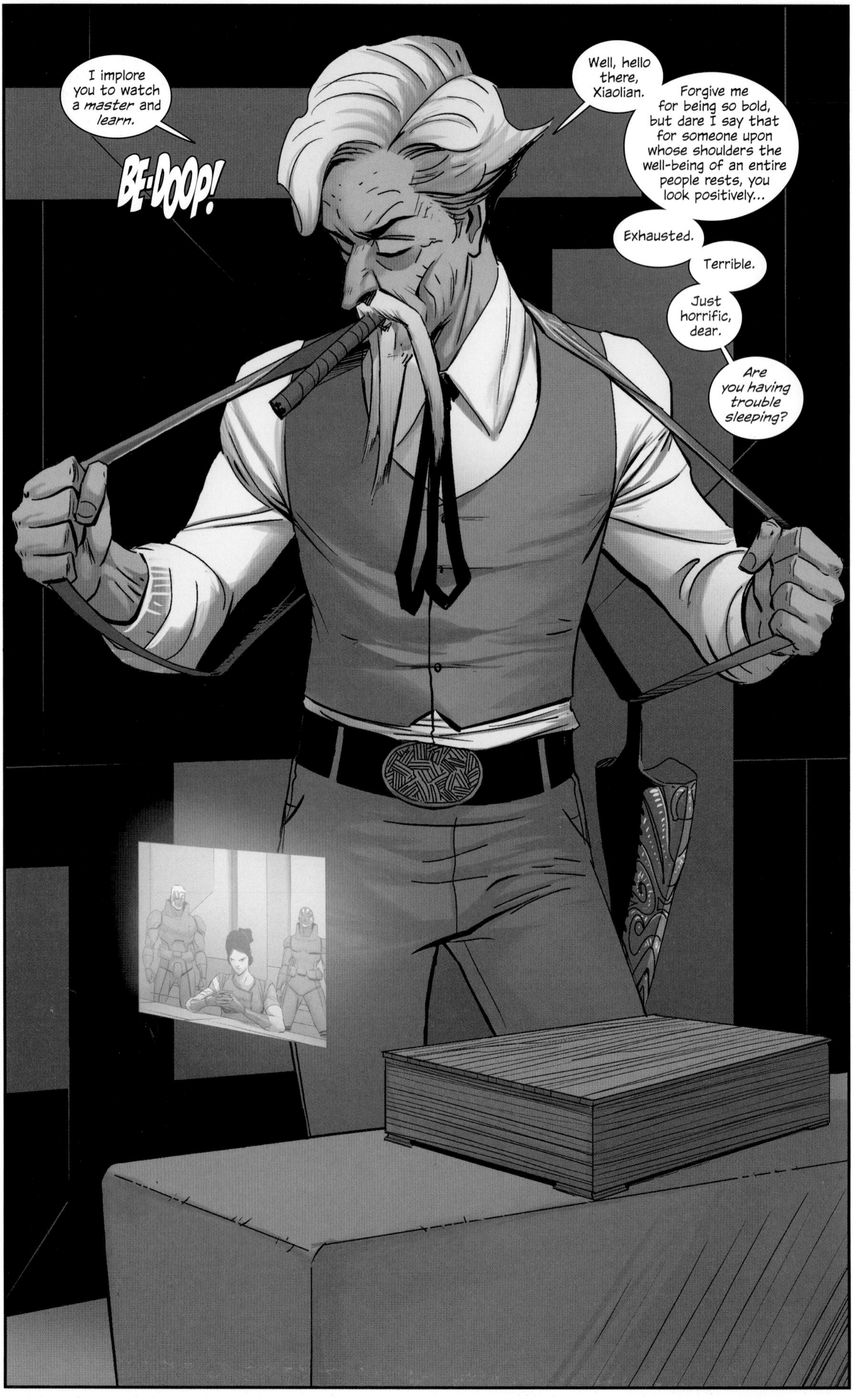
I implore you to watch a *master* and *learn.*
BE-DOOP!
Well, hello there, Xiaolian.
Forgive me for being so bold, but dare I say that for someone upon whose shoulders the well-being of an entire people rests, you look positively...
Exhausted.
Terrible.
Just horrific, dear.
Are you having trouble sleeping?

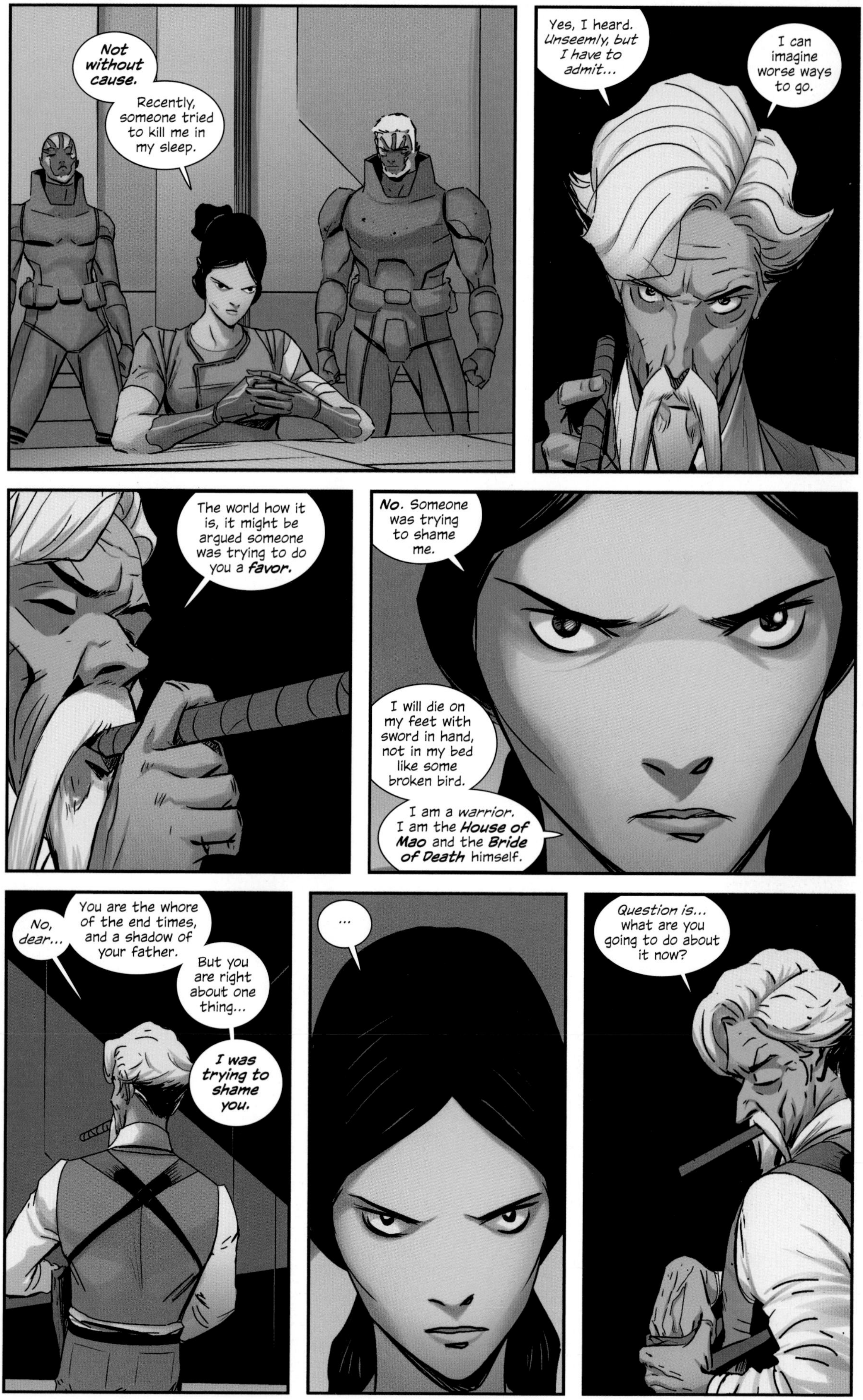
Not without cause.
Recently, someone tried to kill me in my sleep.
Yes, I heard. *Unseemly, but I have to admit...*
I can imagine worse ways to go.
The world how it is, it might be argued someone was trying to do you a *favor.*
No. Someone was trying to shame me.
I will die on my feet with sword in hand, not in my bed like some broken bird.
I am a *warrior.* I am the *House of Mao* and the *Bride of Death* himself.
No, dear...
You are the whore of the end times, and a shadow of your father.
But you are right about one thing...
I was trying to shame you.
...
Question is... what are you going to do about it now?

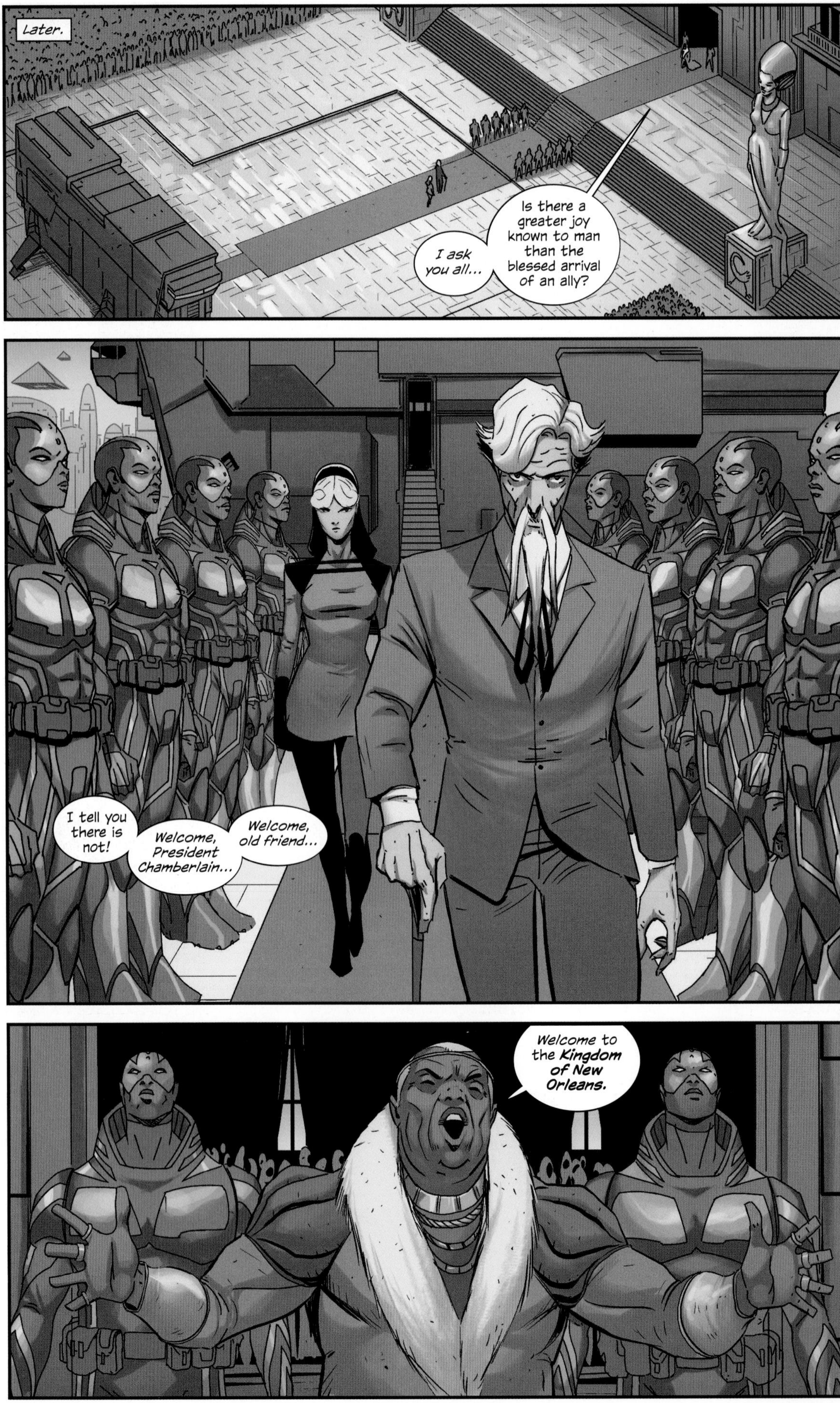
Later.
I ask you all...
Is there a greater joy known to man than the blessed arrival of an ally?
I tell you there is not!
Welcome, President Chamberlain...
Welcome, old friend...
Welcome to the **Kingdom of New Orleans.**

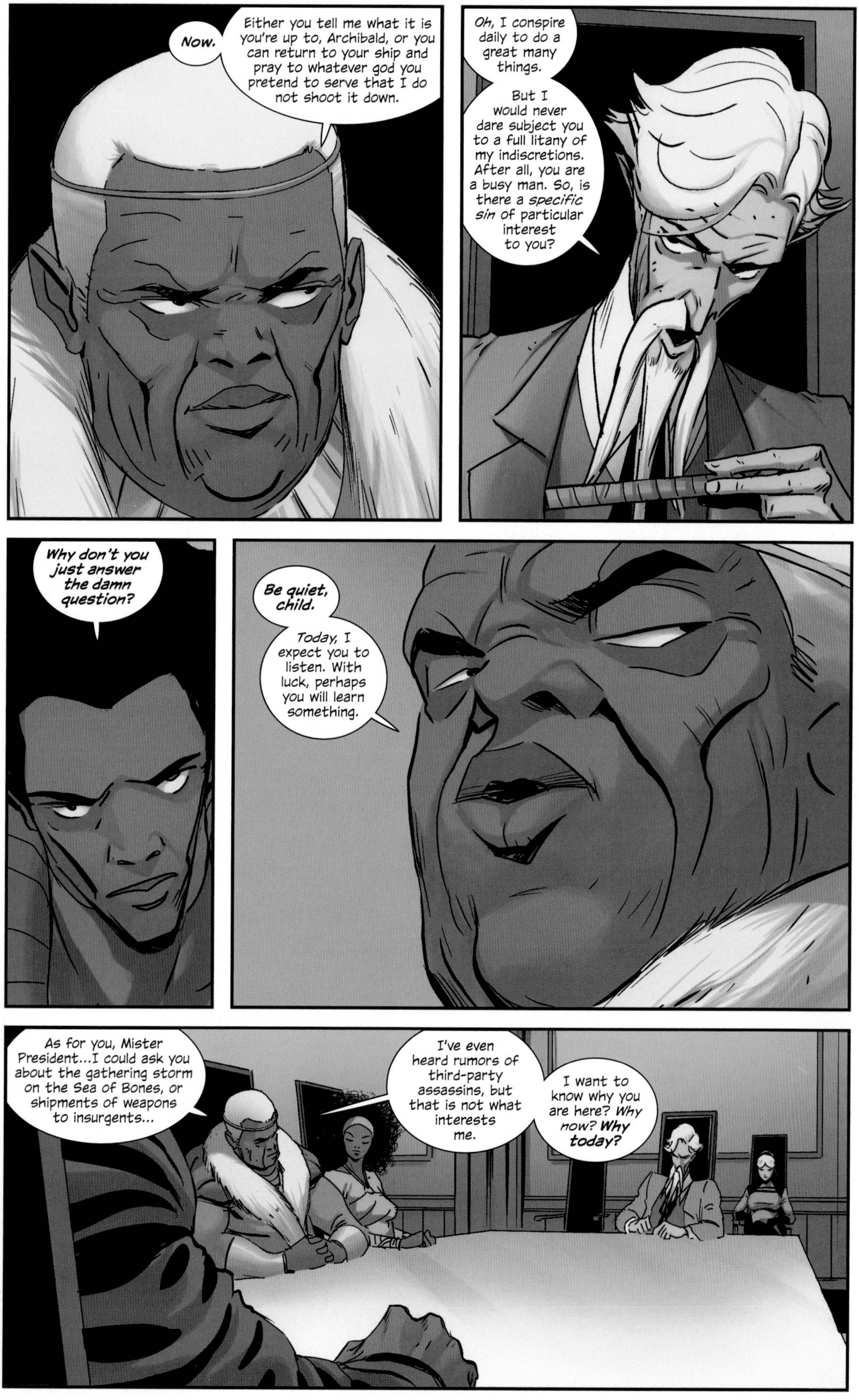
Now.
Either you tell me what it is you're up to, Archibald, or you can return to your ship and pray to whatever god you pretend to serve that I do not shoot it down.
Oh, I conspire daily to do a great many things.
But I would never dare subject you to a full litany of my indiscretions. After all, you are a busy man. So, is there a *specific sin* of particular interest to you?
Why don't you just answer the damn question?
Be quiet, child.
Today, I expect you to listen. With luck, perhaps you will learn something.
As for you, Mister President...I could ask you about the gathering storm on the Sea of Bones, or shipments of weapons to insurgents...
I've even heard rumors of third-party assassins, but that is not what interests me.
I want to know why you are here? *Why now?* ***Why today?***

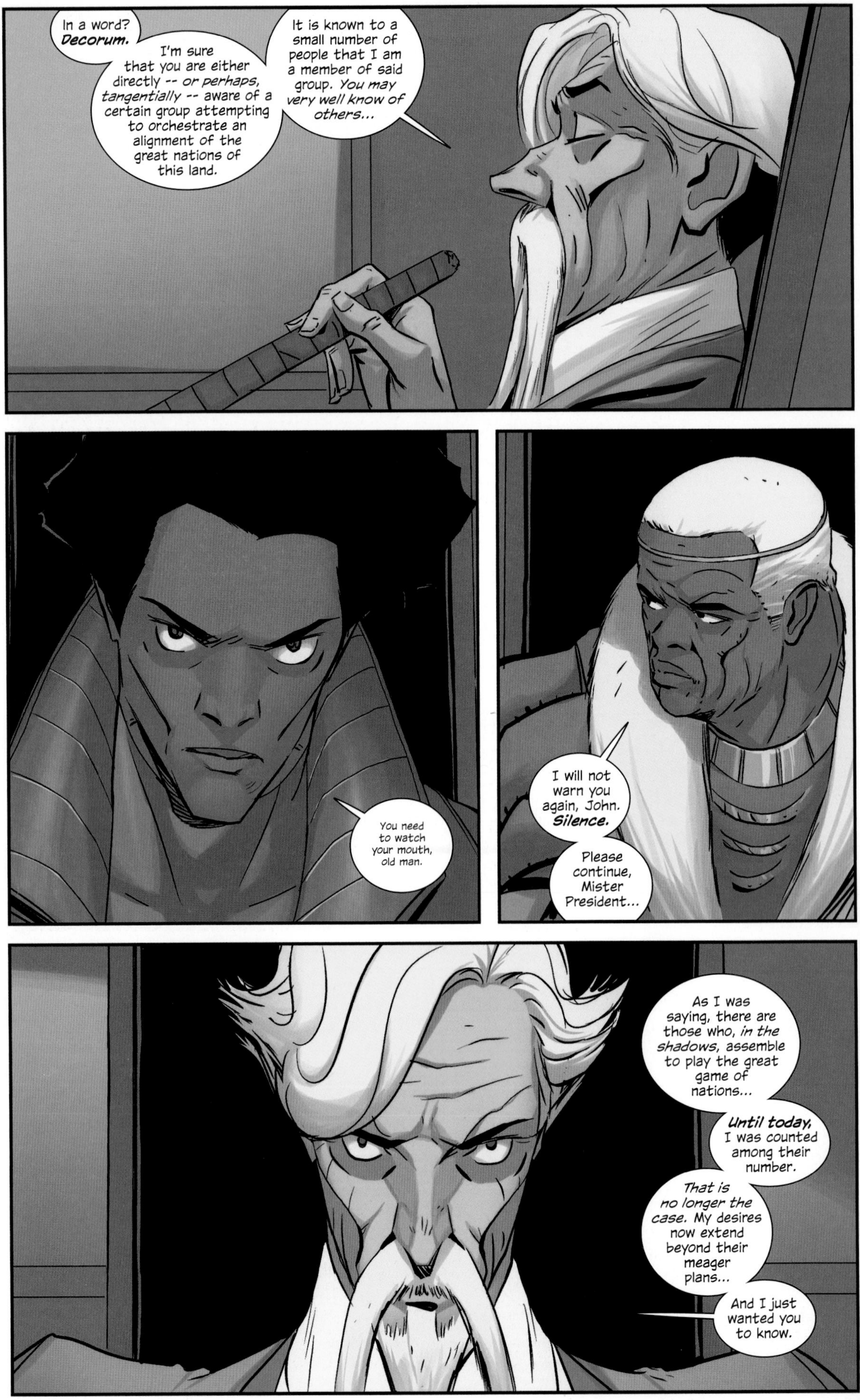
In a word? **Decorum.**
I'm sure that you are either directly -- *or perhaps, tangentially* -- aware of a certain group attempting to orchestrate an alignment of the great nations of this land.
It is known to a small number of people that I am a member of said group. *You may very well know of others...*
You need to watch your mouth, old man.
I will not warn you again, John. ***Silence.***
Please continue, Mister President...
As I was saying, there are those who, *in the shadows*, assemble to play the great game of nations...
Until today, I was counted among their number.
That is no longer the case. My desires now extend beyond their meager plans...
And I just wanted you to know.

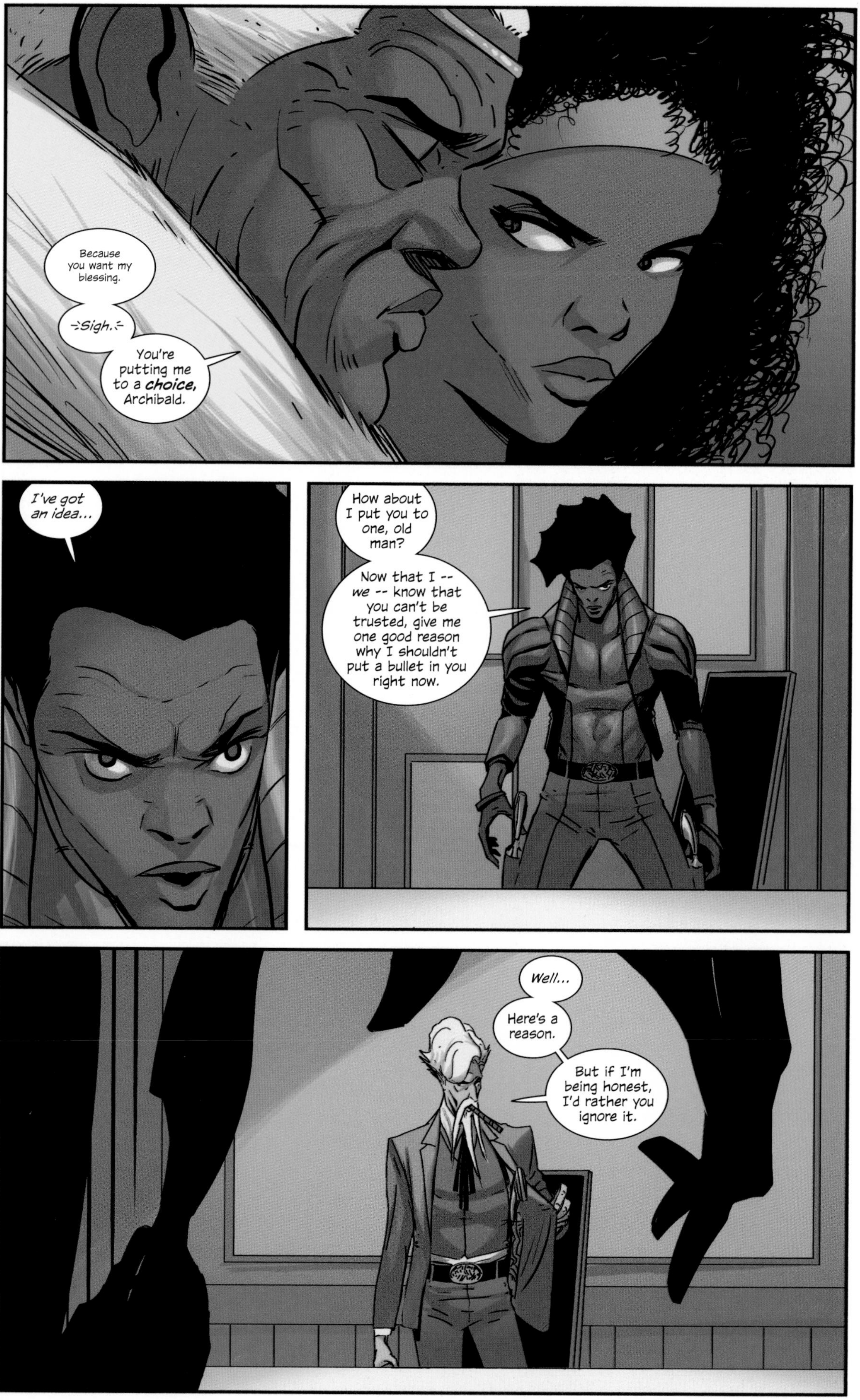
Because you want my blessing.
-Sigh.-
You're putting me to a **choice,** Archibald.
I've got an idea...
How about I put you to one, old man?
Now that I -- *we* -- know that you can't be trusted, give me one good reason why I shouldn't put a bullet in you right now.
Well...
Here's a reason.
But if I'm being honest, I'd rather you ignore it.

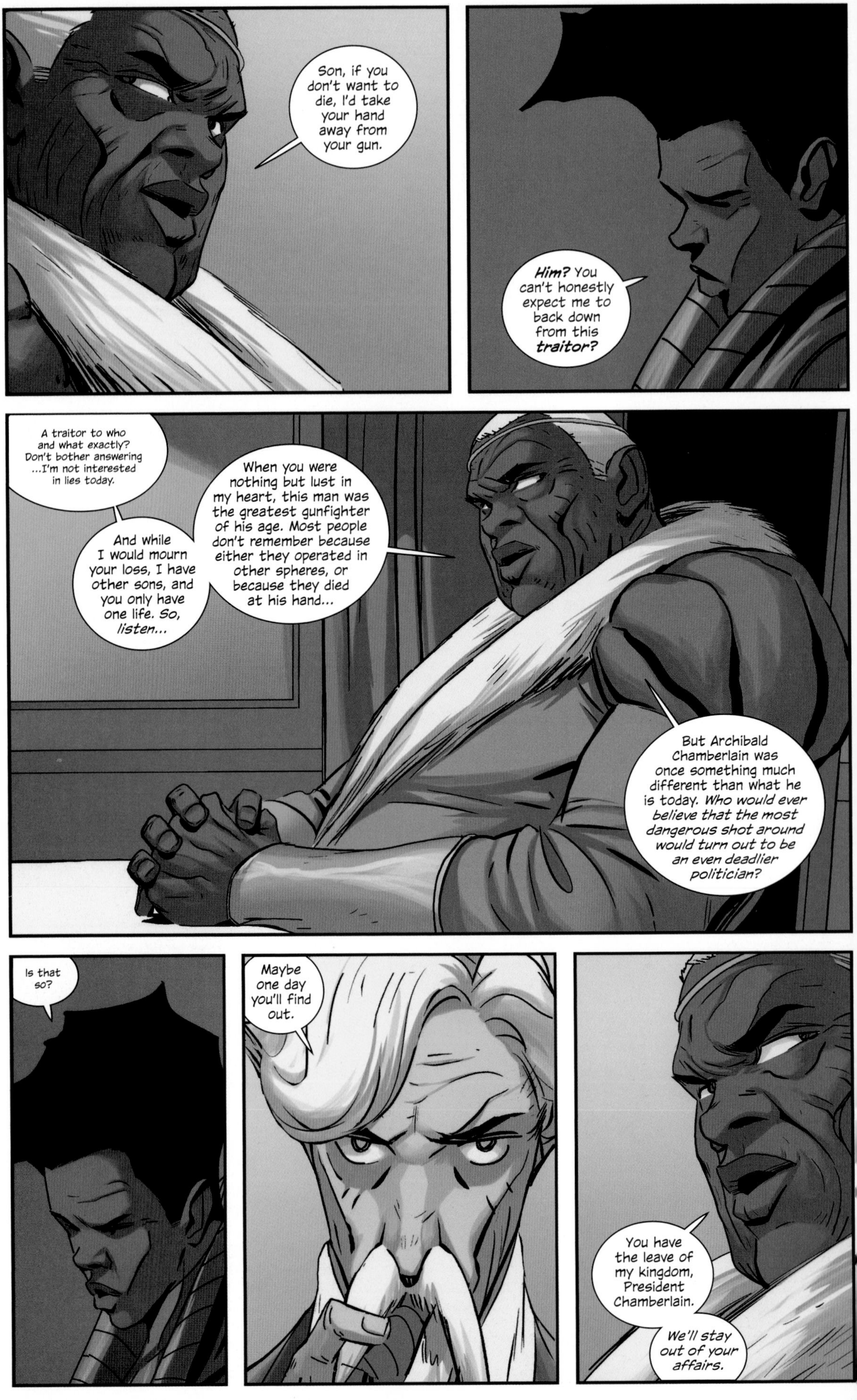
Son, if you don't want to die, I'd take your hand away from your gun.
Him? You can't honestly expect me to back down from this traitor?
A traitor to who and what exactly? Don't bother answering ...I'm not interested in lies today.
And while I would mourn your loss, I have other sons, and you only have one life. So, listen...
When you were nothing but lust in my heart, this man was the greatest gunfighter of his age. Most people don't remember because either they operated in other spheres, or because they died at his hand...
But Archibald Chamberlain was once something much different than what he is today. Who would ever believe that the most dangerous shot around would turn out to be an even deadlier politician?
Is that so?
Maybe one day you'll find out.
You have the leave of my kingdom, President Chamberlain.
We'll stay out of your affairs.

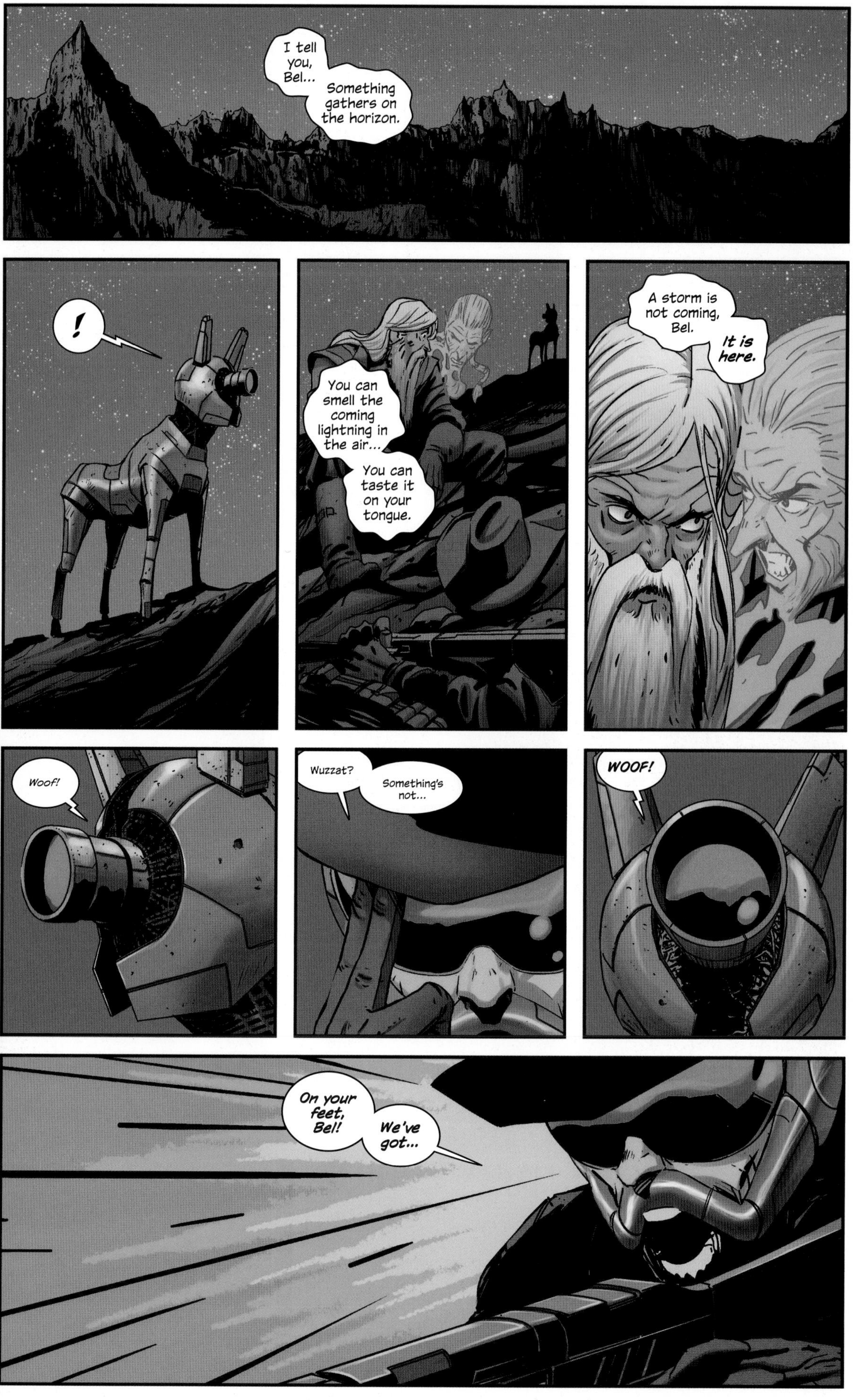
I tell you, Bel...
Something gathers on the horizon.
!
You can smell the coming lightning in the air...
You can taste it on your tongue.
A storm is not coming, Bel.
It is here.
Woof!
Wuzzat?
Something's not...
WOOF!
On your feet, Bel!
We've got...

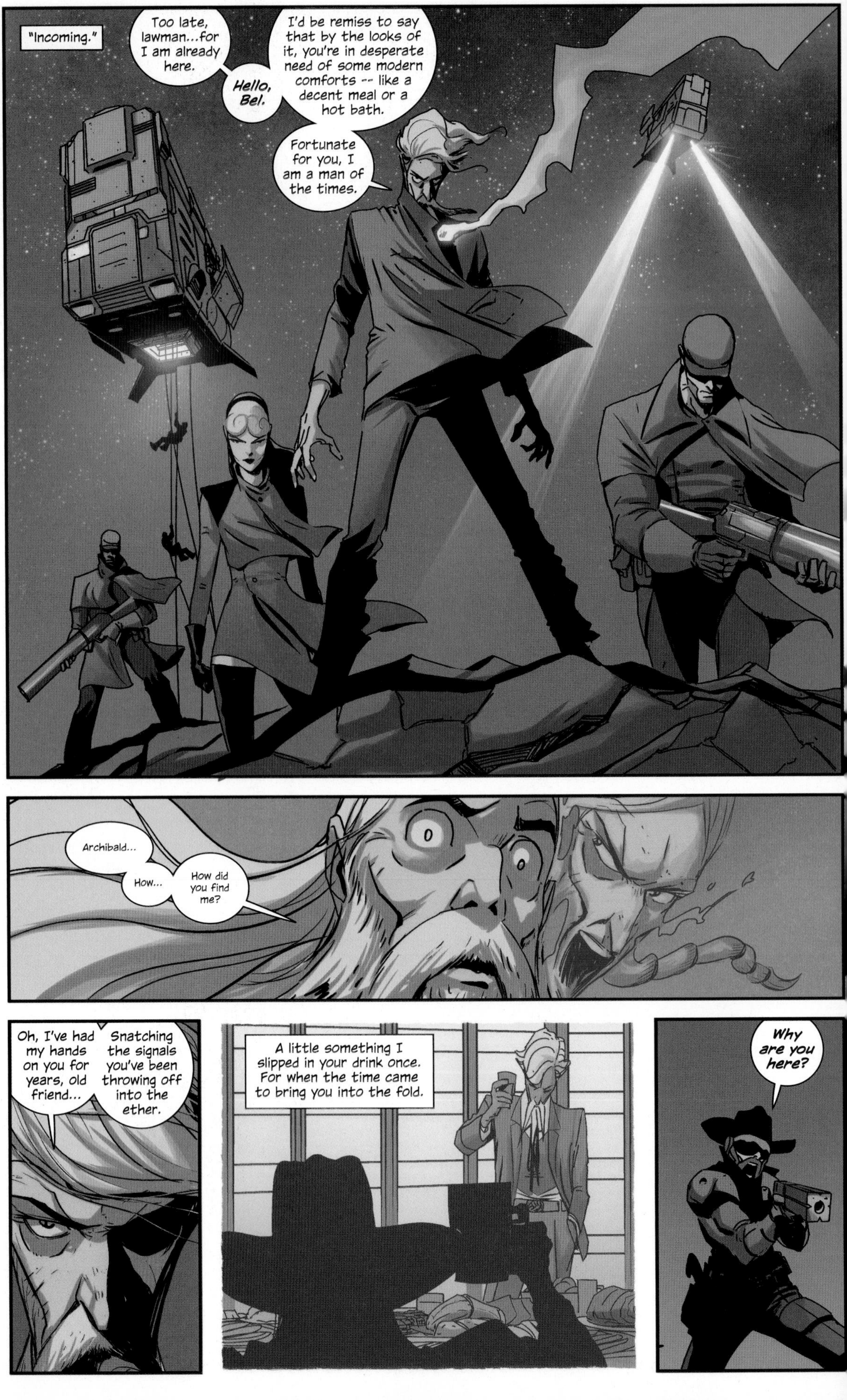
"Incoming."
Too late, lawman...for I am already here.
Hello, Bel.
I'd be remiss to say that by the looks of it, you're in desperate need of some modern comforts -- like a decent meal or a hot bath.
Fortunate for you, I am a man of the times.
Archibald...
How...
How did you find me?
Oh, I've had my hands on you for years, old friend...
Snatching the signals you've been throwing off into the ether.
A little something I slipped in your drink once. For when the time came to bring you into the fold.
Why are you here?

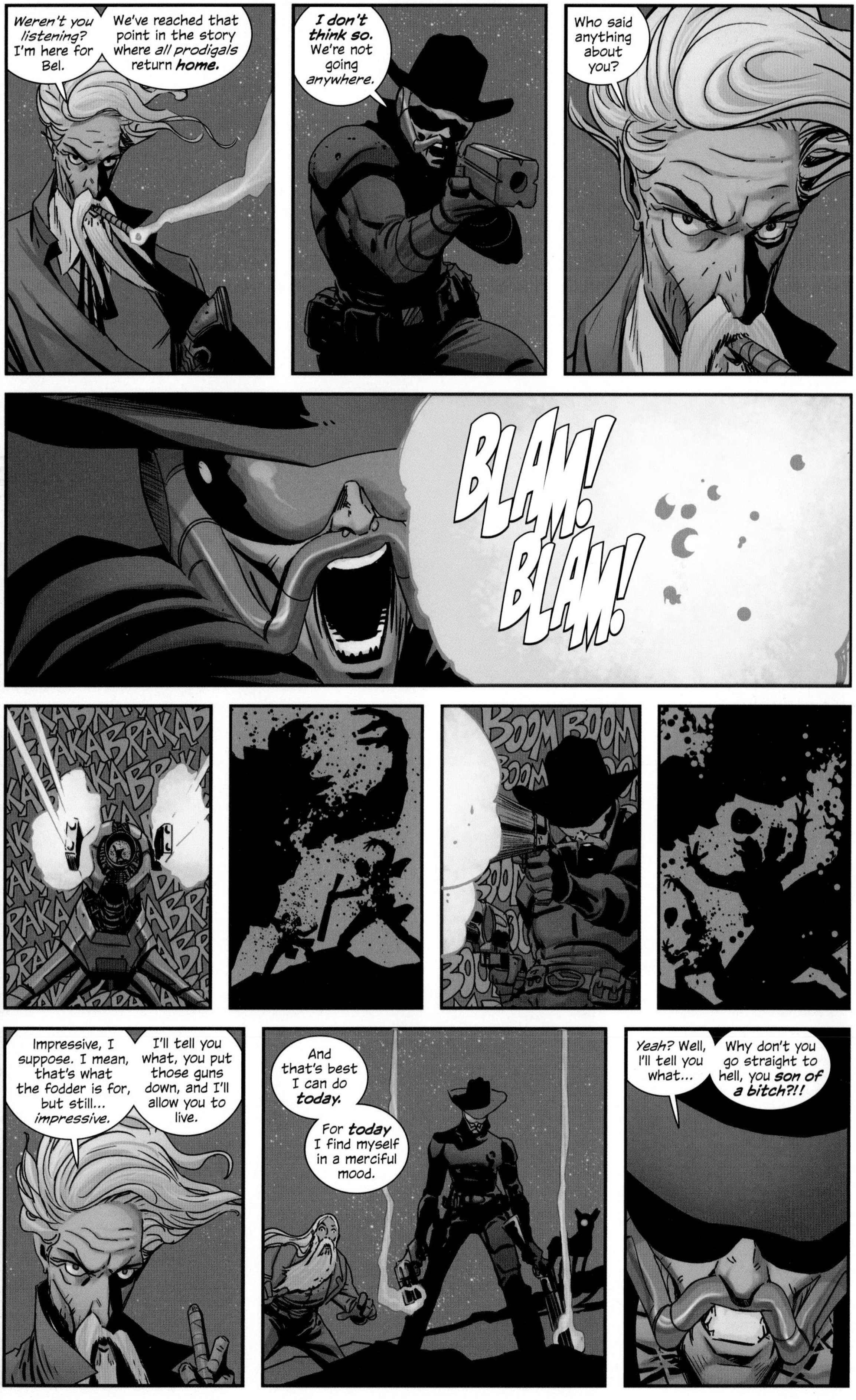

Weren't you listening? I'm here for Bel.
We've reached that point in the story where *all prodigals* return ***home.***
I don't think so. We're not going *anywhere.*
Who said anything about you?
BLAM! BLAM!
BOOM BOOM
Impressive, I suppose. I mean, that's what the fodder is for, but still... *impressive.*
I'll tell you what, you put those guns down, and I'll allow you to live.
And that's best I can do ***today.***
For ***today*** I find myself in a merciful mood.
Yeah? Well, I'll tell you what...
Why don't you go straight to hell, you ***son of a bitch?!!***

Just remember... I did offer.

KA-POOOWWWWWWWK
KA-POOOWWWWWWT
KA-POOOWWWWWWT

THURP

SPRT

CRAK

Uhhhhhhh...

Next time...you might want to be more appreciative when a man like myself is feeling generous.

Understand?

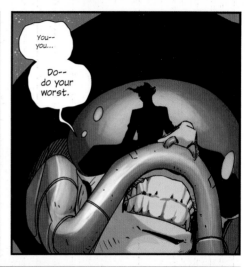

You-- you...

Do-- do your worst.

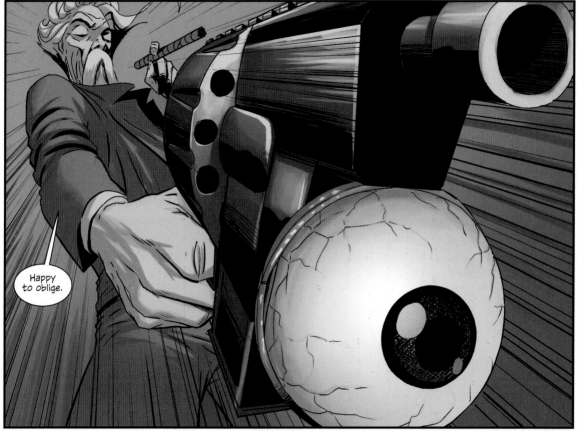

Happy to oblige.

Woof!

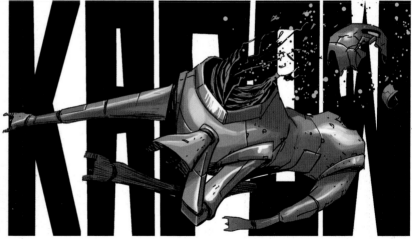

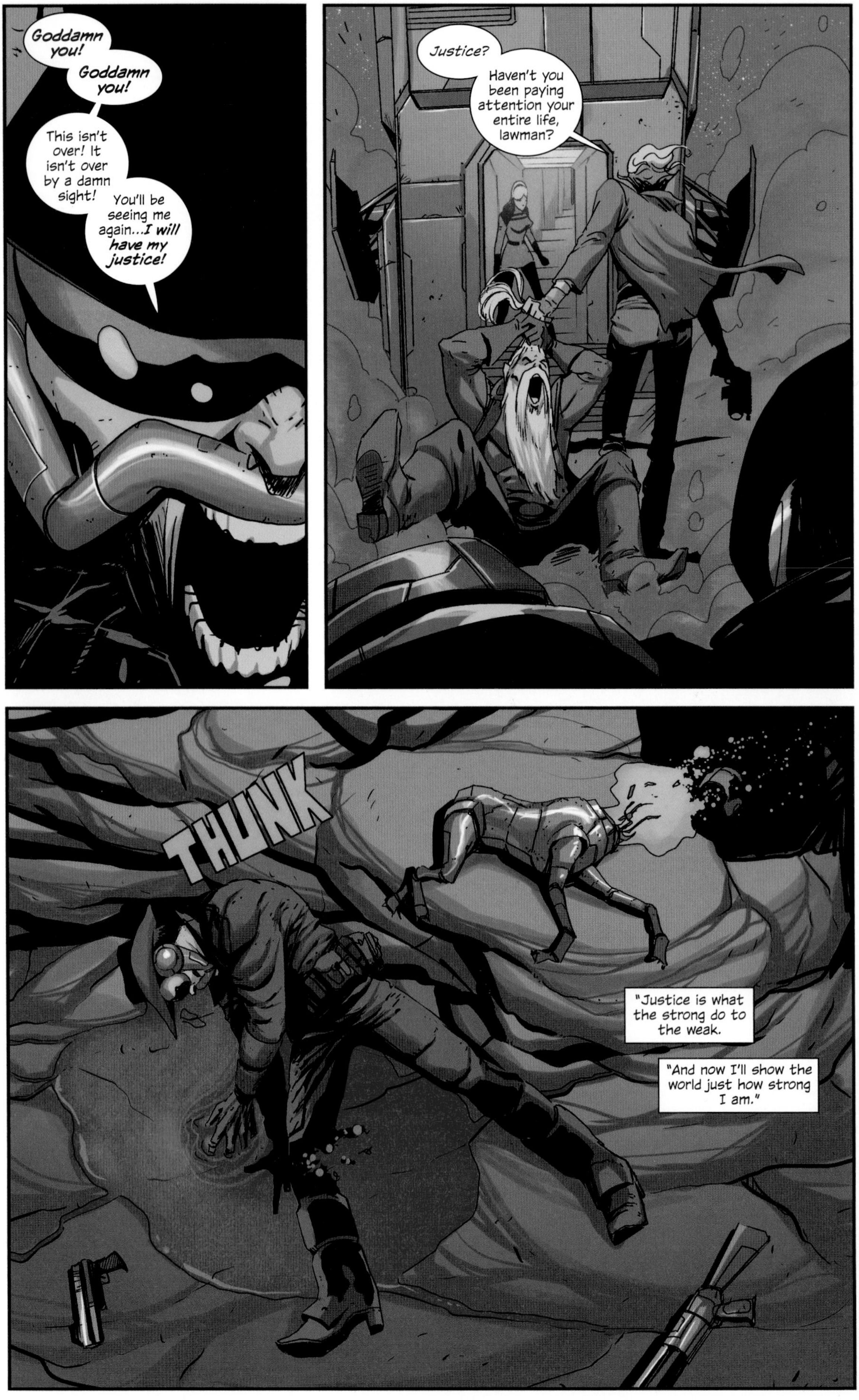
Goddamn you!
Goddamn you!
This isn't over! It isn't over by a damn sight!
You'll be seeing me again...I will have my justice!
Justice?
Haven't you been paying attention your entire life, lawman?
THUNK
"Justice is what the strong do to the weak.
"And now I'll show the world just how strong I am."

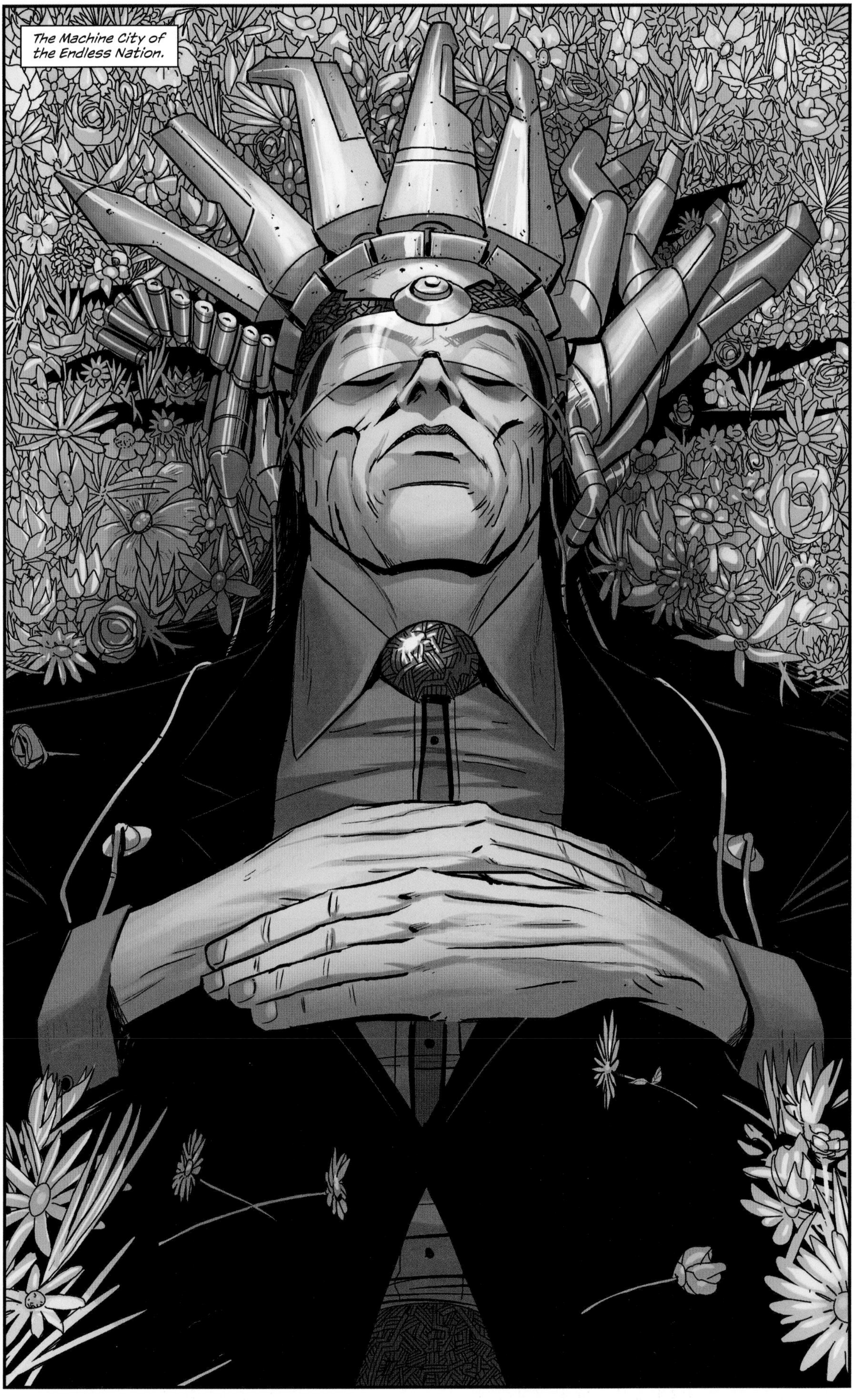
The Machine City of the Endless Nation.

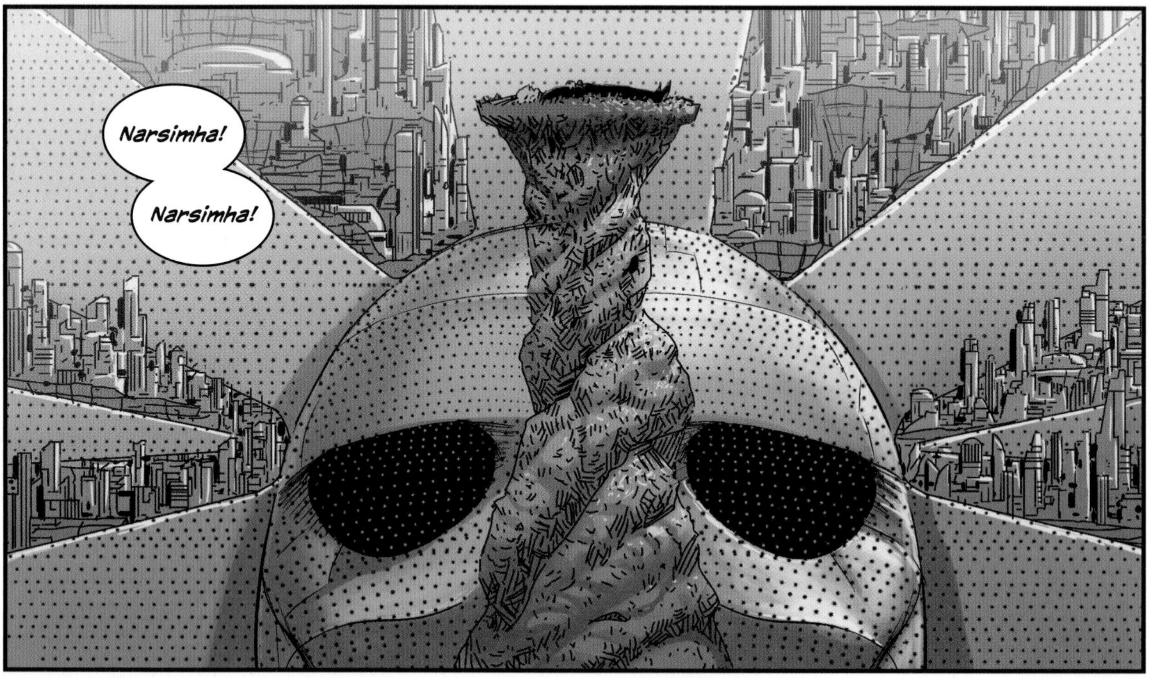
Narsimha!
Narsimha!

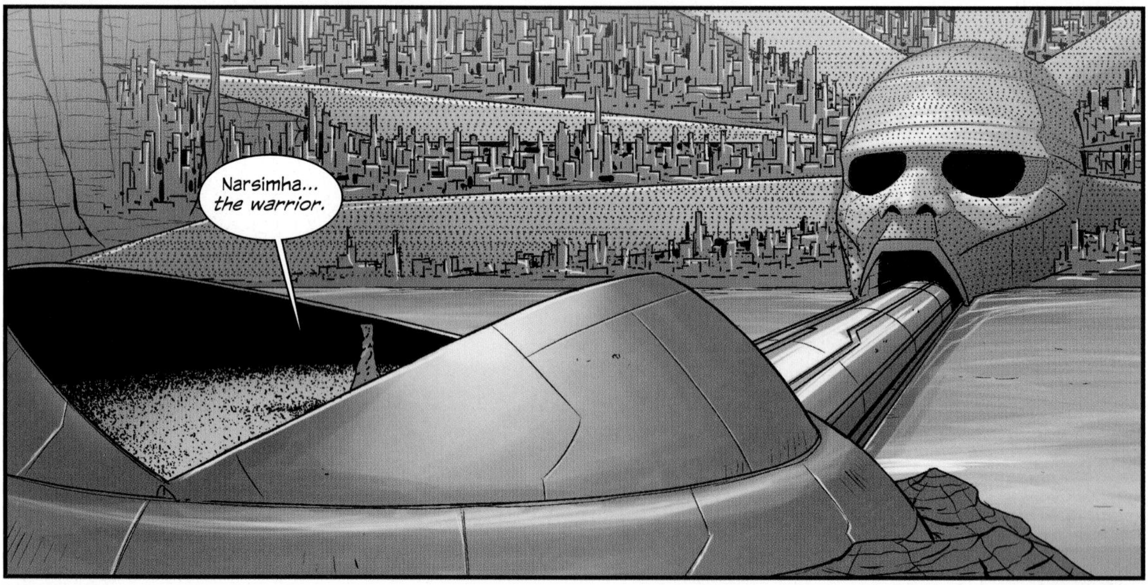
Narsimha... the warrior.

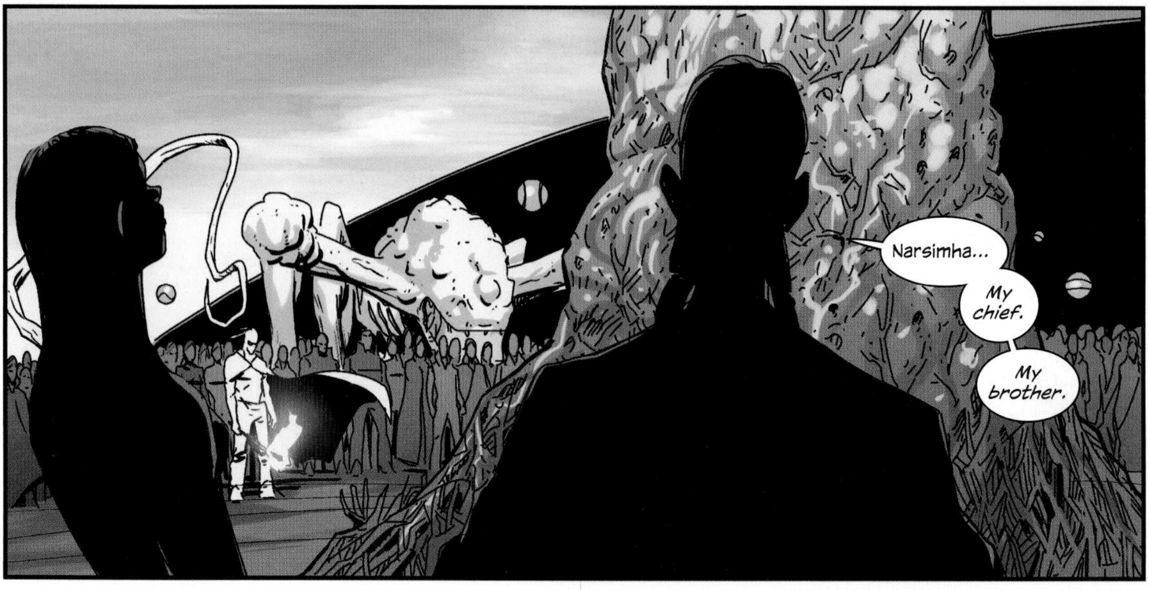
Narsimha...
My chief.
My brother.

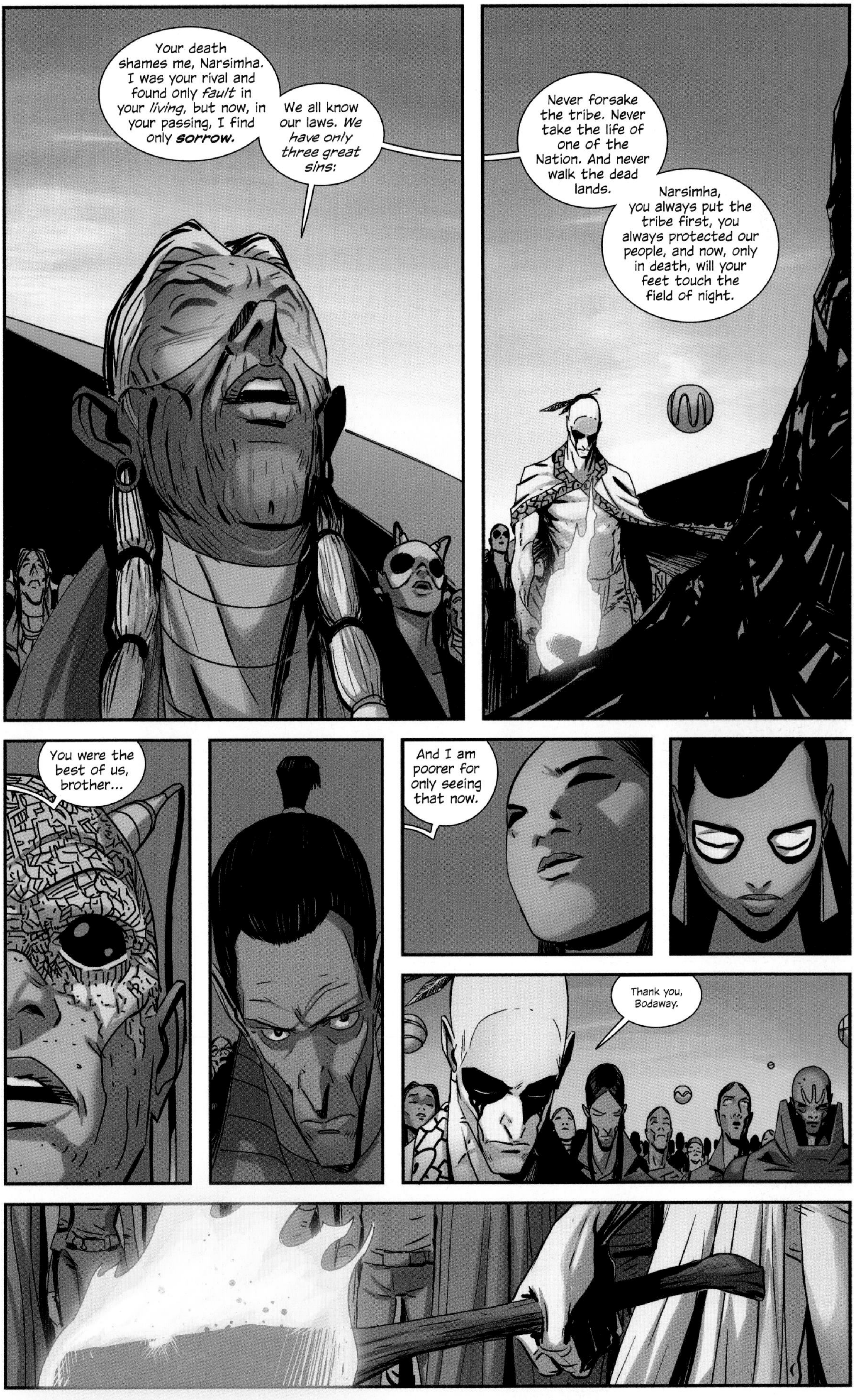

Your death shames me, Narsimha. I was your rival and found only *fault* in your *living*, but now, in your passing, I find only **sorrow.**
We all know our laws. *We have only three great sins:*
Never forsake the tribe. Never take the life of one of the Nation. And never walk the dead lands.
Narsimha, you always put the tribe first, you always protected our people, and now, only in death, will your feet touch the field of night.
You were the best of us, brother...
And I am poorer for only seeing that now.
Thank you, Bodaway.

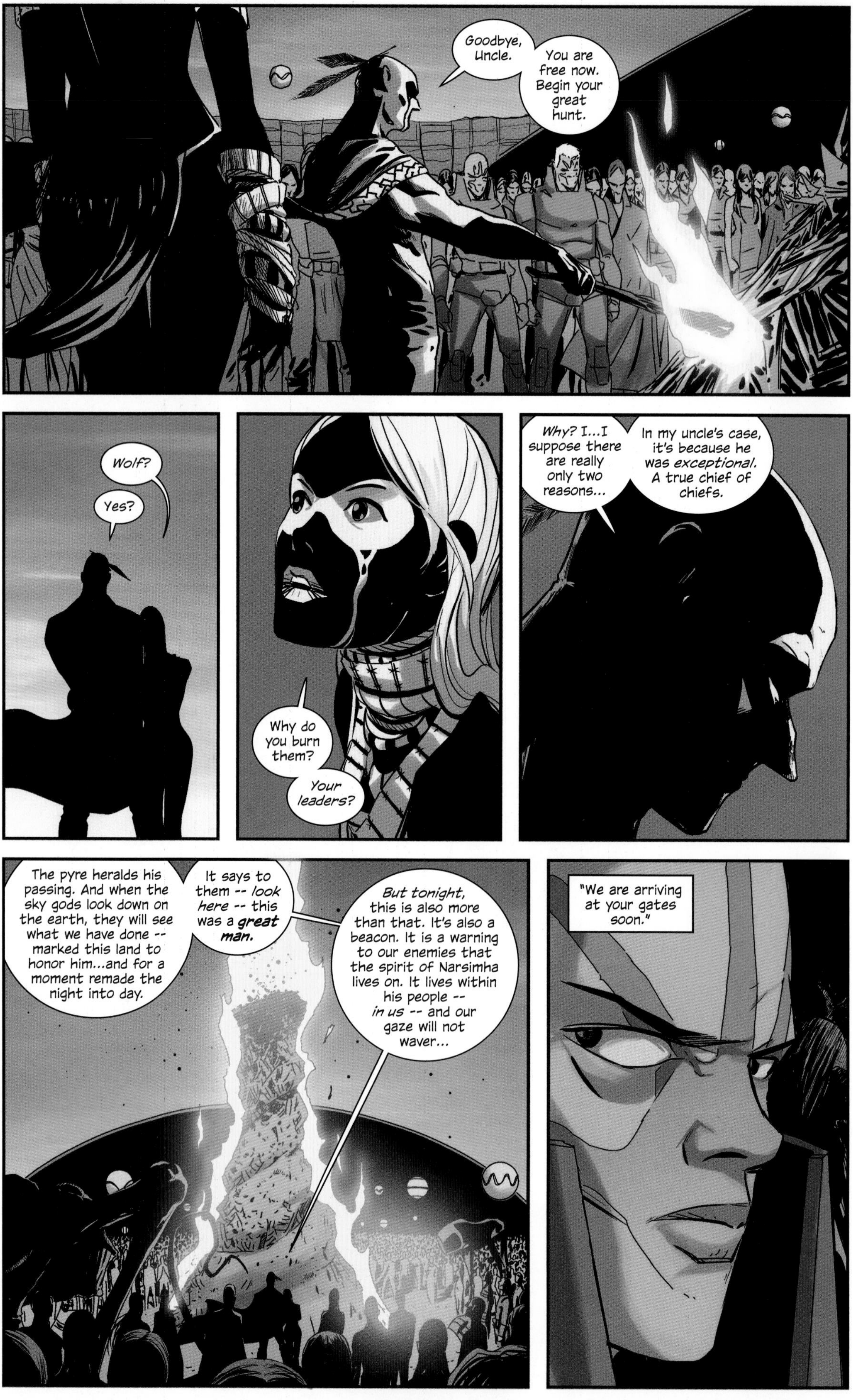
Goodbye, Uncle.
You are free now. Begin your great hunt.
Wolf?
Yes?
Why do you burn them?
Your leaders?
Why? I...I suppose there are really only two reasons...
In my uncle's case, it's because he was exceptional. A true chief of chiefs.
The pyre heralds his passing. And when the sky gods look down on the earth, they will see what we have done -- marked this land to honor him...and for a moment remade the night into day.
It says to them -- look here -- this was a great man.
But tonight, this is also more than that. It's also a beacon. It is a warning to our enemies that the spirit of Narsimha lives on. It lives within his people -- in us -- and our gaze will not waver...
"We are arriving at your gates soon."

SEE US WITH THE
COMING SUN.

WE ARE HERE FOR THE
UNION.

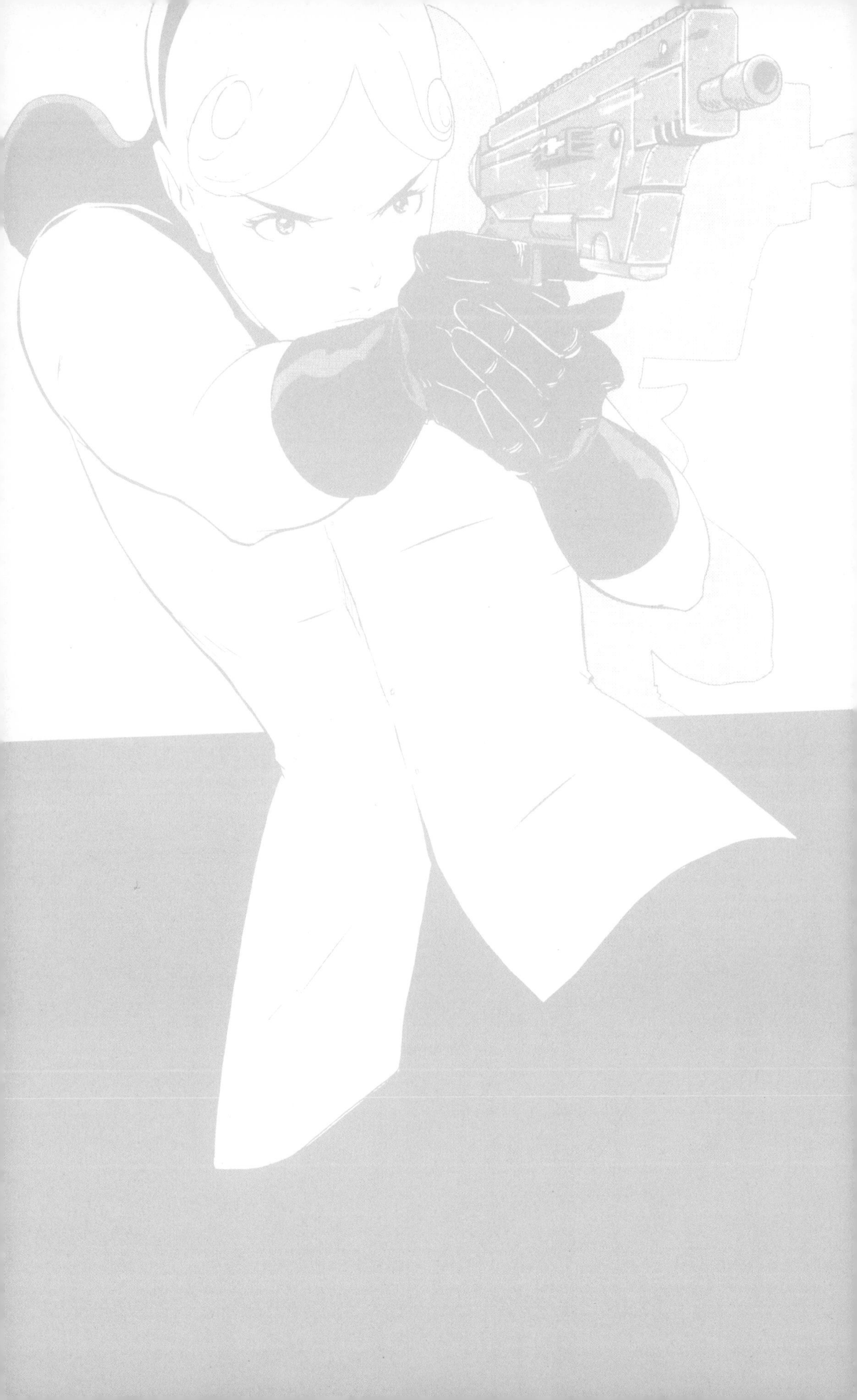

 THIRTY-THREE:
A **SIGNAL** TO **FIRE**

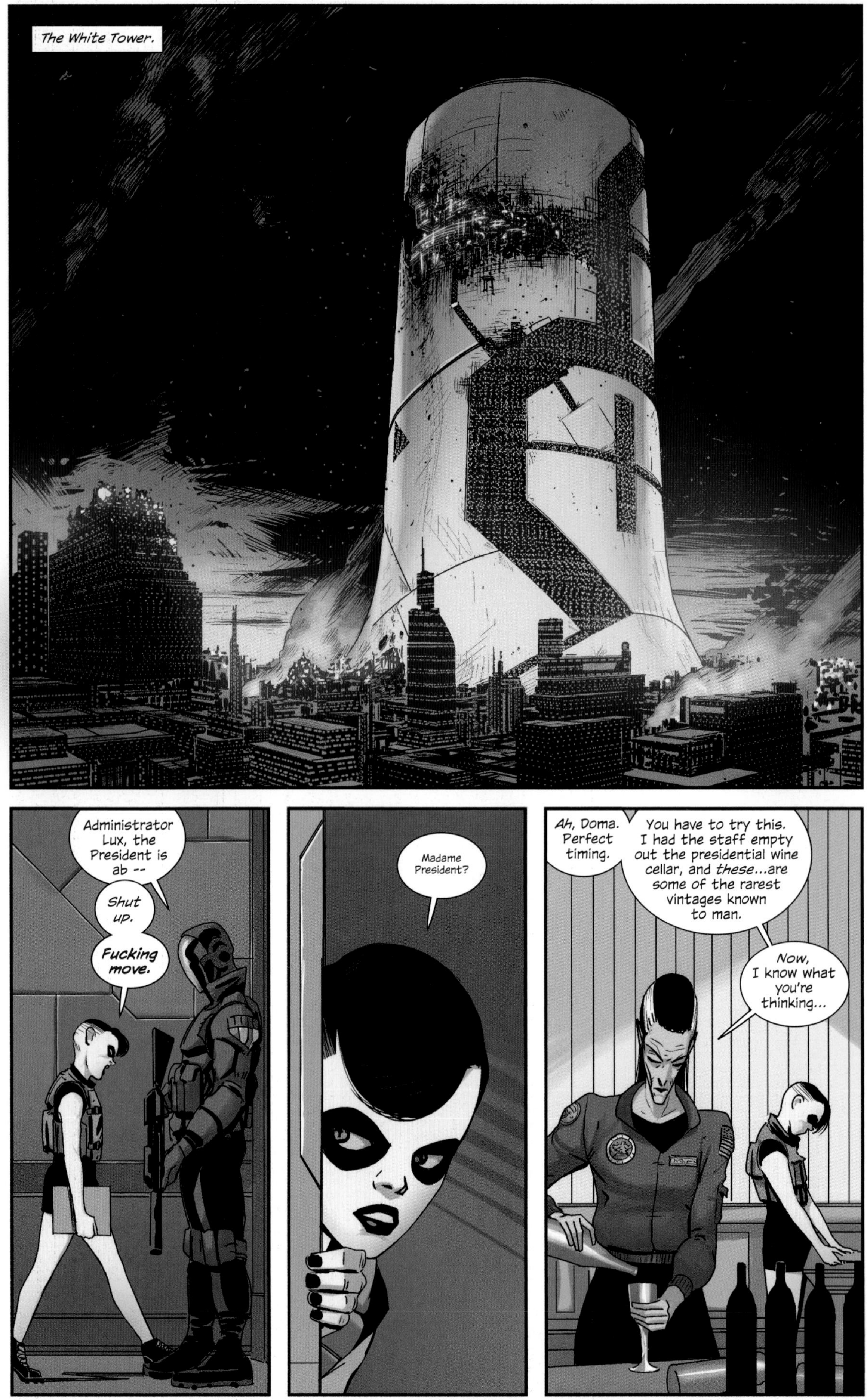
The White Tower.
Administrator Lux, the President is ab --
Shut up.
Fucking move.
Madame President?
Ah, Doma. Perfect timing.
You have to try this. I had the staff empty out the presidential wine cellar, and these...are some of the rarest vintages known to man.
Now, I know what you're thinking...

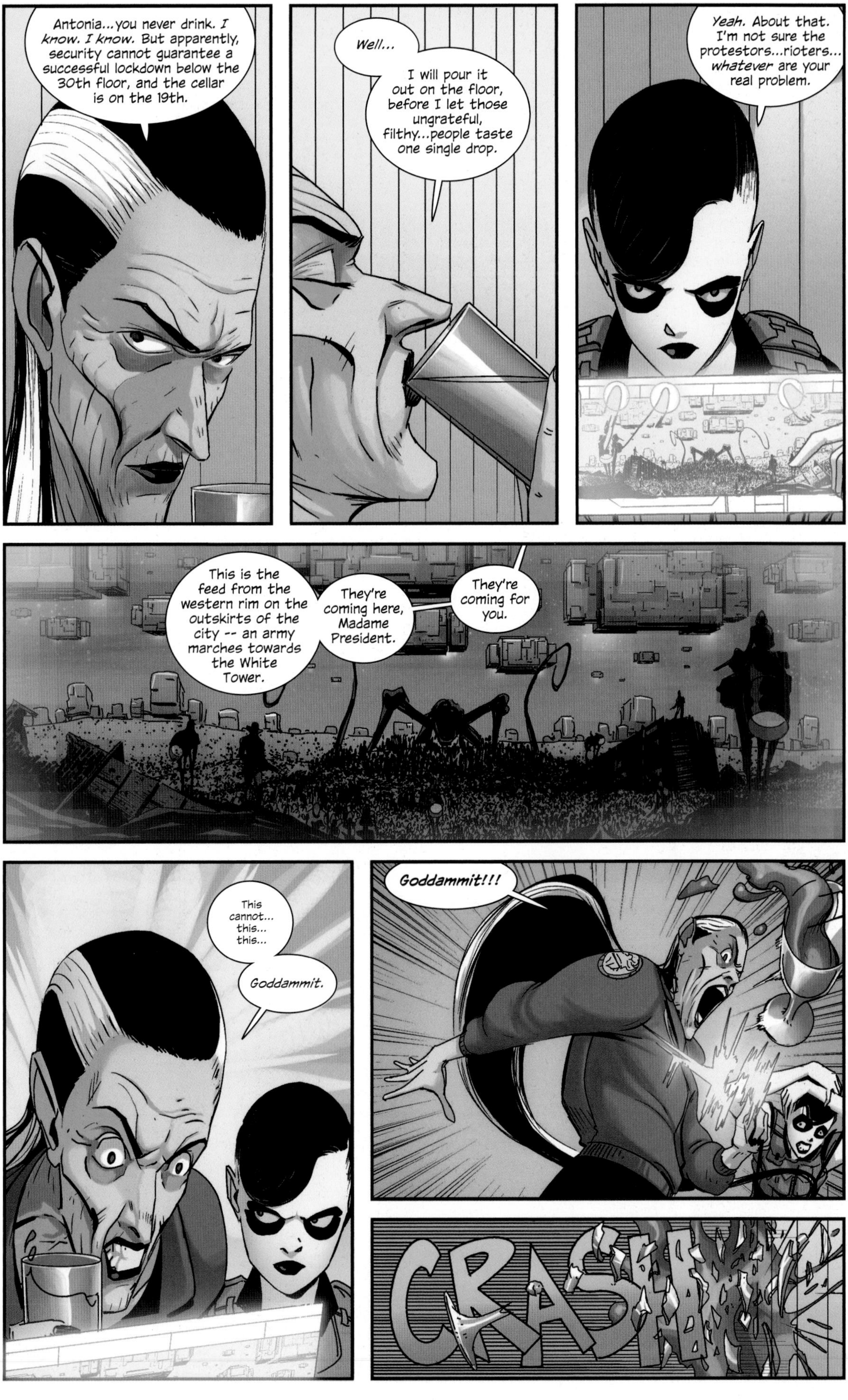
Antonia...you never drink. *I know. I know.* But apparently, security cannot guarantee a successful lockdown below the 30th floor, and the cellar is on the 19th.
Well...
I will pour it out on the floor, before I let those ungrateful, filthy...people taste one single drop.
Yeah. About that. I'm not sure the protestors...rioters... *whatever* are your real problem.
This is the feed from the western rim on the outskirts of the city -- an army marches towards the White Tower.
They're coming here, Madame President.
They're coming for you.
This cannot... this... this...
Goddammit.
Goddammit!!!
CRASH

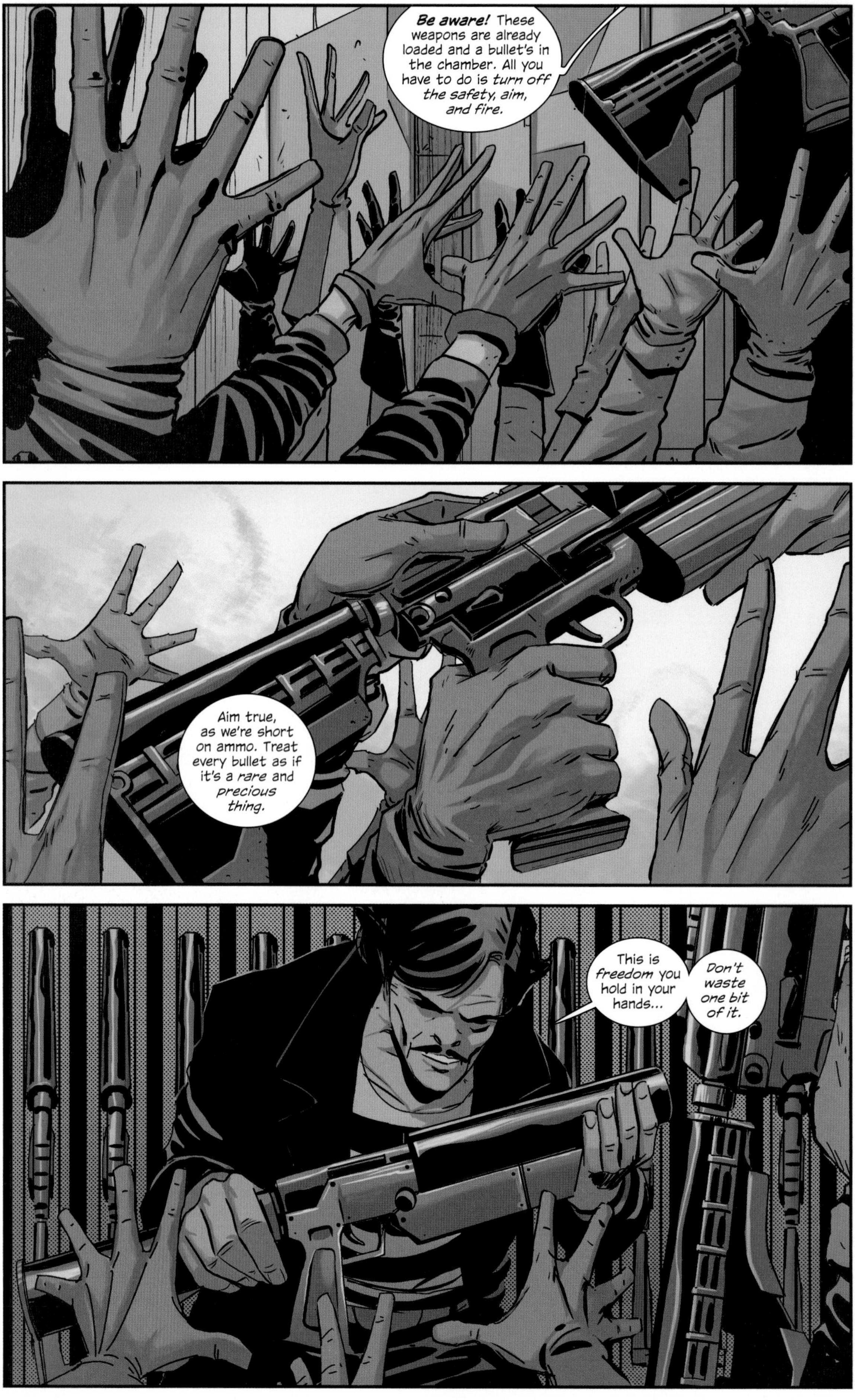

Be aware! These weapons are already loaded and a bullet's in the chamber. All you have to do is *turn off the safety, aim, and fire.*
Aim true, as we're short on ammo. Treat every bullet as if it's a *rare* and *precious* thing.
This is *freedom* you hold in your hands...
Don't waste one bit of it.

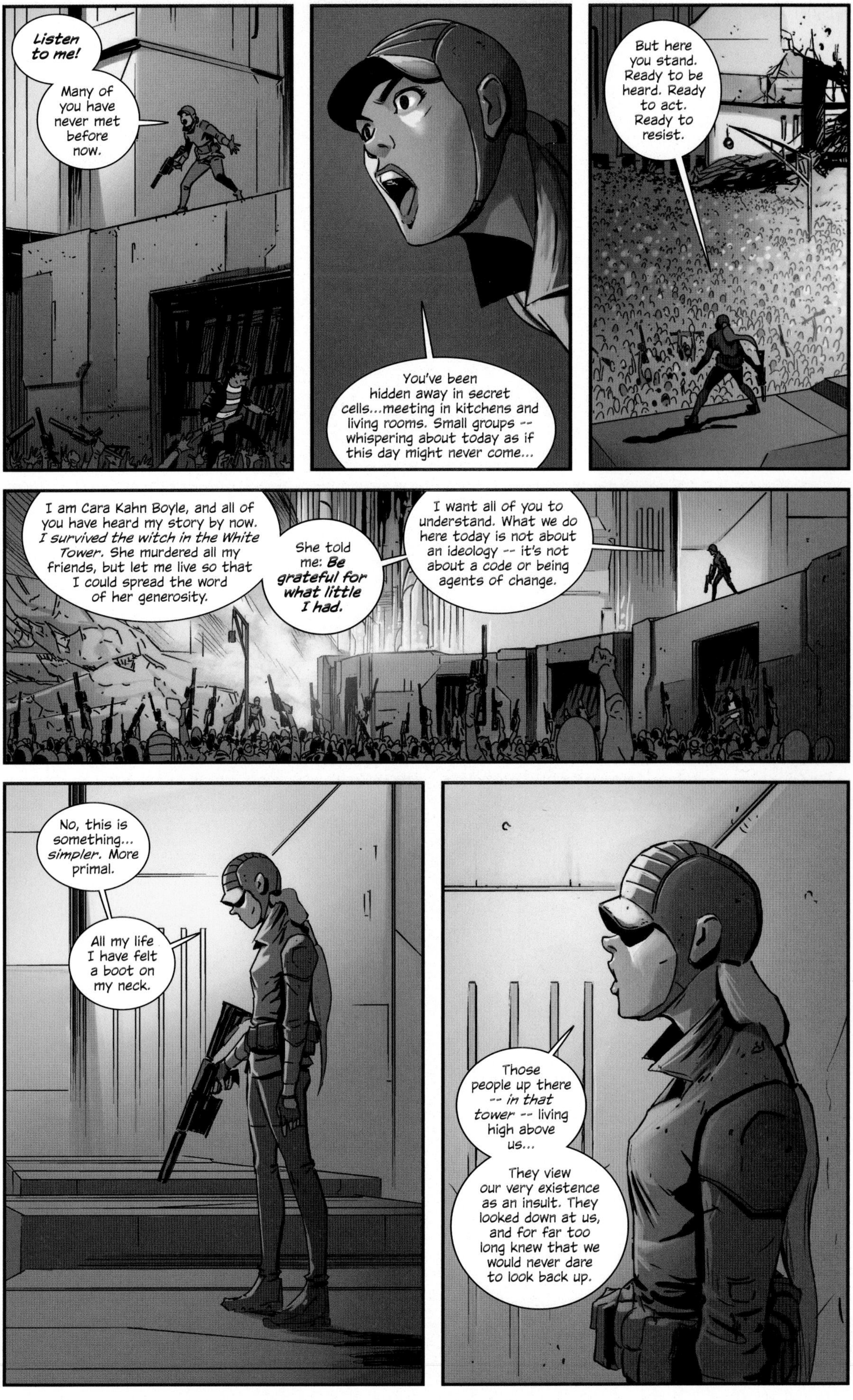
Listen to me!
Many of you have never met before now.
You've been hidden away in secret cells...meeting in kitchens and living rooms. Small groups -- whispering about today as if this day might never come...
But here you stand. Ready to be heard. Ready to act. Ready to resist.
I am Cara Kahn Boyle, and all of you have heard my story by now. I survived the witch in the White Tower. She murdered all my friends, but let me live so that I could spread the word of her generosity.
She told me: Be grateful for what little I had.
I want all of you to understand. What we do here today is not about an ideology -- it's not about a code or being agents of change.
No, this is something... simpler. More primal.
All my life I have felt a boot on my neck.
Those people up there -- in that tower -- living high above us...
They view our very existence as an insult. They looked down at us, and for far too long knew that we would never dare to look back up.

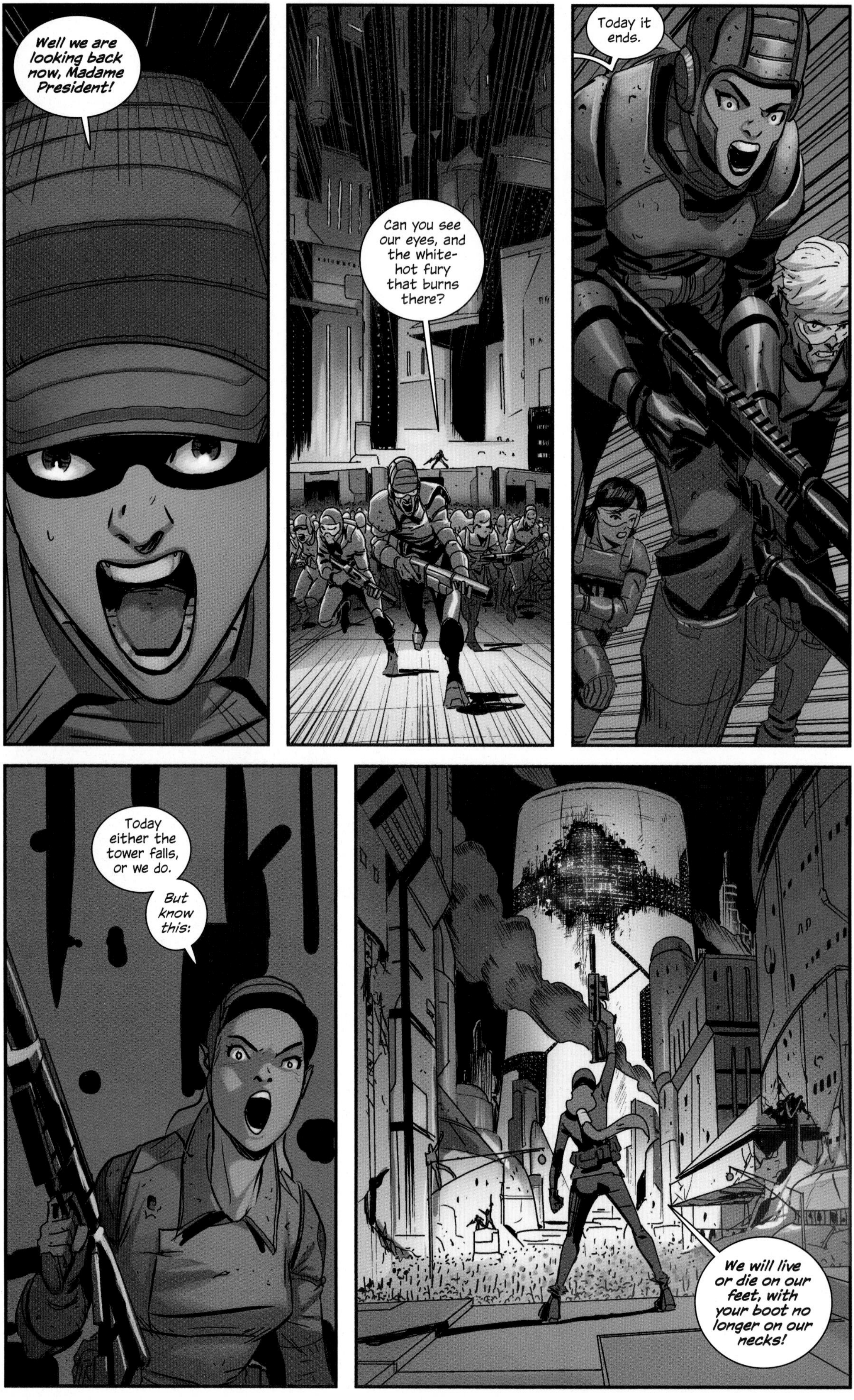

Well we are looking back now, Madame President!
Can you see our eyes, and the white-hot fury that burns there?
Today it ends.
Today either the tower falls, or we do.
But know this:
We will live or die on our feet, with your boot no longer on our necks!

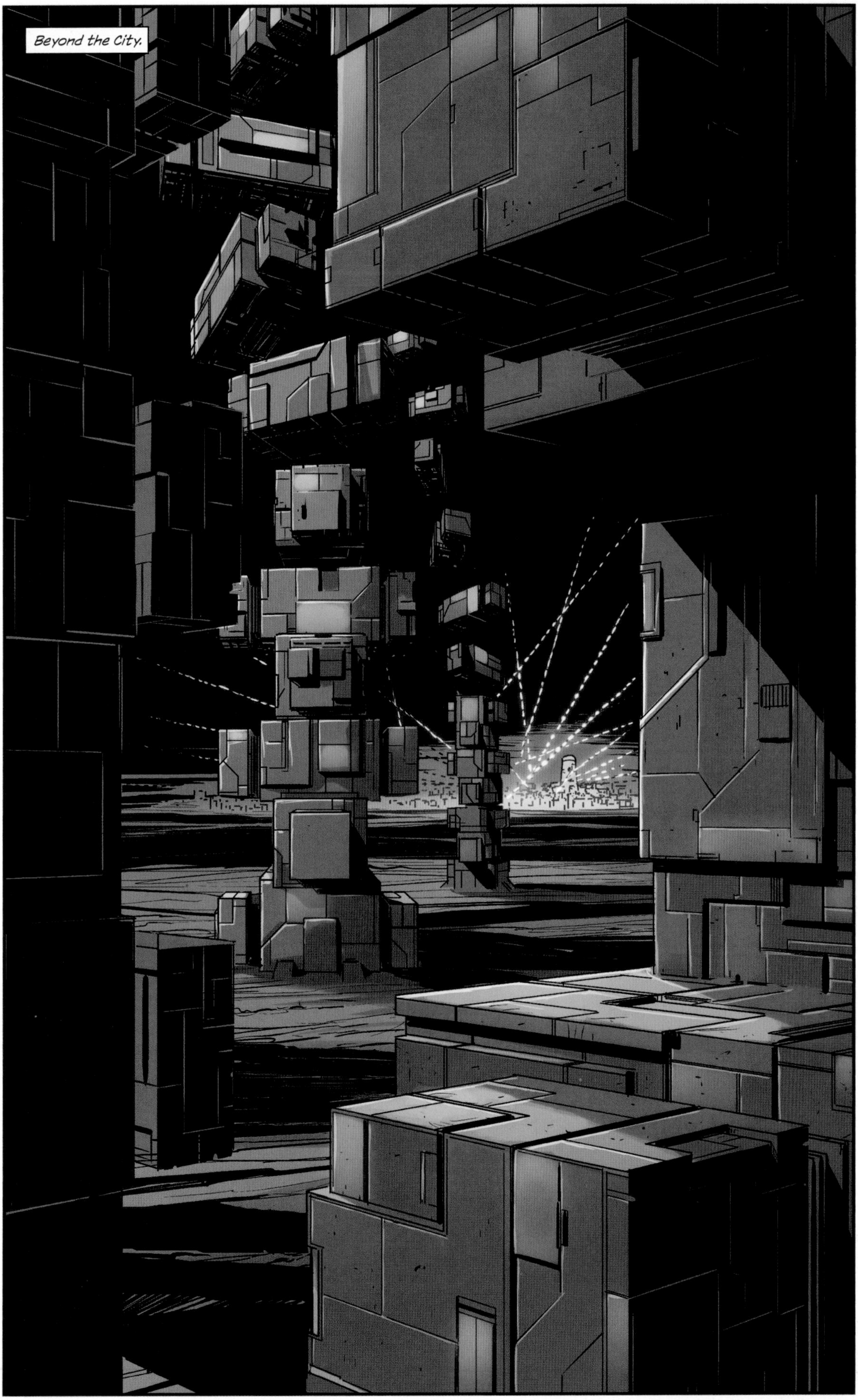
Beyond the City.

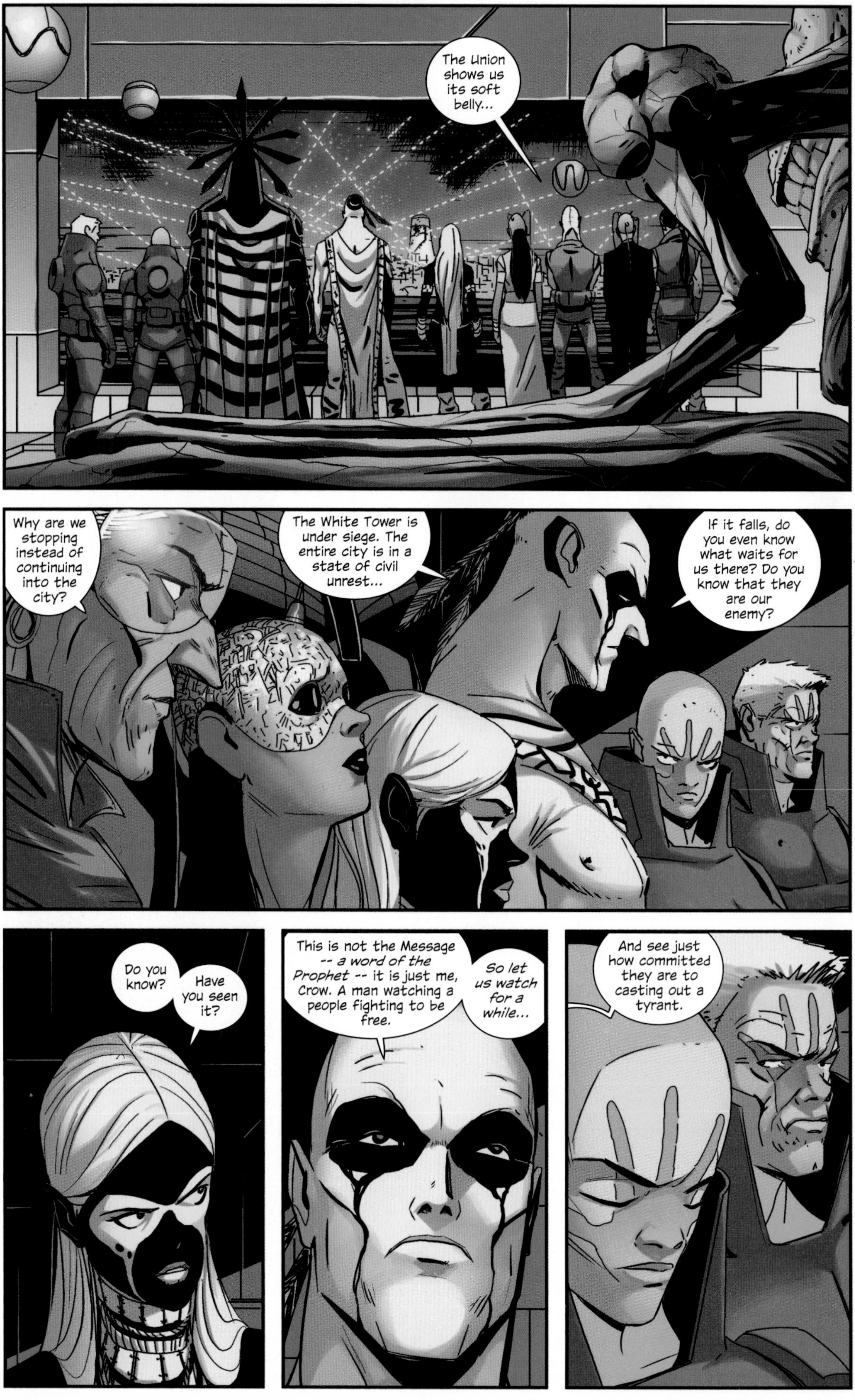

The Union shows us its soft belly...
Why are we stopping instead of continuing into the city?
The White Tower is under siege. The entire city is in a state of civil unrest...
If it falls, do you even know what waits for us there? Do you know that they are our enemy?
Do you know?
Have you seen it?
This is not the Message -- *a word of the Prophet* -- it is just me, Crow. A man watching a people fighting to be free.
So let us watch for a while...
And see just how committed they are to casting out a tyrant.

Brother Dragon... It's time to let the House of Mao know what is happening here.

And will it be a favorable report, Little Sister?

Hmmm. How could it not be?

BE— DOOP.

Sacred Mao... It is w--

DONK

What the...

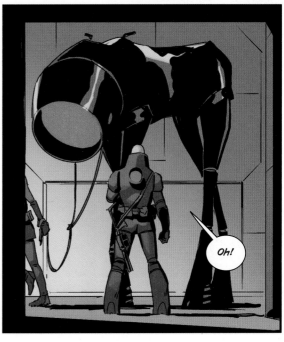

Oh!

New Shanghai.

What is it?

A report from the field, Premier.

From the Widowmaker embedded with the Endless Nation.

Play it.

Sacred Mao...

It is with a heavy heart that I make this report.

Your family lifted me up from nothing. You gave me purpose beyond any I could ever dare to dream.

I revered your father...

But that reverence pales in comparison to my feelings for you.

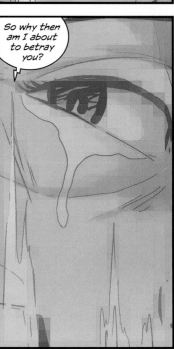

So why then am I about to betray you?

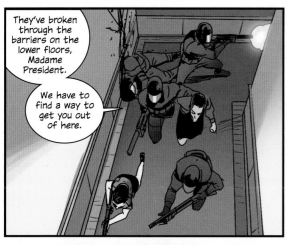

They've broken through the barriers on the lower floors, Madame President.

We have to find a way to get you out of here.

"I never thought that there could be something I believed in more than your great house."

"Your father showed me my calling."

"He gave me a place."

"And you, Xiaolian..."

"You gave me a purpose."

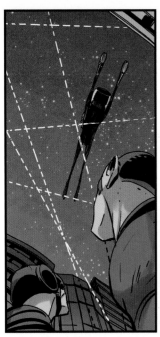

I'm sorry, Antonia. It's over.

NO!

Yes. All this...

For nothing...

"I swear, I thought I would die in your service."

"I believed I would die for you."

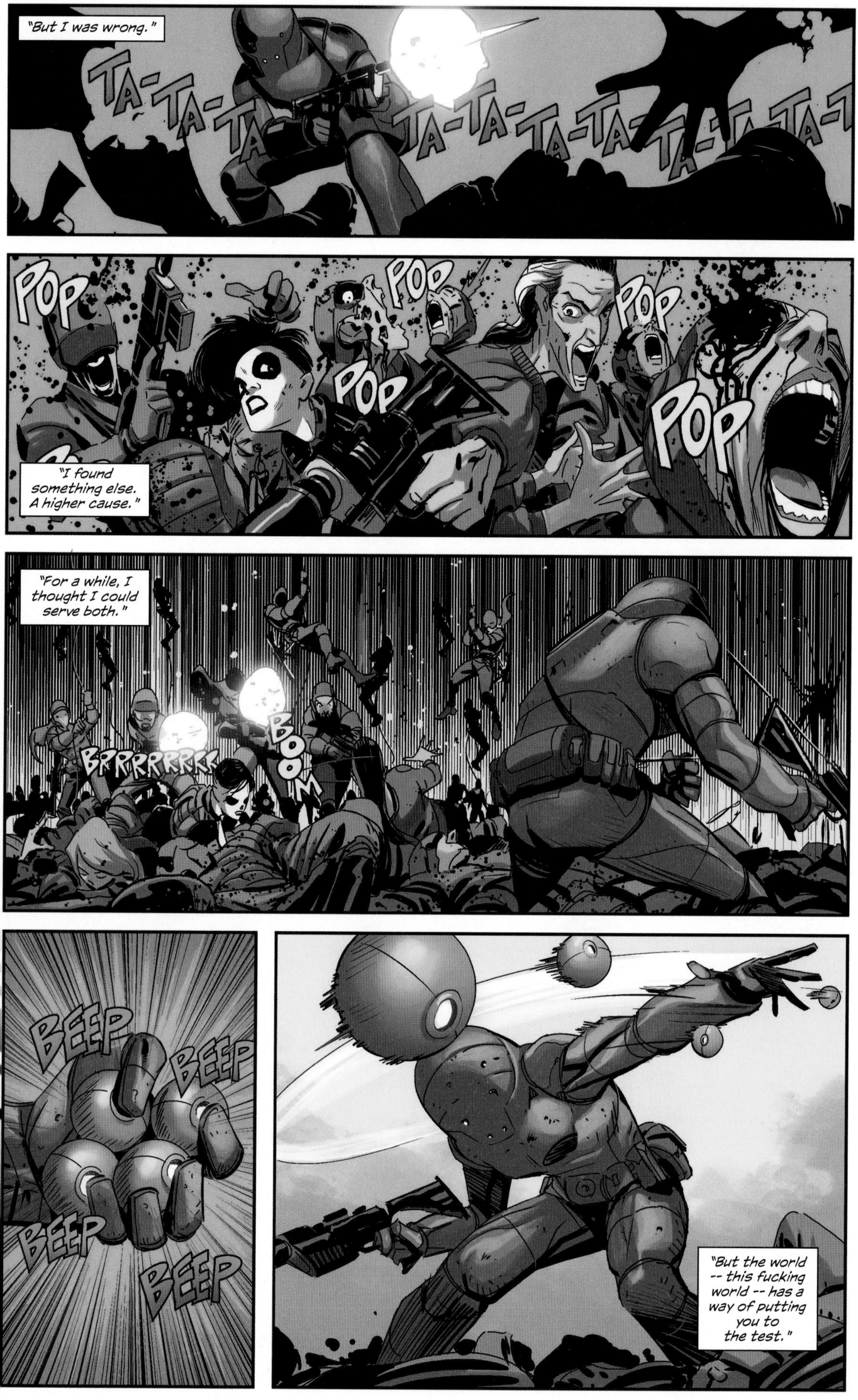
"But I was wrong."
TA-TA-TA-TA-TA-TA-TA-TA-TA-TA-TA-TA-T
POP
POP
POP
POP
POP
"I found something else. A higher cause."
"For a while, I thought I could serve both."
BRRRRRRRR
BOOM
BEEP
BEEP
BEEP
BEEP
"But the world -- this fucking world -- has a way of putting you to the test."

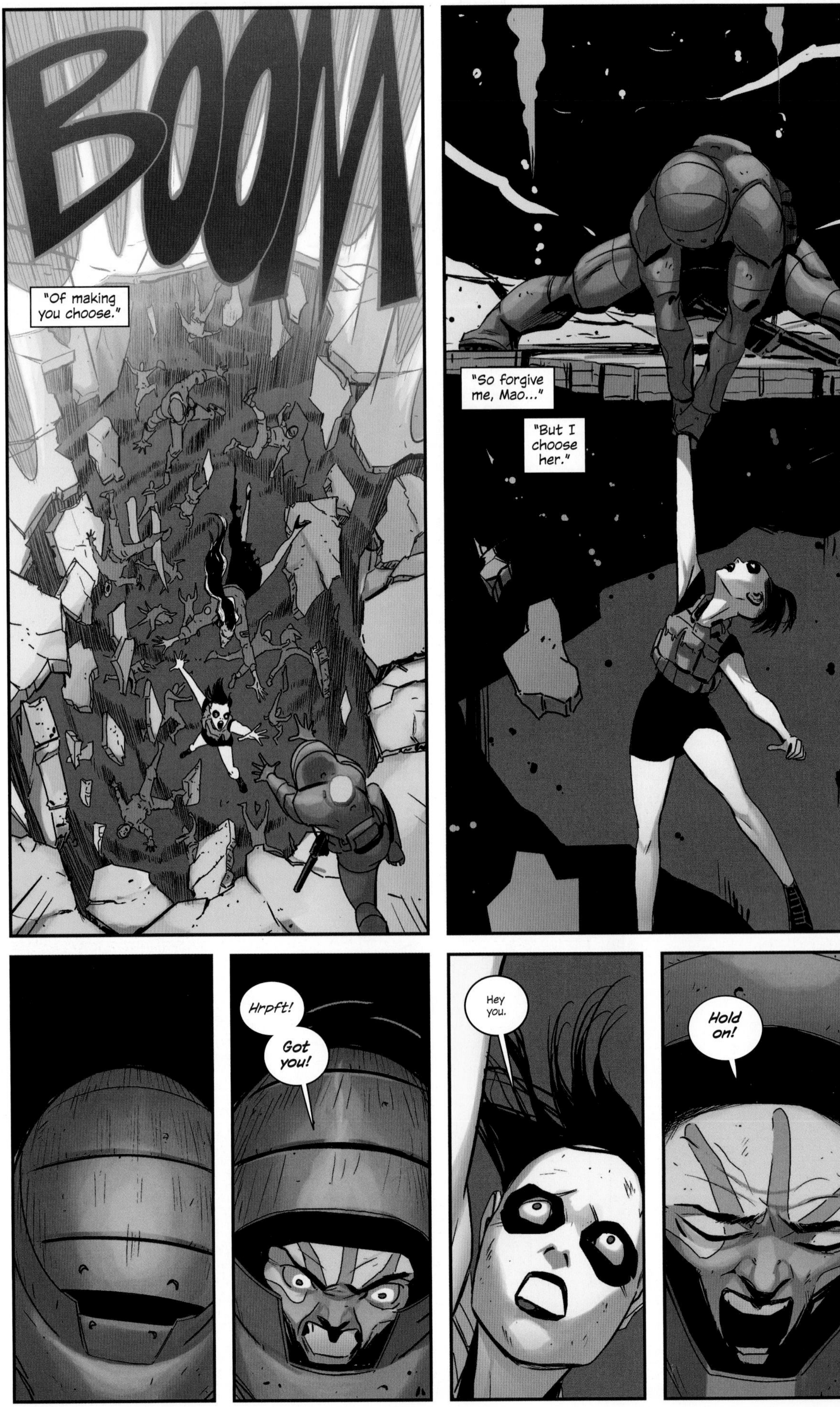
BOOM
"Of making you choose."
"So forgive me, Mao..."
"But I choose her."
Hrpft!
Got you!
Hey you.
Hold on!

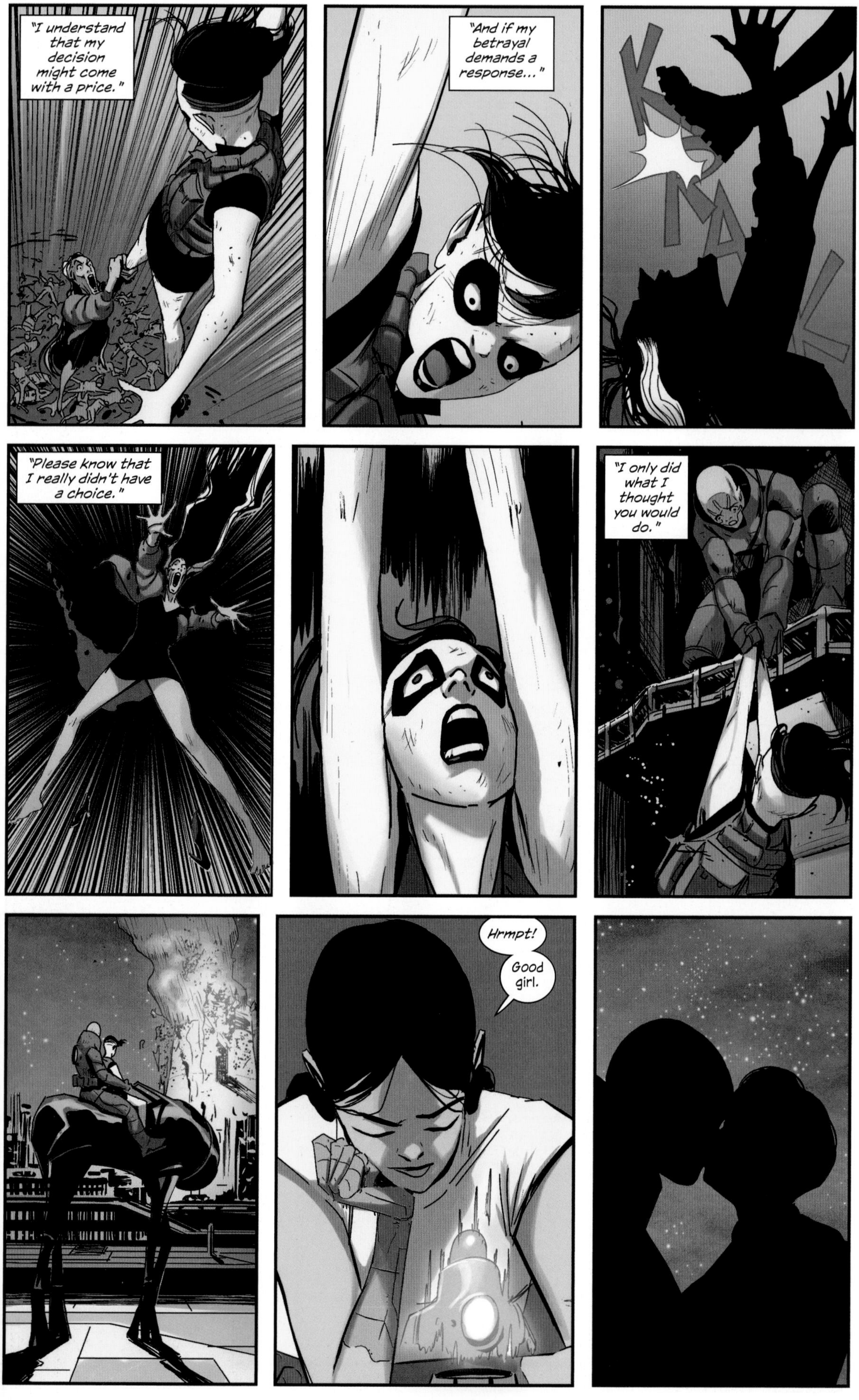
"I understand that my decision might come with a price."
"And if my betrayal demands a response..."
"Please know that I really didn't have a choice."
"I only did what I thought you would do."
Hrmpt!
Good girl.

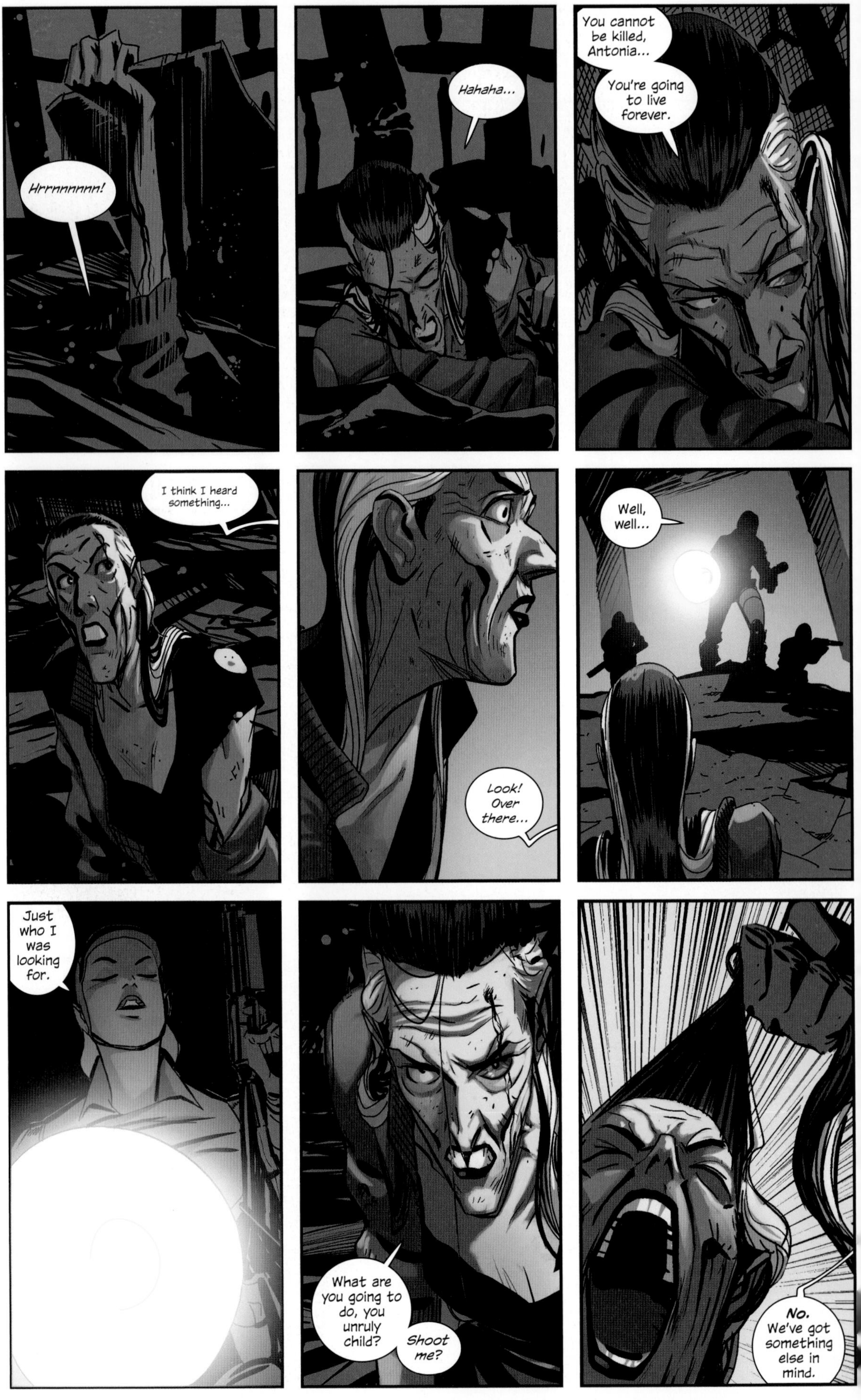
Hrrnnnnnnn!
Hahaha...
You cannot be killed, Antonia...
You're going to live forever.
I think I heard something...
Look! Over there...
Well, well...
Just who I was looking for.
What are you going to do, you unruly child?
Shoot me?
No. We've got something else in mind.

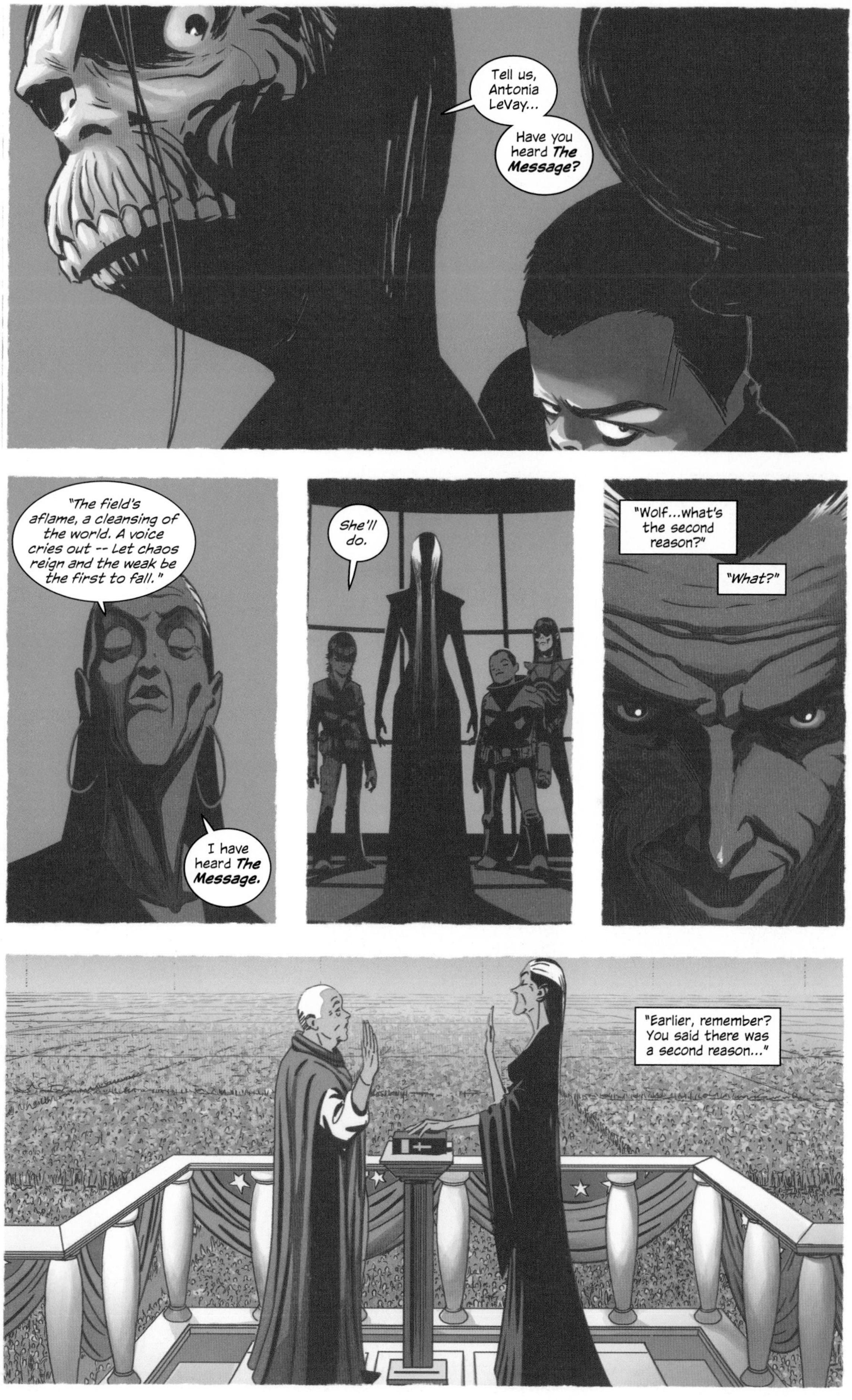
Tell us, Antonia LeVay...
Have you heard *The Message?*
"The field's aflame, a cleansing of the world. A voice cries out -- Let chaos reign and the weak be the first to fall."
I have heard *The Message.*
She'll do.
"Wolf...what's the second reason?"
"What?"
"Earlier, remember? You said there was a second reason..."

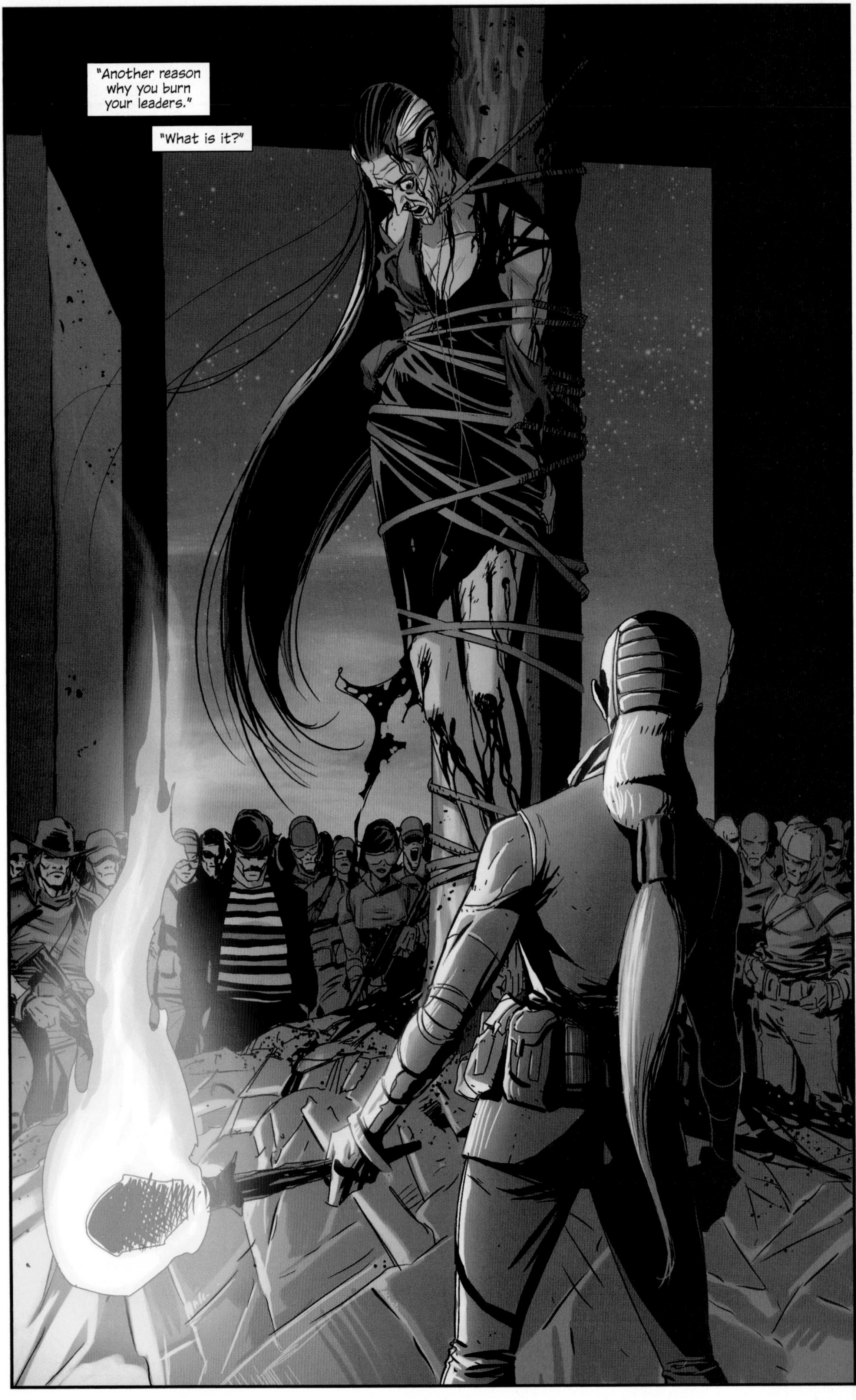
"Another reason why you burn your leaders."
"What is it?"

"Oh, that..."

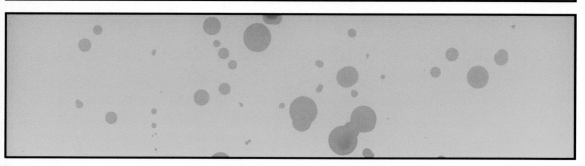

"We burn them...
because they
had it coming."

SILENCE...

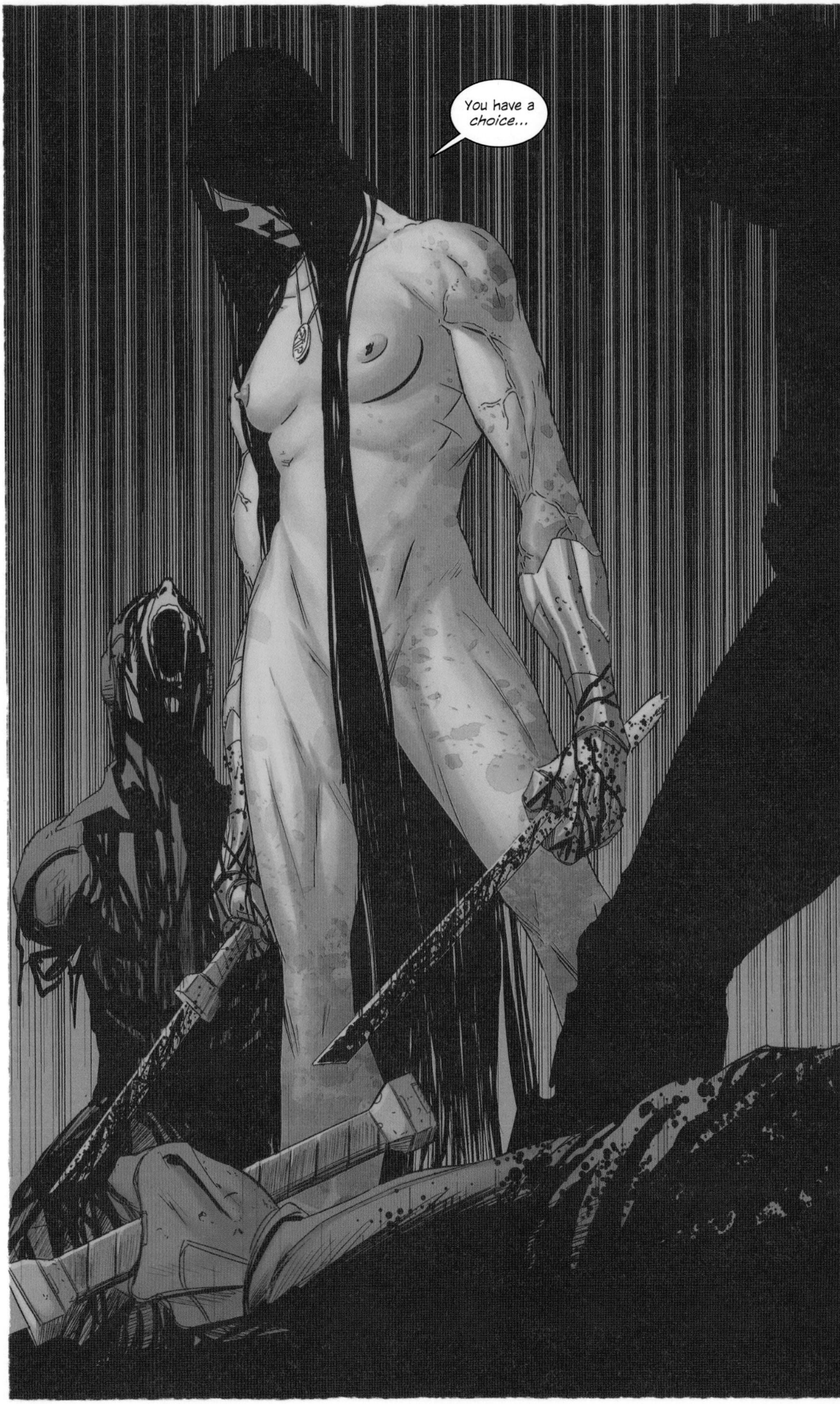
You have a choice...

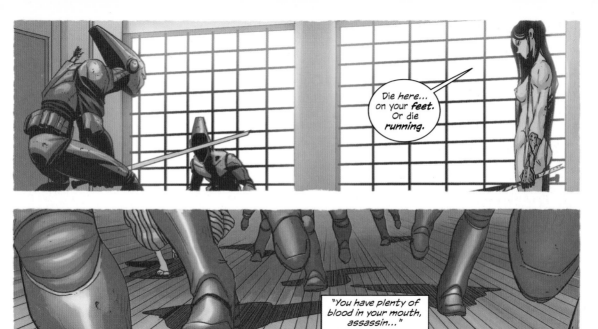

Die here... on your **feet.** Or die **running.**

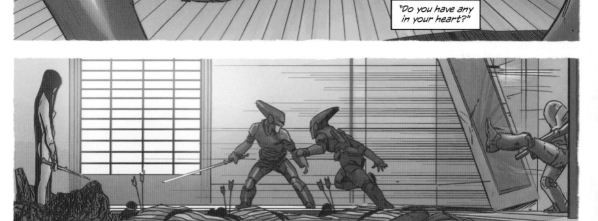

"You have plenty of blood in your mouth, assassin..."

"Do you have any in your heart?"

Go.

I want them taken alive.

Premier?

"I suppose not."

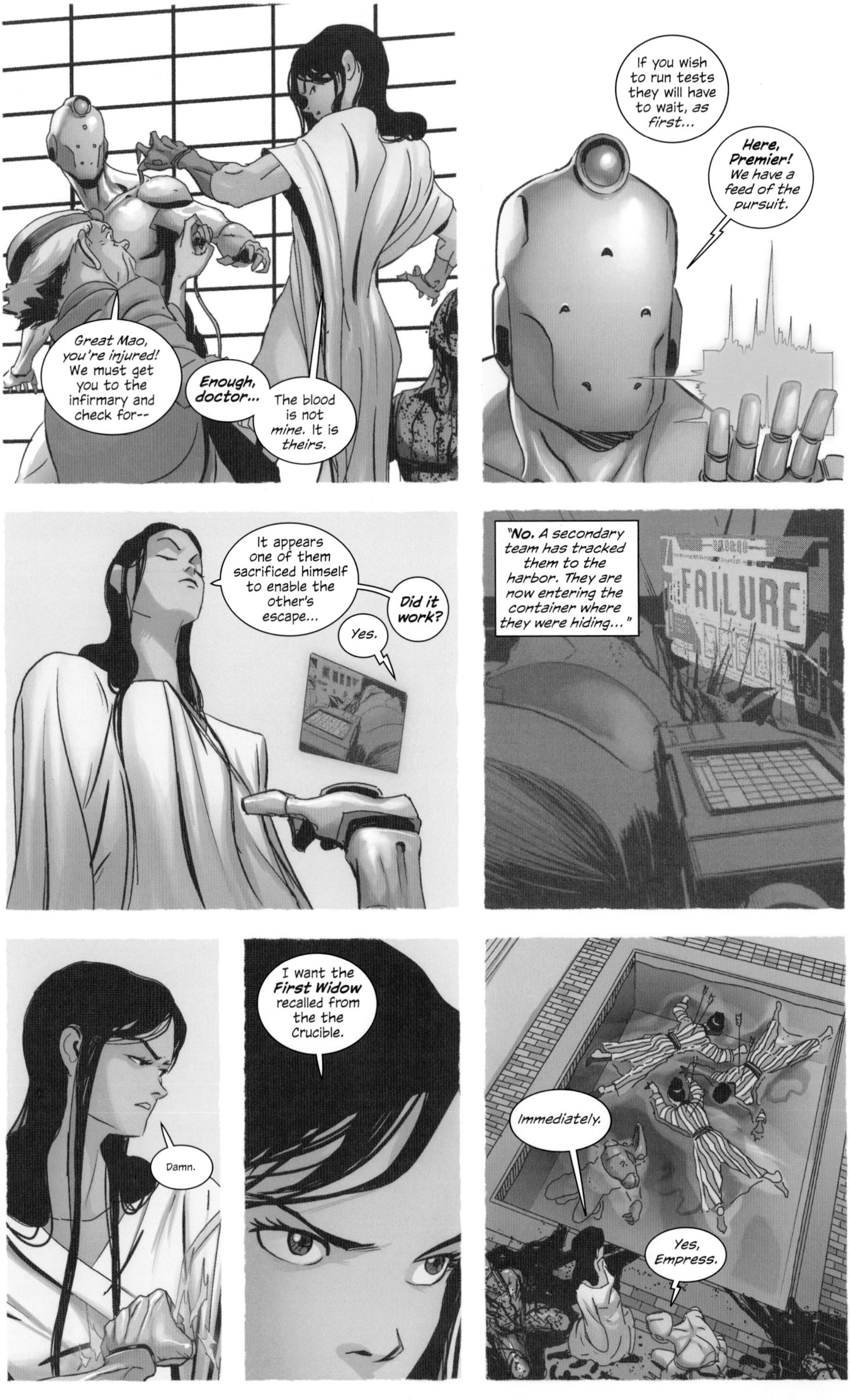
Great Mao, you're injured! We must get you to the infirmary and check for--
Enough, doctor...
The blood is not mine. It is theirs.
If you wish to run tests they will have to wait, as first...
Here, Premier! We have a feed of the pursuit.
It appears one of them sacrificed himself to enable the other's escape...
Did it work?
Yes.
"No. A secondary team has tracked them to the harbor. They are now entering the container where they were hiding..."
FAILURE
Damn.
I want the First Widow recalled from the the Crucible.
Immediately.
Yes, Empress.

AND THEN **THUNDER.**

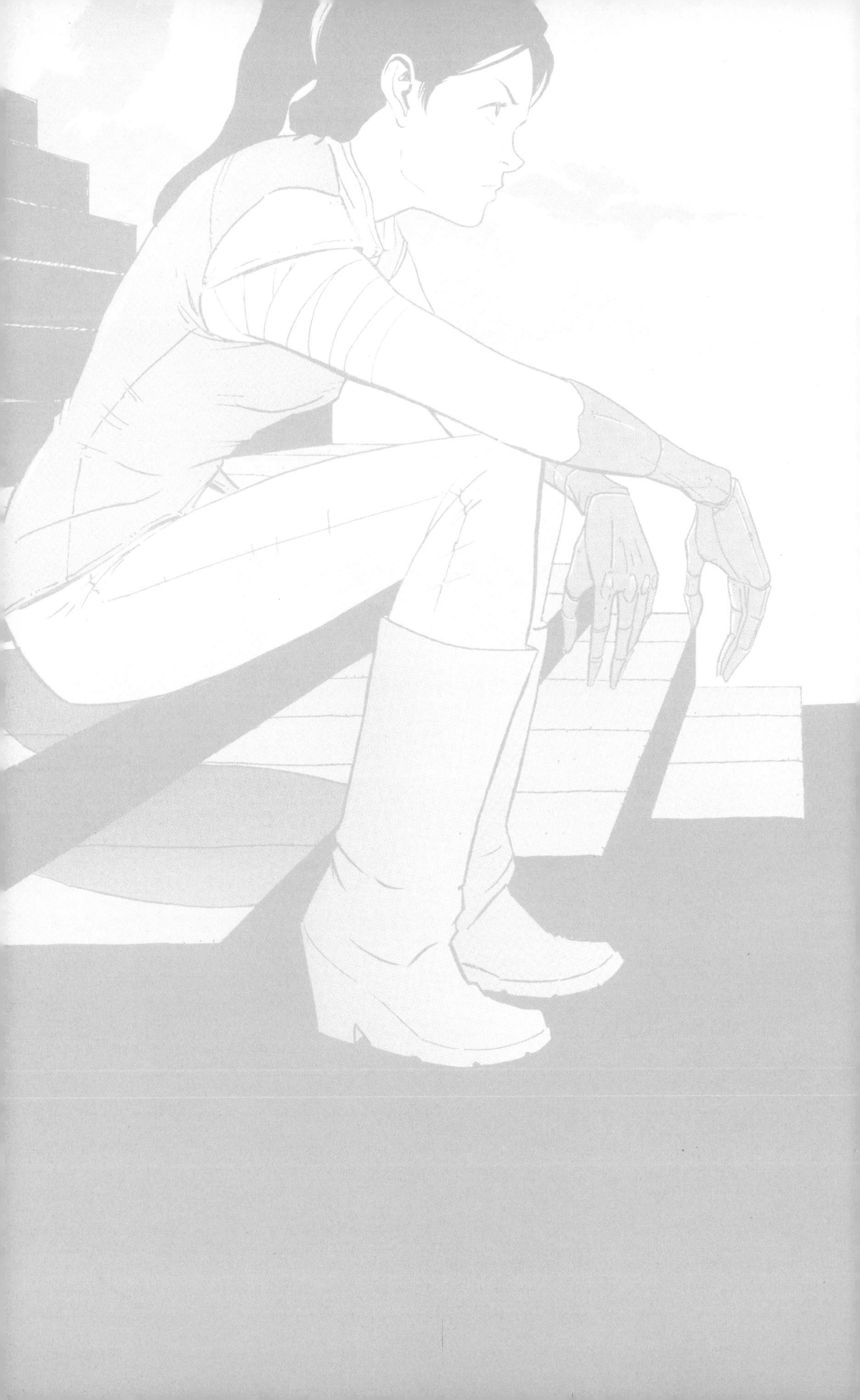

THIRTY-FOUR:
THIS NEVER-
ENDING **CYCLE** OF
VIOLENCE

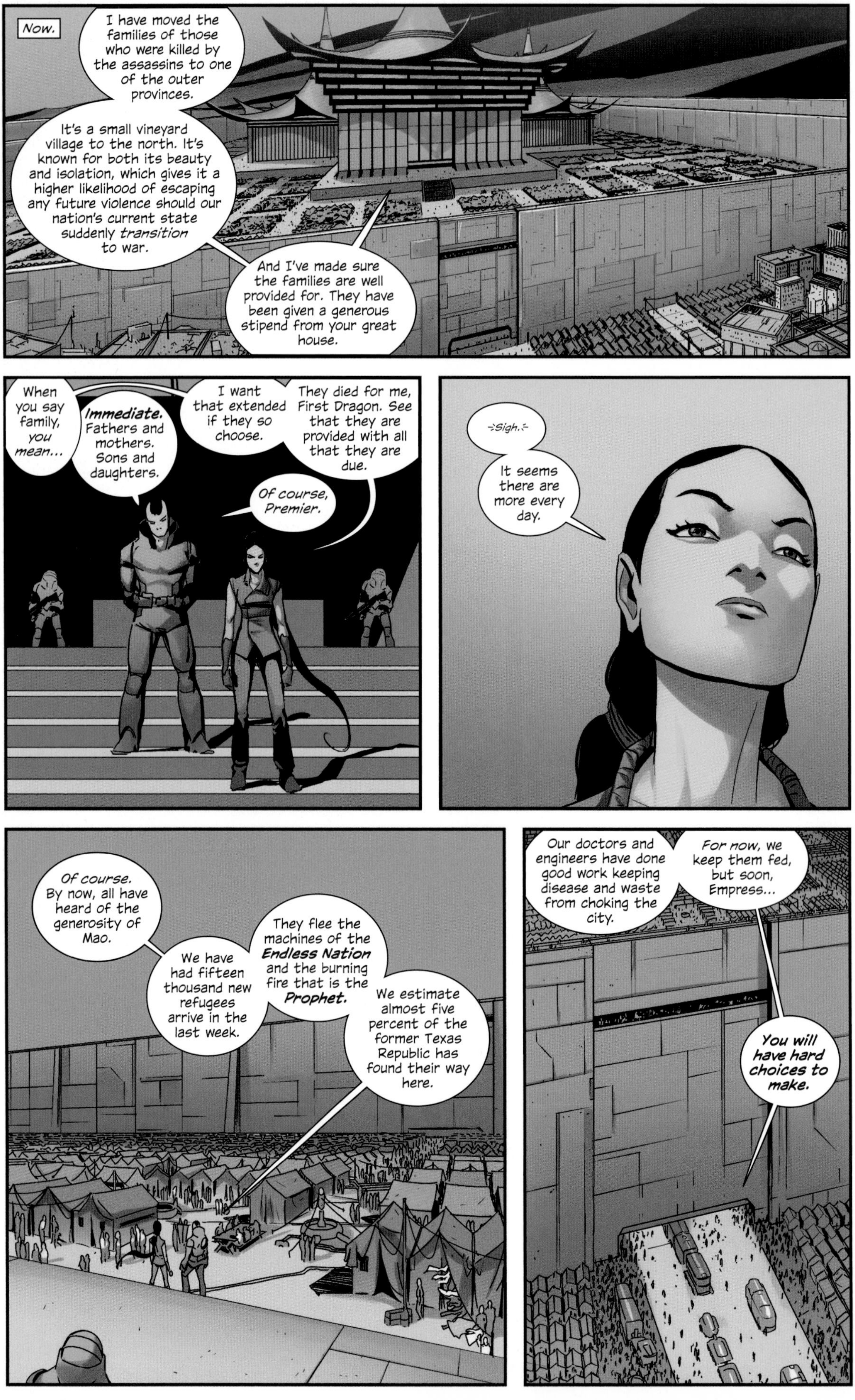
Now.
I have moved the families of those who were killed by the assassins to one of the outer provinces.
It's a small vineyard village to the north. It's known for both its beauty and isolation, which gives it a higher likelihood of escaping any future violence should our nation's current state suddenly *transition* to war.
And I've made sure the families are well provided for. They have been given a generous stipend from your great house.
When you say family, *you mean...*
Immediate. Fathers and mothers. Sons and daughters.
I want that extended if they so choose.
They died for me, First Dragon. See that they are provided with all that they are due.
Of course, Premier.
Sigh.
It seems there are more every day.
Of course. By now, all have heard of the generosity of Mao.
We have had fifteen thousand new refugees arrive in the last week.
They flee the machines of the ***Endless Nation*** and the burning fire that is the ***Prophet.***
We estimate almost five percent of the former Texas Republic has found their way here.
Our doctors and engineers have done good work keeping disease and waste from choking the city.
For now, we keep them fed, but soon, Empress...
You will have hard choices to make.

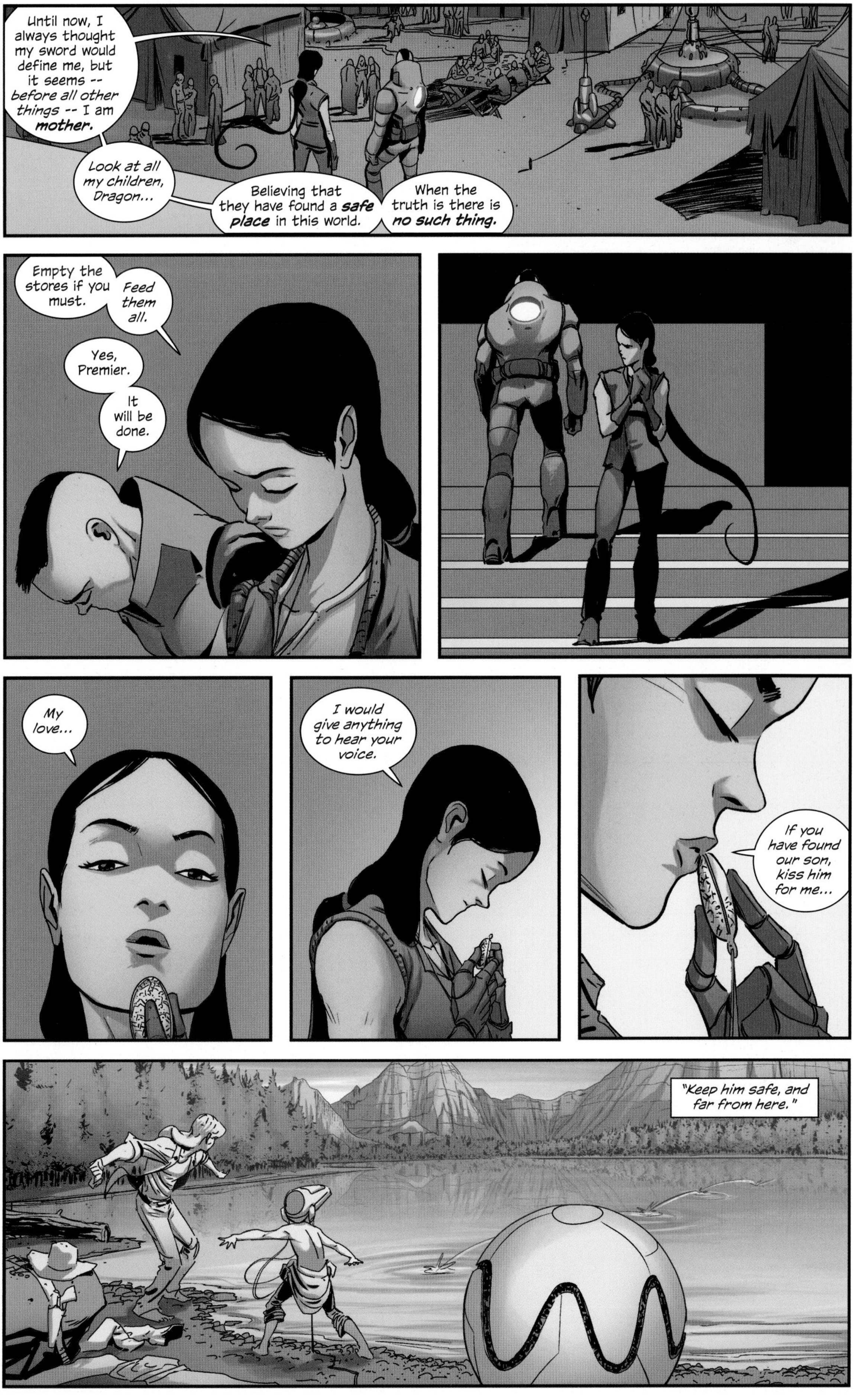
Until now, I always thought my sword would define me, but it seems -- *before all other things* -- I am ***mother.***
Look at all my children, Dragon...
Believing that they have found a ***safe place*** in this world.
When the truth is there is ***no such thing.***
Empty the stores if you must.
Feed them all.
Yes, Premier.
It will be done.
My love...
I would give anything to hear your voice.
If you have found our son, kiss him for me...
"Keep him safe, and far from here."

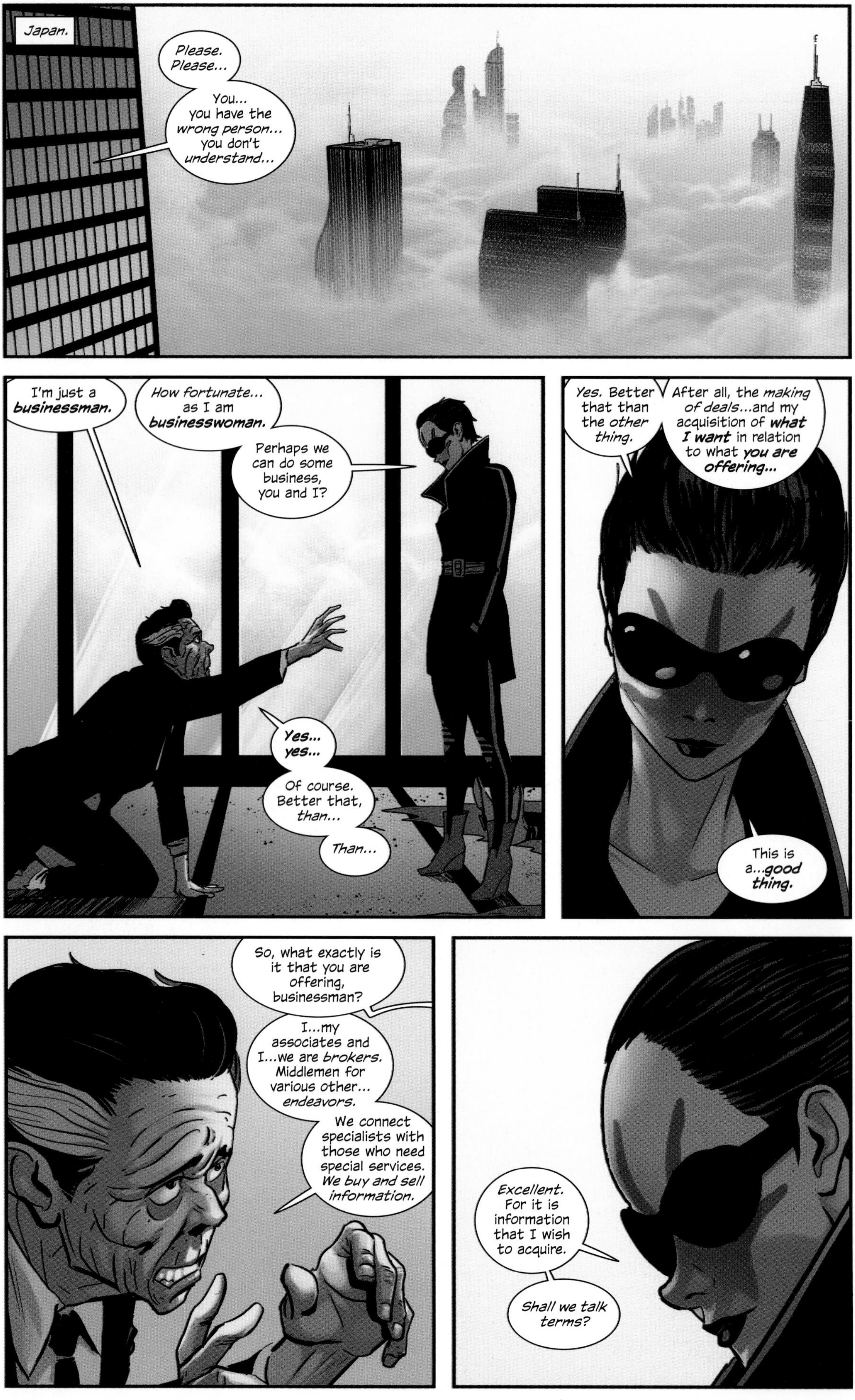
Japan.
Please. Please...
You... you have the wrong person... you don't understand...
I'm just a businessman.
How fortunate... as I am businesswoman.
Perhaps we can do some business, you and I?
Yes... yes...
Of course. Better that, than...
Than...
Yes. Better that than the other thing.
After all, the making of deals...and my acquisition of what I want in relation to what you are offering...
This is a...good thing.
So, what exactly is it that you are offering, businessman?
I...my associates and I...we are brokers. Middlemen for various other... endeavors.
We connect specialists with those who need special services. We buy and sell information.
Excellent. For it is information that I wish to acquire.
Shall we talk terms?

What are your... what are you offering?

My *abstention* from engaging in my *normal* business.

Would you like to know what business that is?

Yes.

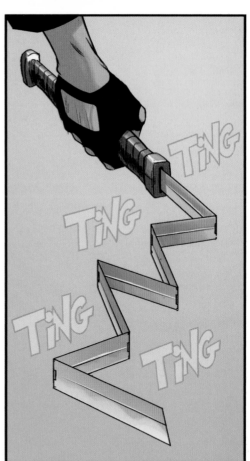

TING TING TING TING TING

I am the *First Widow* of the *House of Mao*...

SHHHIK

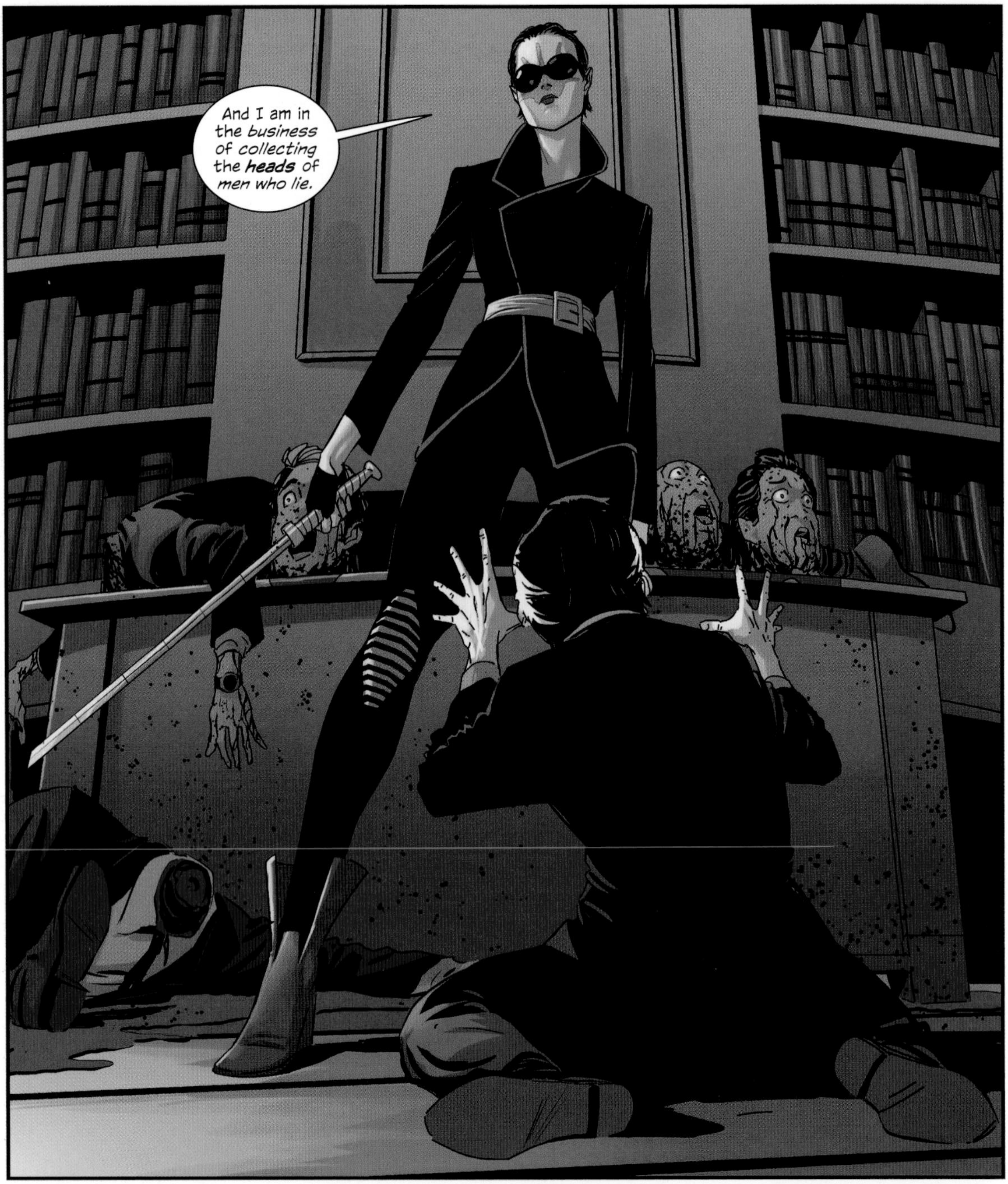
And I am in the *business* of collecting the ***heads*** of *men who lie.*

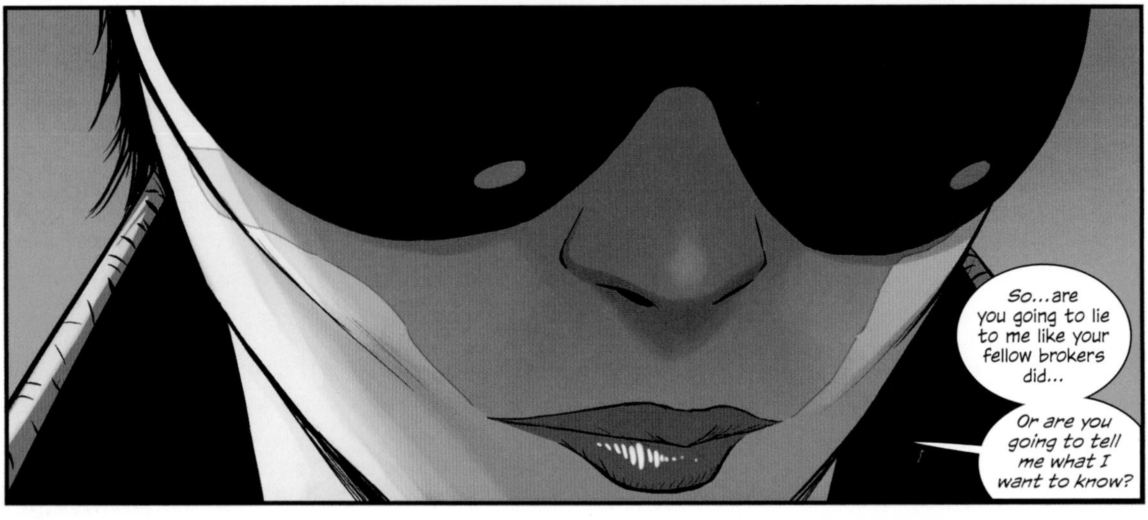
So...are you going to lie to me like your fellow brokers did...
Or are you going to tell me what I want to know?

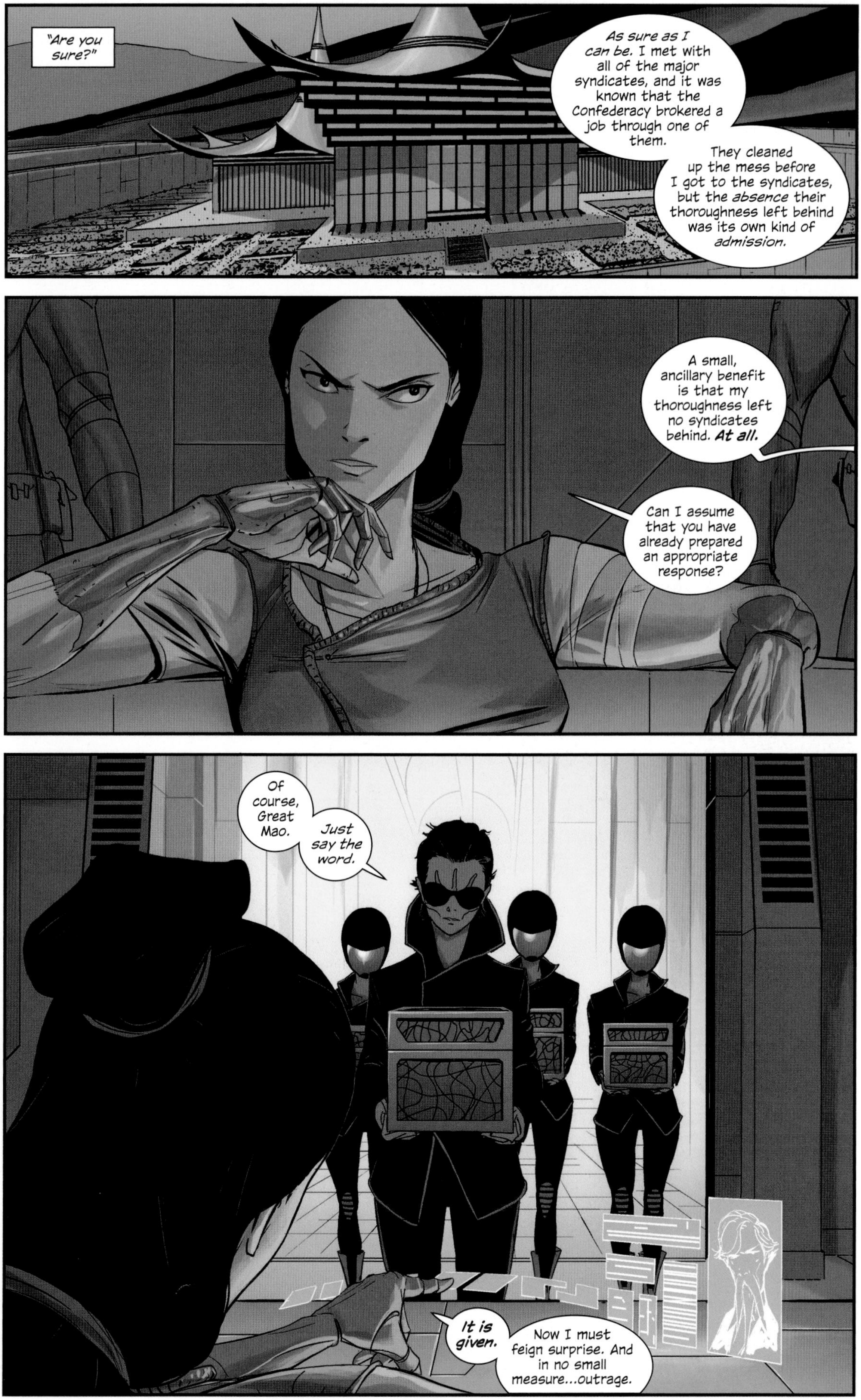
"Are you sure?"
As sure as I can be. I met with all of the major syndicates, and it was known that the Confederacy brokered a job through one of them.
They cleaned up the mess before I got to the syndicates, but the absence their thoroughness left behind was its own kind of admission.
A small, ancillary benefit is that my thoroughness left no syndicates behind. At all.
Can I assume that you have already prepared an appropriate response?
Of course, Great Mao.
Just say the word.
It is given.
Now I must feign surprise. And in no small measure...outrage.

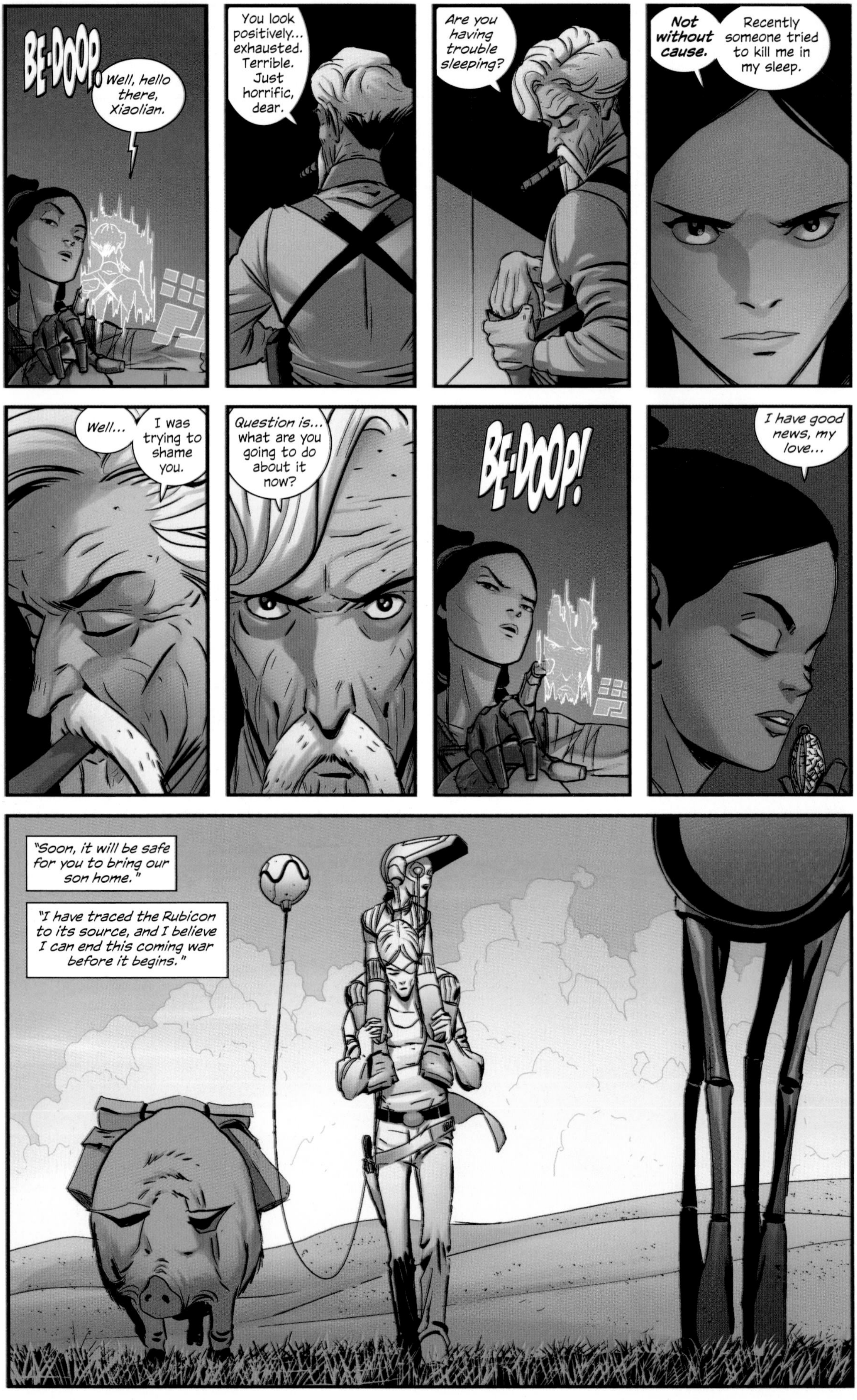
BE-DOOP.
Well, hello there, Xiaolian.
You look positively... exhausted. Terrible. Just horrific, dear.
Are you having trouble sleeping?
Not without cause.
Recently someone tried to kill me in my sleep.
Well...
I was trying to shame you.
Question is... what are you going to do about it now?
BE-DOOP!
I have good news, my love...
"Soon, it will be safe for you to bring our son home."
"I have traced the Rubicon to its source, and I believe I can end this coming war before it begins."

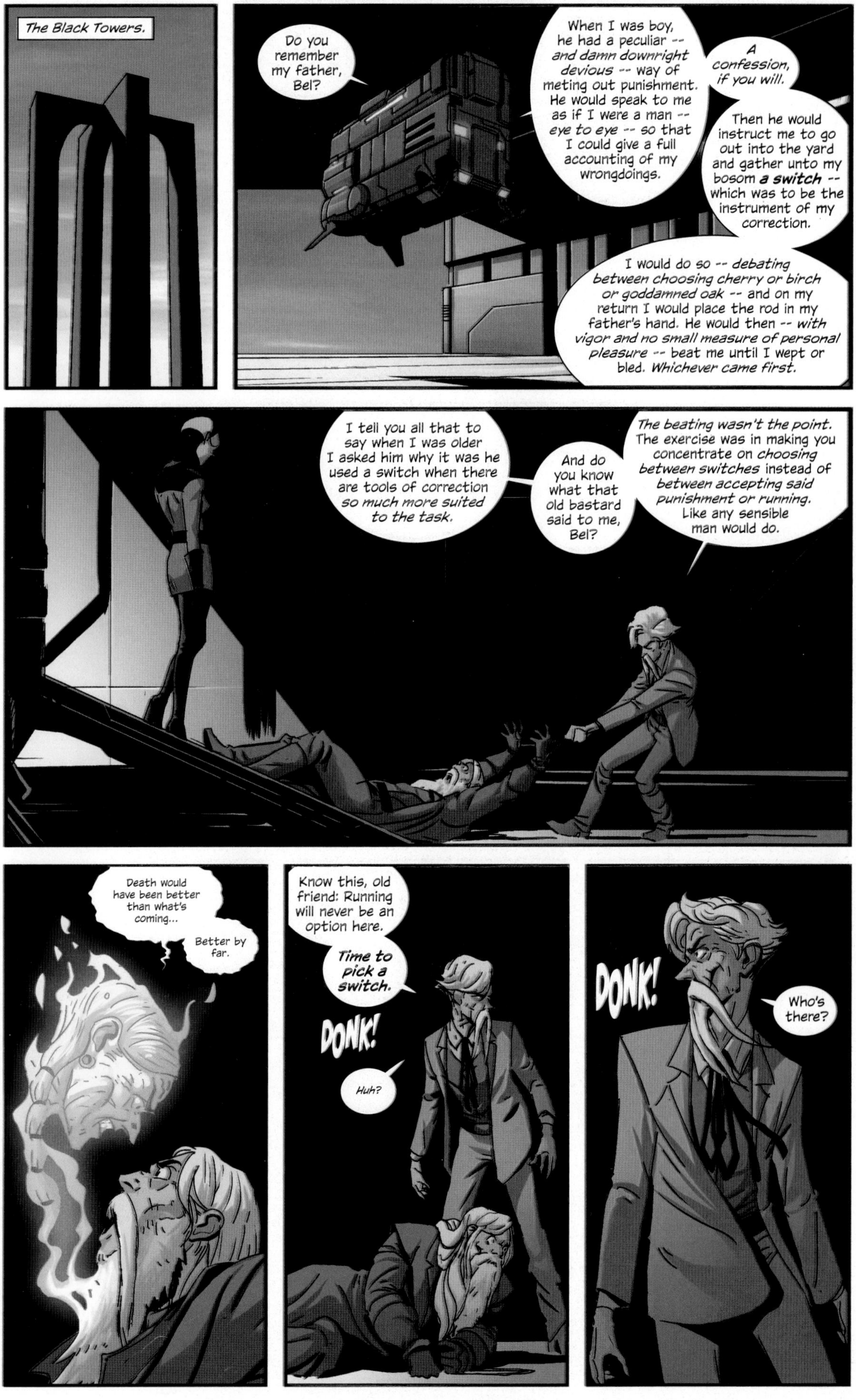

The Black Towers.
Do you remember my father, Bel?
When I was boy, he had a peculiar -- and damn downright devious -- way of meting out punishment. He would speak to me as if I were a man -- eye to eye -- so that I could give a full accounting of my wrongdoings.
A confession, if you will.
Then he would instruct me to go out into the yard and gather unto my bosom a switch -- which was to be the instrument of my correction.
I would do so -- debating between choosing cherry or birch or goddamned oak -- and on my return I would place the rod in my father's hand. He would then -- with vigor and no small measure of personal pleasure -- beat me until I wept or bled. Whichever came first.
I tell you all that to say when I was older I asked him why it was he used a switch when there are tools of correction so much more suited to the task.
And do you know what that old bastard said to me, Bel?
The beating wasn't the point. The exercise was in making you concentrate on choosing between switches instead of between accepting said punishment or running. Like any sensible man would do.
Death would have been better than what's coming...
Better by far.
Know this, old friend: Running will never be an option here.
Time to pick a switch.
DONK!
Huh?
DONK!
Who's there?

Call me *vengeance*. Call me *revenge*.

Call me the answer to an insult.

Well, that's a bit melodramatic.

Don't you think?

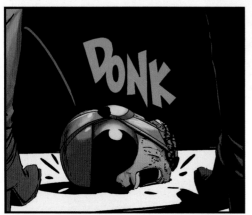

DONK

DONK

I stand corrected.

DONK

You tried to kill Mao.

Know this, old man: Running will never be an option here.

Time to pick a blade.

Hrmpt!

Normally I'm not a fan of others' flamboyance in the face of my own, but I think I like you. *You and your whole show.*

Pray tell, might I know your name before I summarily dismiss you? *For all eternity.*

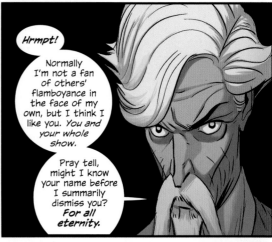

Ha ha.

Posturing is deception...

And *deception* is a *lie.*

I am the First Widow of the Crucible.

The knife of Xiaolian...

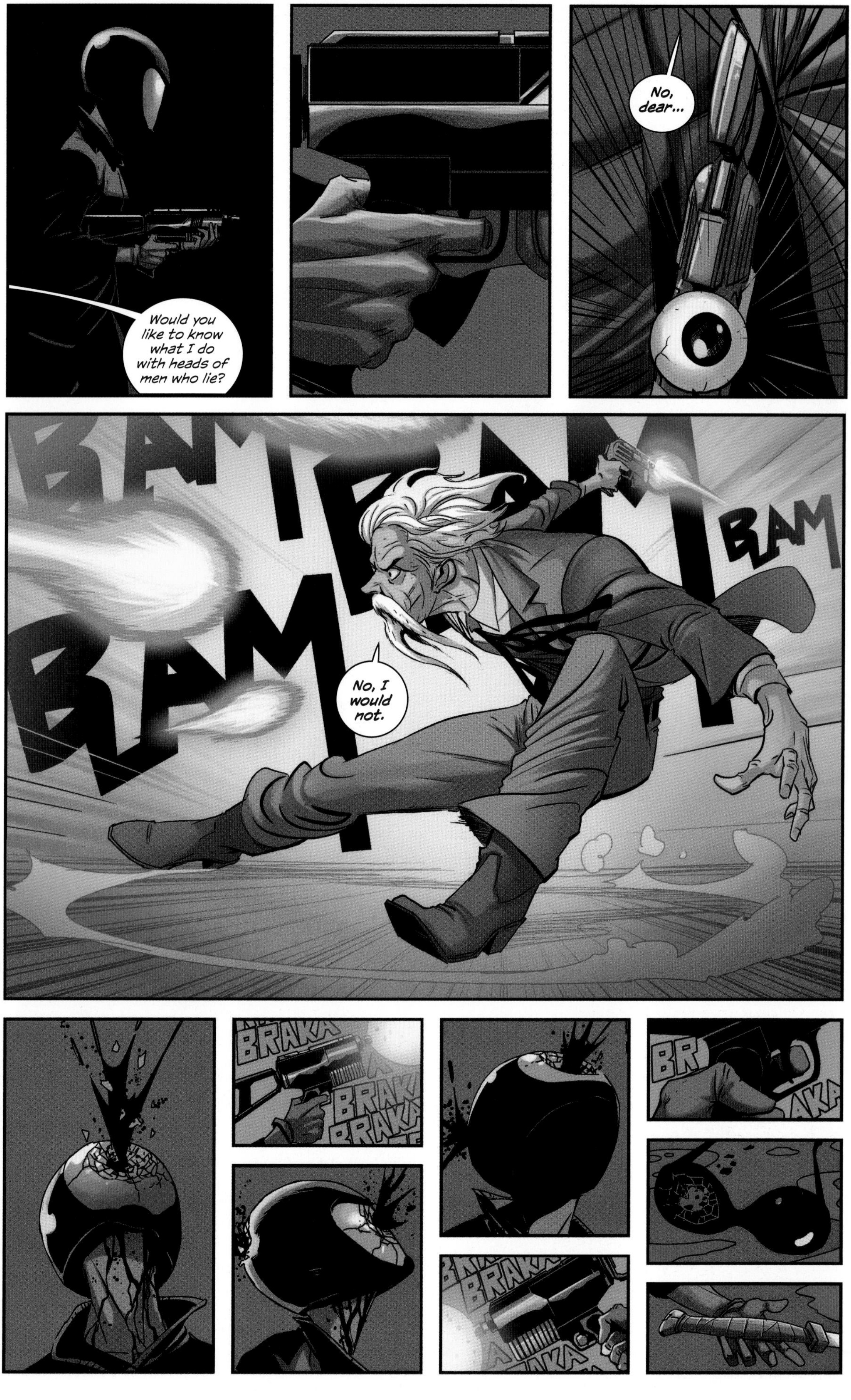
Would you like to know what I do with heads of men who lie?
No, dear...
BAM
BAM
BAM
BAM
No, I would not.
BRAKA
BRAKA
BRAKA
BR
AKA
BRAKA

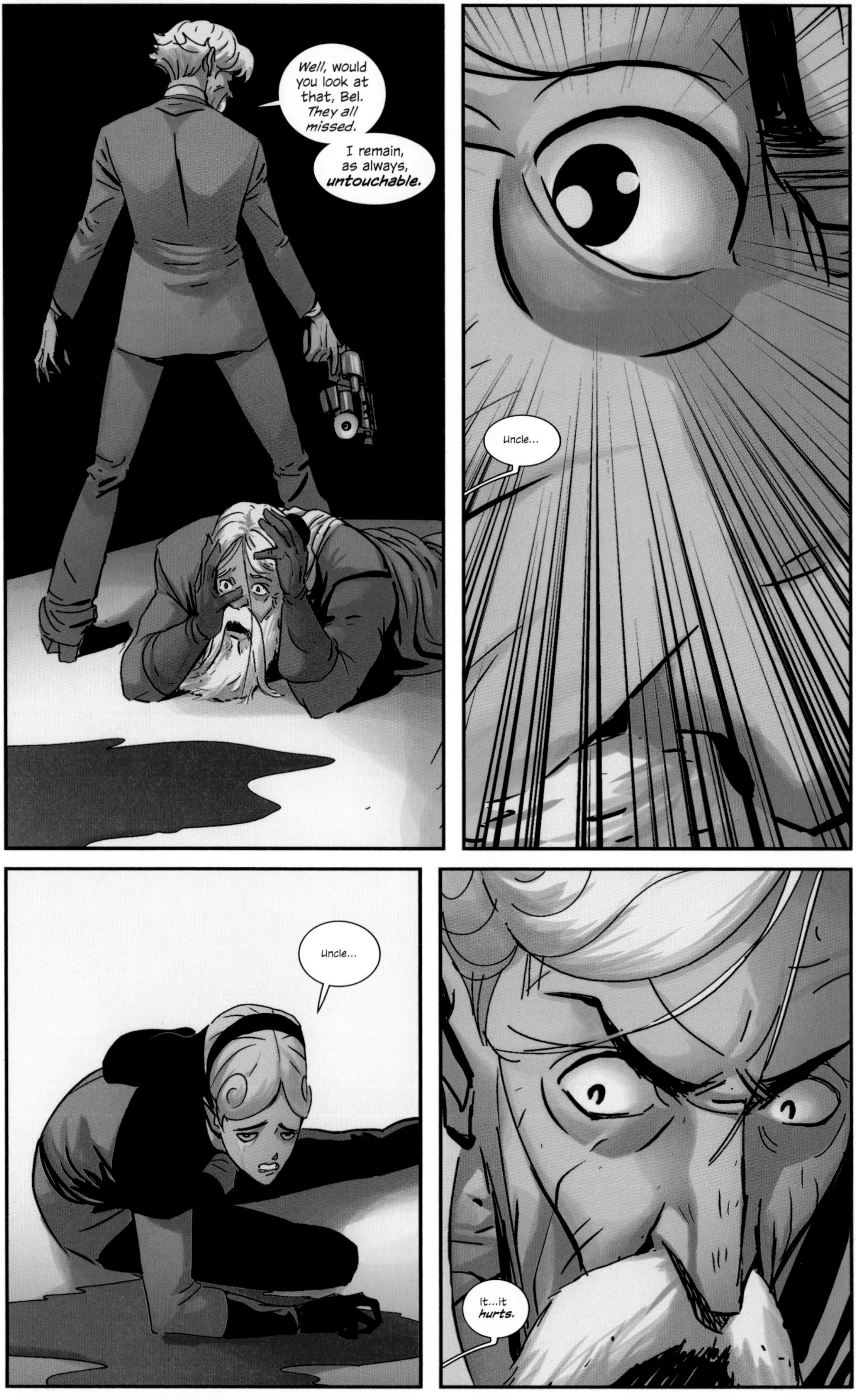

Well, would you look at that, Bel. *They all missed.*
I remain, as always, ***untouchable.***
Uncle...
Uncle...
It...it ***hurts.***

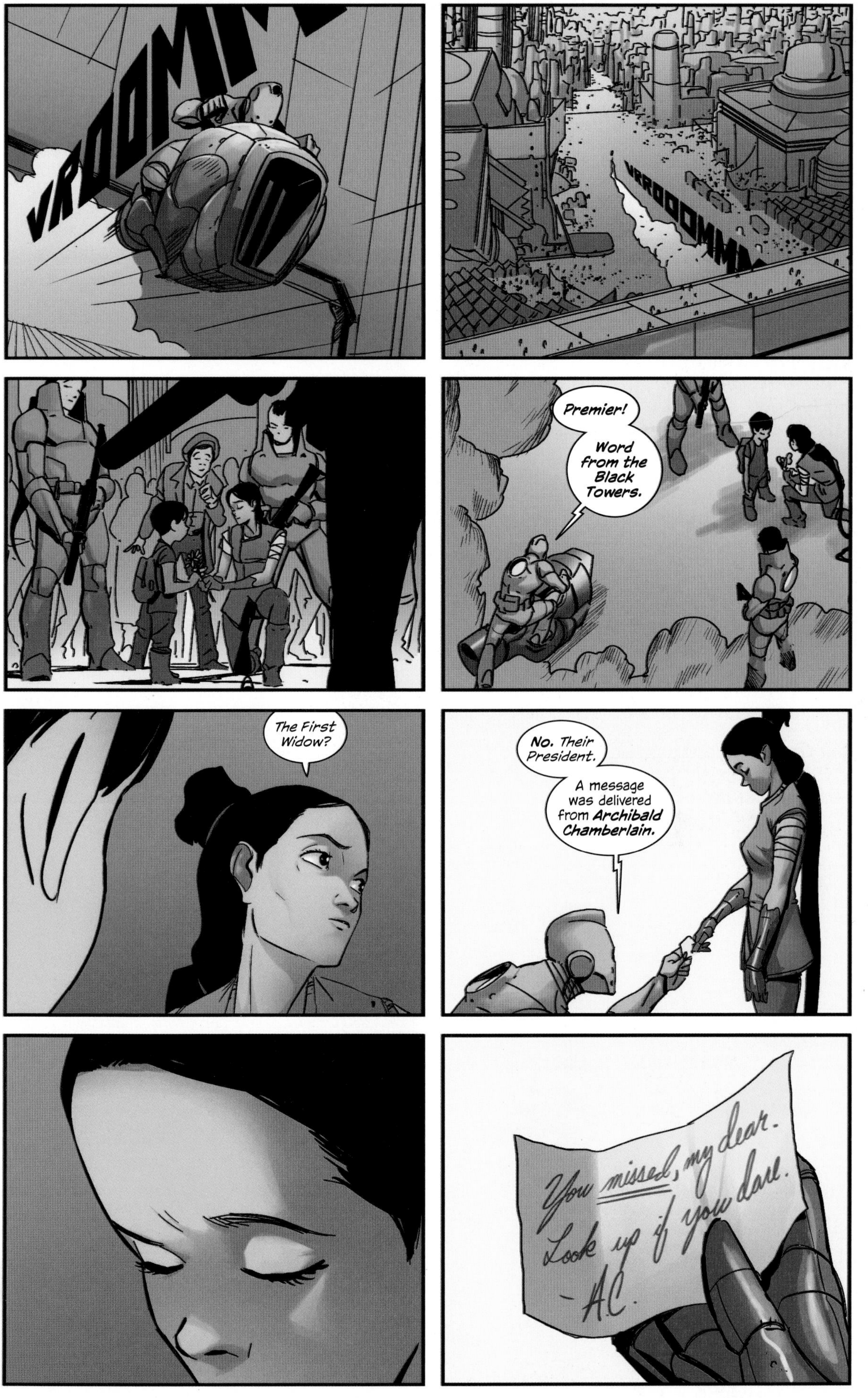
VROOM
VRROOOMM
Premier!
Word from the Black Towers.
The First Widow?
No. Their President.
A message was delivered from Archibald Chamberlain.
You missed, my dear.
Look up if you dare.
- A.C.

Oh, no...

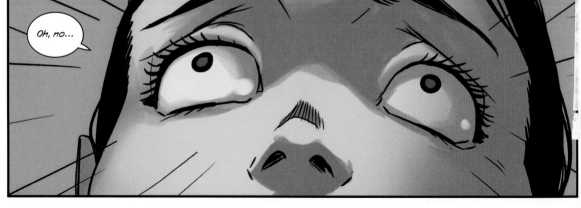

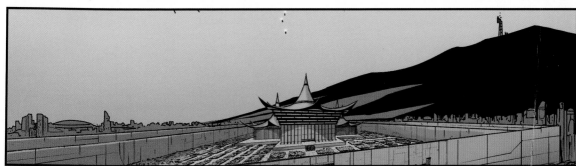

Alert the guard!

Raise the shields! Do it!

Do it NOW!!

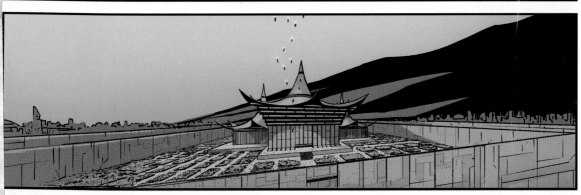

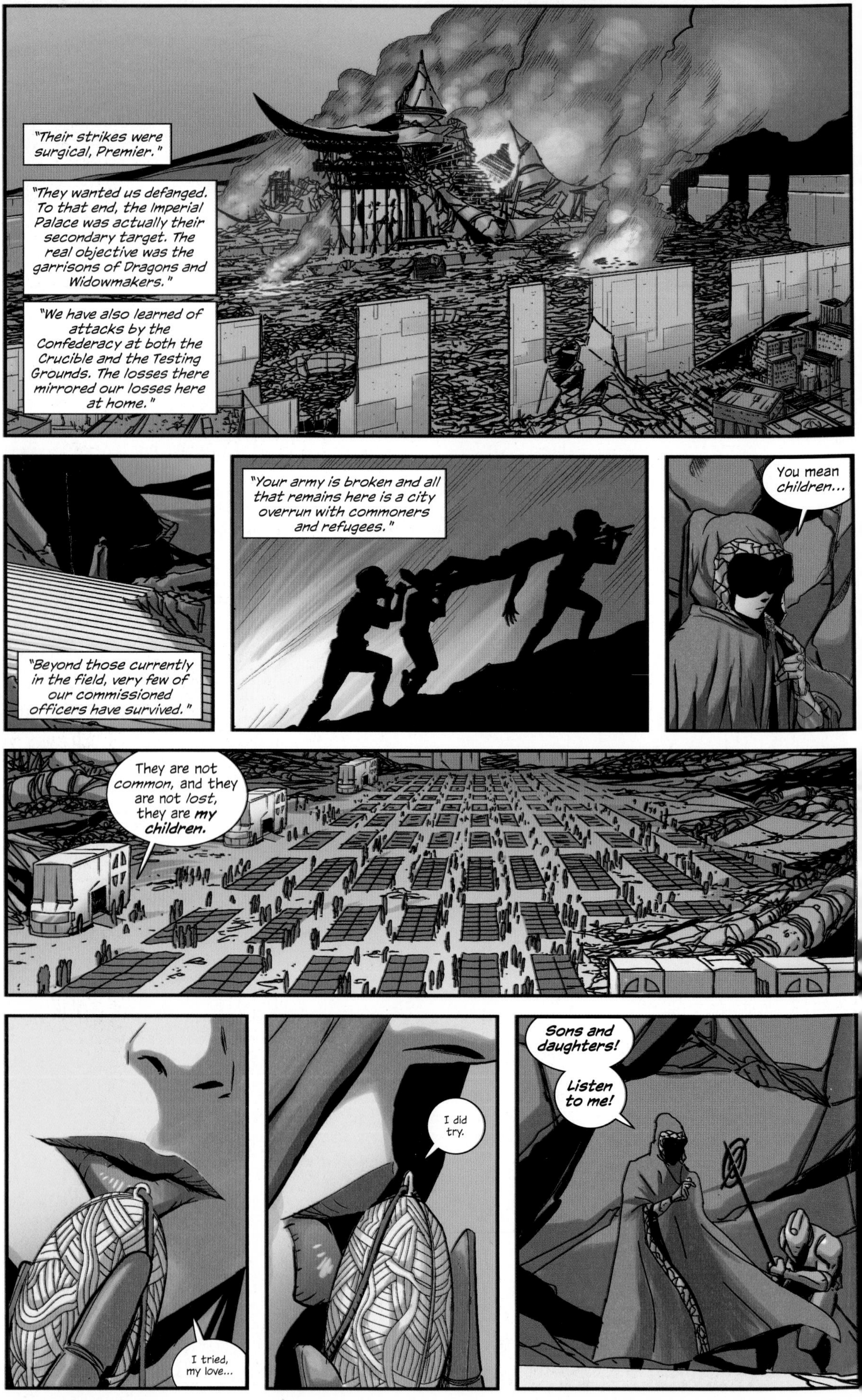
"Their strikes were surgical, Premier."
"They wanted us defanged. To that end, the Imperial Palace was actually their secondary target. The real objective was the garrisons of Dragons and Widowmakers."
"We have also learned of attacks by the Confederacy at both the Crucible and the Testing Grounds. The losses there mirrored our losses here at home."
"Beyond those currently in the field, very few of our commissioned officers have survived."
"Your army is broken and all that remains here is a city overrun with commoners and refugees."
You mean children...
They are not common, and they are not lost, they are my children.
I tried, my love...
I did try.
Sons and daughters!
Listen to me!

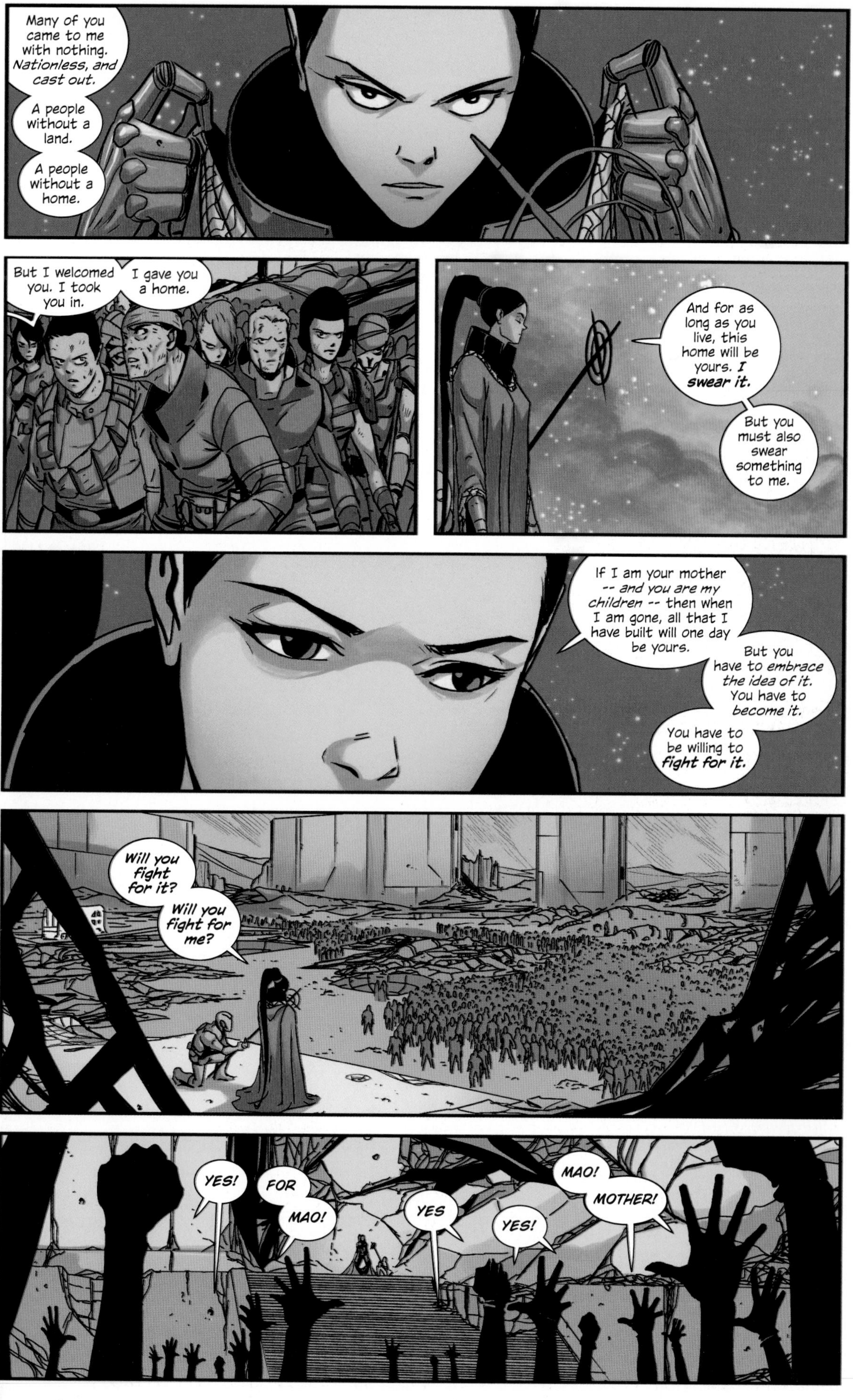
Many of you came to me with nothing. *Nationless, and cast out.*
A people without a land.
A people without a home.
But I welcomed you. I took you in.
I gave you a home.
And for as long as you live, this home will be yours. ***I swear it.***
But you must also swear something to me.
If I am your mother -- *and you are my children* -- then when I am gone, all that I have built will one day be yours.
But you have to *embrace the idea of it.* You have to *become it.*
You have to be willing to ***fight for it.***
Will you fight for it?
Will you fight for me?
YES!
FOR
MAO!
YES
YES!
MAO!
MOTHER!

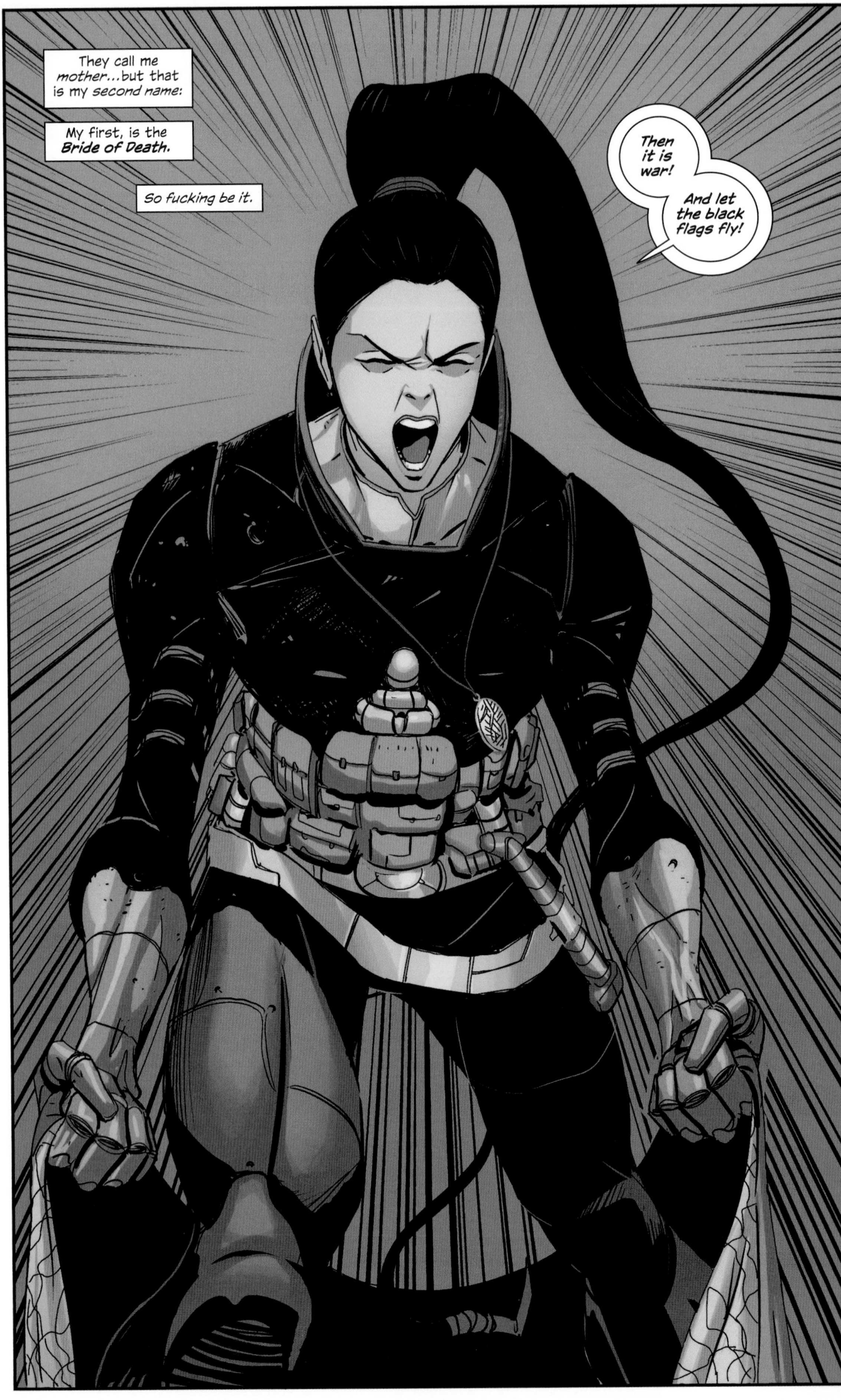
They call me *mother*...but that is my *second name:*
My first, is the ***Bride of Death.***
So fucking be it.
Then it is war!
And let the black flags fly!

ALL MEN TELL **LIES.**
THESE ARE A **FEW** OF
THEM.

Jonathan Hickman is the visionary talent behind such works as the Eisner-nominated **NIGHTLY NEWS, THE MANHATTAN PROJECTS** and **PAX ROMANA**. He also plies his trade at MARVEL working on books like **FANTASTIC FOUR** and **THE AVENGERS**.

His twin brother, Marc, was just named the PGA caddie of the year.

Jonathan lives in South Carolina except when he doesn't.

You can visit his website: *www.pronea.com*, or email him at: *jonathan@pronea.com*.

•

Nick Dragotta's career began at Marvel Comics working on titles as varied as **X-STATIX, THE AGE OF THE SENTRY, X-MEN: FIRST CLASS, CAPTAIN AMERICA: FOREVER ALLIES** and **VENGEANCE**.

In addition, Nick is the co-creator of **HOWTOONS,** a comic series teaching kids how to build things and explore the world around them. **EAST OF WEST** is Nick's first creator-owned project at Image.